Leadership as Identity

Also by Jackie Ford, Nancy Harding and Mark Learmonth
CRITICAL PUBLIC SECTOR MANAGEMENT: A New Approach (*co-edited with Graeme Currie*)

Also by Nancy Harding and Mark Learmonth
UNMASKING HEALTH MANAGEMENT (*edited*)

Also by Nancy Harding
THE SOCIAL CONSTRUCTION OF MANAGEMENT: Texts and Identities

CONFUSED PROFESSIONALS: The Social Construction of Dementia (*with Colin Palfrey*)

Leadership as Identity

Constructions and Deconstructions

Jackie Ford
Professor of Leadership and Organization Studies

Nancy Harding
Senior Lecturer in Organization Studies

Mark Learmonth
Associate Professor of Organization Theory

palgrave
macmillan

First published 2008 by
PALGRAVE MACMILLAN

Palgrave Macmillan in the UK is an imprint of Macmillan Publishers Limited, registered in England, company number 785998, of Houndmills, Basingstoke, Hampshire RG21 6XS.

Palgrave Macmillan in the US is a division of St Martin's Press LLC, 175 Fifth Avenue, New York, NY 10010.

Palgrave Macmillan is the global academic imprint of the above companies and has companies and representatives throughout the world.

Palgrave® and Macmillan® are registered trademarks in the United States, the United Kingdom, Europe and other countries.

ISBN-13: 978-0-230-51632-8   hardback
ISBN-10: 0-230-51632-7   hardback

This book is printed on paper suitable for recycling and made from fully managed and sustained forest sources. Logging, pulping and manufacturing processes are expected to conform to the environmental regulations of the country of origin.

A catalogue record for this book is available from the British Library.

A catalog record for this book is available from the Library of Congress.

10 9 8 7 6 5 4 3 2 1
17 16 15 14 13 12 11 10 09 08

Printed and bound in Great Britain by
CPI Antony Rowe, Chippenham and Eastbourne

Jackie Ford dedicates this book to Chris, Claire and Mikey.

Nancy Harding dedicates it to Brychan James Harding and Dylan Thomas Harding.

Mark Learmonth dedicates it to Glynis, James and Katie.

Contents

Table

Acknowledgements

Earlier versions of several chapters have appeared elsewhere, as follows:

Chapter 2: Leadership As Performative: Or How The Words 'Leader' and 'Leadership' *Do* Things
Learmonth, M. 2005. Doing things with words: the case of 'management' and 'administration'. *Public Administration* 83, 3, 617–37.

Chapter 3: The Leader as Hero
Learmonth, M. (2001) NHS Trust Chief Executives as Heroes? *Health Care Analysis* 9 (4) 417–36.

Chapter 4: Learning to be a Leader – Training Courses
Ford, Jackie and Harding, Nancy. (2007) 'Move Over Management: We're all Leaders Now.' *Management Learning* 38, 5, 475–93.

Chapter 6: Gendering Leadership
Ford, Jackie. (2007) 'Managers As Leaders: Towards A Post-Structuralist Feminist Analysis Of Leadership Dynamics In UK Local Government', Unpublished PhD thesis.

Chapter 7: The Psyche and Leadership
Ford, Jackie and Harding, Nancy. Leadership Theory: A Promise of Happiness and Goodness or a Threat of Sado-Machochism? Paper presented at Academy of Management Conference, Philadelphia, August 2007, and submitted to Organization Studies September 2007.

Part I Constructions

Opening Notes

This book aims to

1. develop a way of thinking about leadership which will allow those charged with the task of being leaders to reflect upon how they are changed by taking on that very task;
2. offer managers and leaders a language and a set of ideas they may not previously have come across, so as to facilitate their reflection upon how they are treated when they are at work;
3. make post-structuralist ideas accessible to readers new to post-structuralism through careful attention to the language we use, but without compromising the integrity of the theories themselves. We have attempted to explain the complicated terminology used in post-structural theories in ways that make it interesting and relevant to a broader audience than those accustomed to reading the often-convoluted language of post-structuralist theory. Post-structuralist theory offers a way of thinking that may be hugely insightful for people who are exploring how to become leaders and who may perhaps feel some uncertainty about the whole endeavour but may not know how to articulate those feelings. This book aims to provide that language. At the same time we do not wish to compromise the power of the language used in post-structuralist texts, for reasons that become self-explanatory as the chapters proceed;
4. contribute to the rather small body of critical work on leadership.

Leadership is lauded as the contemporary, superior successor to management. Management, with its aura of failed expectations, is regarded as belonging to a past century; leadership promises a bright new tomorrow. Publications on leadership, both academic and popular, are growing exponentially. Large proportions of managers in the UK, USA and other countries are studying university degree programmes in leadership, attending leadership training courses and are, in other ways, being prepared to adopt the mantle and identity of leader. There is a presumption that this outpouring of publications and the investment in training will produce persons with the skills and characters of leaders, able to guide organisations through the turmoil of the twenty-first-century global market. The theory underpinning this appears to be straightforward: there is this thing called 'leadership', but it is in short supply. Through identifying what good leadership *is*, education and training courses can help those charged with the task of leadership to develop their skills and practices, and organisations will benefit in various ways.

That is one perspective. Post-structuralist theories which have influenced thinking in academia in the arts, humanities and social sciences, and in the cultural world in films, novels and other forms of art, suggest the outcome of all this activity may differ from that anticipated; indeed the very acts of writing or representation may be producing something. In the words of Gibson-Graham (1996) who draws upon this form of post-structuralist theorising, social representations have a performative effect, they are *constitutive* of the worlds they describe Gibson-Graham (1996, p. ix). In other words, representations bring things into being. Thus,

> When theorists depict patriarchy, or racism, or compulsory hetero-sexuality, or capitalist hegemony they are not only delineating a formation they hope to see destabilized or replaced. They are also generating a representation of the social world and endowing it with performative force. To the extent that this representation becomes influential it may contribute to the hegemony of a 'hegemonic formation' and it will undoubtedly influence people's ideas about the possibilities of difference and change, including the potential for successful political interventions.
>
> (Gibson-Graham, 1996, p. x)

More simply, when something is brought into being it can come to dominate the ways in which we think so that it seems as if there is no other way of being. Our stance in this book, which is informed throughout by post-structuralist theories, is to acknowledge the existence of this thing called 'leadership' but to argue that it has been brought into being through the very repetition of the word, that is, the performative effect of the repeated representations of the word in the huge number of texts published on leadership.

We use the word 'performative' often in this book. It tends to have two meanings. In management studies, critical or otherwise, it tends to refer to the search for knowledge about how to maximise output for minimum input (Fournier and Grey, 2000). In post-structuralist theory, however, it has a different meaning. It is found notably in the work of Judith Butler (1993) whose argument is that forms of authoritative speech perform certain actions that cause things to have an existence. In other words, it is through acts of speaking and writing that things come into existence. Sex and gender are the foci of Butler's most famous works. In these she critiques the dominant assumptions that both sex and gender are given (by biology) and unchangeable. Instead, she shows, following Foucault, that both sex and gender are achieved through discourses and the repeated performance, from minute to minute, of the actions that (per)form sex and gender. We will discuss the meaning of 'the performative' in more depth in later chapters in this book.

By the performative impact of *words* we are harking back to the theories of J. L. Austin who argued that language is not neutral, nor merely descriptive, but actively brings something into being. The most famous example is the marriage ceremony: by pronouncing two people husband and wife a married couple is brought into being. Austin's work has proved influential in post-structuralist theories, notably in the works of Jacques Derrida (1988) and Judith Butler (1990, 1993, 1997, 2004), whose writings inform much of what follows in this book.

In post-structuralist perspectives that build on the performative effect of language, there is no such thing as a passive reading of a text or looking at a film: the 'gaze' is actively engaged both in interpreting the text (and thus the reader becomes part of the text) and in the production of the self, or subjectivity, through the very act of looking (Fuery and Mansfield, 2000). Thus reader and text are caught up in one another— the text confers subjectivity (Silverman, 1988; Harding, 2003).

We are dealing in this book with a topic that has a remarkable number of texts devoted to its study and dissemination, so our concern is partly with the impact of these innumerable texts upon readers. It is commonly assumed that readers of leadership books will learn about leadership and perhaps they will be inspired to become leaders and carry out the tasks of leadership, using the information they have been given. In post-structuralist terms far more happens between reader and text. Each reader will interpret a text differently from any other reader, as they will bring with them to the reading their own unique histories, their own cultures, backgrounds, educational experiences, etc. Further, the texts will work on the readers in different, but active ways—through the reading each reader will be somehow changed. The argument here is that texts are located within discourses, and discourses have a *performative* impact (Butler, 1993, 1997a, 1997b).

Discourses govern what is sayable and what can therefore be thought. They do not work in a straightforward way: it cannot be said that because there is a word 'leader' leaders can therefore exist. Just because people read about leadership does not mean the texts construct them as leaders. Rather, discourses intersect, interweave, inform each other, so the term 'leader' will be informed by overlapping discourses: the meaning of what appears to be such an easily apprehended term as 'leader', therefore, becomes so complex and so elusive that it always slips out of our grasp. How texts on leadership work on readers then, that is, how they construct the subject as leader, must be in ways that are utterly convoluted and complex. The one thing that is certain is that the assumptions in mainstream theory of a straightforward transmission between text (or training course) and reader (or student) is misplaced. By 'mainstream' we mean theories and perspectives that are devoted to finding ways of making organisations more efficient and effective. Our perspective is one that has a political intent and is regarded as 'critical', that is, it is concerned with exploring organisations as places in which people work, the lives they live there, the oppressive nature of work, how organisation is 'achieved', etc.

Now, it could be that in this book we are inevitably doing the same: constituting something called 'leadership', albeit that our intent is to destabilise. As noted above, our aims in writing this book are to offer an alternative way of thinking about leadership which will allow those charged with the task of being leaders to reflect upon how they are changed by taking on that very task. We are offering leaders a language or set of ideas many may not previously have come across, one which we hope will facilitate their reflection upon how they are treated when they are at work. The language used by many post-structuralist theorists is complex, deliberately so in the works of such theorists as Derrida, Lacan and Butler, who wish to slow down our reading and make us think about what it is that we are absorbing from the text. In this book we try to explain the more complicated or unusual terms we use. Our aim in doing this is to make powerful ideas accessible to readers new to such ways of thinking, reading and writing.

We are, furthermore, drawing upon a range of studies into leadership that we three authors have undertaken, individually and jointly, over the last ten years. Much current research into leadership is located in a very narrow perspective, and is based on large, quantitative surveys which are uncritical and can, at best, report statistical information. Although statistics can be extremely useful they tell us little about people's subjective experiences nor about their beliefs and their ideas. As leadership's focus is very much upon subjectively located interactions, there is a need for studies that tell us something about the subjective and the personal, about ideas and beliefs, about how people talk and dream about leadership, the stories and narratives they construct in their talking and dreaming, etc. Qualitative research allows us to explore something about these things. The studies we draw upon are based upon work we have carried out at different times and for different purposes over the years, but the interview transcripts and observations we made in each study seemed, when we examined our group data banks, to tell us more than they had as discrete studies. We have interviews with chief executives talking about their leadership roles; a mixed method study of 30 UK organisations into leadership development; an in-depth analysis of an organisation which had carried out an intensive leadership development programme; an autoethnographic study of working as leadership trainers and, in addition, two chapters based on an analysis of written texts. We give brief information about the studies drawn upon in each chapter.

In Part II of this book we will explore critically some of the complexities of the formation of the identity of 'leader'. Part I lays the foundations for that analysis through firstly, in Chapter 1, setting out what is contained in what we are calling 'mainstream theory'. This is a summary of the history of thinking about leadership, and the phenomenal amount of publications on the subject. The exploration of the literature on leadership in Chapter 1 shows how this body of writing constructs a homogeneous model of leadership despite its uncertainty as to what leadership is. It develops what we call 'a mainstream theory of leadership'. It shows how organisations are adapting this theory through the production of competences or sets of behaviours in leadership. Through developing a critique of this mainstream model the chapter begins to complicate the concept of leadership. Chapter 2 introduces post-structuralist theory by using a Derridean-based analysis to explore how chief executives discuss leadership, while Chapter 3 continues that exploration through analysing how the idea of 'the hero' informs their talk about themselves. Chapter 4 turns to training courses in leadership to develop a theory of what happens when people participate in leadership training courses.

The four chapters in Part I therefore explore how the identity of 'the leader' is constructed. This opens the way for the three chapters of Part II, which turn a more critical eye upon this thing, 'the leader', and the negative aspects of its construction.

1
Texts

The surfeit of publications on leadership

An average of ten articles a day were published on leadership in the 1990s, a figure that had doubled from the five per day of the 1980s (Grint, 2000). The continuing emphasis upon leadership in the noughties suggests that the rate of output will not have decreased. It may, indeed, have continued to rise; for organisations around the world, in the public and private sectors, have been searching for that elusive something that will ensure their survival in what is portrayed as the fierce competitive environment of a globalised economy. Excellent leadership is promoted as a vital element in this Darwinian struggle, and there is governmental support for and advocacy of good organisational leadership. In Britain, for example, a government disappointed in the failure of the policy of investing heavily in the managerialisation of the public sector in the 1980s and 1990s has advocated leadership as the means by which it is now trying to achieve the holy grail of efficient and effective public sector organisations. It has, among other things, established a Council for Excellence in Management and Leadership, which, since its founding in April 2000, has been charged with the task of developing a strategy 'to ensure that the UK has the managers and leaders of the future to match the best in the world' (Council for Excellence, 2002, p. 1). We therefore have the classic demand and supply loop beloved of economists: a demand for leadership met by a supply of literature which aims to support developments which will increase the supply of that particular commodity. Training courses, of course, follow.

This vast literature has been summarised, *ad infinitum*, by each author intending to show how his/her paper or book makes a major advance in the understanding of leadership. We are not critical about or cynical towards these aims, for this is what academics, management consultants and training organisations must do: show how they offer something unique that takes forward thinking in their field. In this chapter, we will briefly summarise some of these many summaries. Our intention, though, is not to offer a Major New Way of Thinking About Leadership. Our concern is with the performative effect of this literature, that is, with what it brings into being by the very fact of its being written and read.

Our intention, therefore, is to offer not a thorough review of the literature on leadership in this chapter but instead to explore the theory that underpins the dominant models of leadership and, through the rest of the book, analyse the performative effect of this model. Our approach comes from within a post-structuralist stance which argues that reading, writing and talking are not innocent activities but are actively productive. By this we mean that the very act of reading, writing and talking influences the reader, enters his/her psyche, and brings about changes that, however tiny, contribute to the self who puts down the book and continues practising in the world. Training courses, as we will discuss in Chapter 4, have as their explicit aim a change in the practices of those attending: our approach suggests these changes may be in ways that are unanticipated, perhaps unintended, but never neutral.

What summaries of the leadership literature show is how homogeneous it is; how the thousands of authors draw upon but a single epistemological position that brooks no alternative perspective on how the world is experienced or, in the terms we use in this book, constructed. Two common threads running through this literature are a fruitless search for a definition of leadership and a determination to advocate something that appears to be beyond definition. Now, anyone who has the most fleeting of acquaintanceship with post-structuralist thinking (and indeed many who haven't) will find this absence of definition intriguing: leadership, it would appear, is an 'empty signifier' (Laclau, 1996), that is, it is a term that is not attached to anything in the way a word such as 'table', to use an example, is attached to that thing with a flat surface supported by legs, often made of wood, and on which we rest crockery, papers, etc. An empty signifier is, in other words, a signifier without a signified (Laclau, 1996, p. 36). Empty signifiers are things which cannot be realised, that is, cannot come into being (p. 39) and therefore are impossible objects (p. 40), albeit ones that may be central to a system.

The word 'leadership' thus has a politically significant perfo⌐ effect, if it is an object whose existence is impossible but which is cen ╷ to that discourse of which it is a part. What that performative effect may be, what the discussions of leadership bring into being and what its political significance may be is the exploration we undertake in this book. In doing this, our aim is perhaps an emancipatory one: to provide people who are charged with the task of leadership with a language and with ideas to help them think through *not* how to be good leaders, but instead to look at the demands that have been placed on them and the ways in which those demands may be influencing who they are, as individuals, as subjects, as people involved in the on-going process of constructing the persons who turn up at the workplace each morning.

But to understand the performative effect of the literature we have first to understand what it is which is discussed in that very literature. As noted above, our intention here is to give only a brief summary of how leadership has been approached and understood, a summary sufficient only to support the later arguments of this book. Major reviews of the literature have been undertaken most adroitly by writers such as Stogdill (1974); Bennis (1989); Bass (1990); Goethals, Sorenson and Burns (2004); House et al. (2004); and van Maurik (2001), who have produced a distillation of the insights of a number of influential theorists, gurus and practitioners. We would refer readers who wish to know more to those texts. What we draw from our reading of the literature are the common themes of a search for a definition, a search for an ideal model for implementing leadership and prescriptions as to what characteristics the ideal leader should possess or practise.

So, what then is leadership?

Leadership is classically defined as a process of influencing the activities of an organised group in its efforts towards goal setting and goal achievement (Stogdill, 1950). That classical statement belies a history of fruitless searching for a meaningful definition of leadership. For example, surveying the already extensive literature on leadership, in 1959, Warren Bennis noted that

> always it seems, the concept of leadership eludes us or turns up in another form to taunt us again with its slipperiness and complexity. So, we have invented an endless proliferation of terms to deal with it . . . and still the concept is not sufficiently defined.

(p. 259)

...had reviewed more than 5000 published works on ...d do no more than concur with Bennis's conclusion. ...Bennis, now writing with Nanus, could conclude

...cademic analysis have given us more than 350 defini- ...lership. Literally thousands of empirical investigations of leaders ... /e been conducted in the last 75 years alone, but no clear and unequivocal understanding exists as to what distinguishes leaders from non-leaders and, perhaps more importantly, what distinguishes effective leaders from ineffective leaders.

(Bennis and Nanus, 1985, p. 4)

In the twenty-first century, in a study we will draw on later in this book, Alimo-Metcalfe et al. looked at how this was reflected in the workplace and, in exploring 30 UK-based organisations, found more definitions than organisations, a situation that mimicked the literature. They concluded that leadership is a 'woolly concept' which

is often used as rhetoric and without any significant meaning. The word 'leader' is often a synonym for the word 'manager', but it has become a label that is fashionable and which suggests that the individual is somehow a very special person.

(Alimo-Metcalfe et al., 2000, p. 15)

Still, writers continue to search for the one true definition of leadership (Easterby-Smith et al., 1991), seeking it in much the same way as natural scientists search for a planet, a previously unknown life form or the remains of an ancient civilisation. The reasoning here is that it is known to exist—it is only inadequate tools that prevent our discovering it. This positivist approach, one that emerges out of the physical sciences and is common to much research into organisations (Boje et al. 2001), is also found in the history of theorising about leadership.

A historiography of writing and thinking about leadership

We have called this section a historiography rather than a history for we are summarising the history of writing about leadership. This history is one of categorisation, whereby later generations of writers seek to carve an order out of the maelstrom of ideas circulating in texts on leadership. Any texts that do not conform to later categories disappear from view. Categorisation, however, also has a performative effect, as Foucault notes in *The Order of Things* (1970). He quotes in the Preface (p. xvi) the list from Borges taken from a Chinese encyclopaedia. This list categorises animals as follows: '(a) belonging to the Emperor, (b) embalmed, (c) tame, (d) sucking pigs, (e) sirens, (f) fabulous, (g) stray dogs, (h) included in the present classification, (i) frenzied, (j) innumerable, (k) drawn with a very fine camelhair brush, (l) *et cetera*, (m) having just broken the water pitcher, (n) that from a very long way off look like flies'. Foucault uses this list a few pages later to pose a question: 'When we establish a considered classification, when we say that a cat and a dog resemble each other less than two greyhounds do, even if both are tame or embalmed, even if both are frenzied, even if both have just broken the water pitcher, what is the ground on which we are able to establish the validity of this classification with complete certainty?' (p. xxi). There is, he argues, no such ground; rather there are codes of a culture which allow the ordering of things and disallow other possible orderings.

We could cite here many hundreds of papers on leadership we have read over the years, but it would be to no good purpose for it is a task that has been done before many times (see the references listed above for good examples of summaries of the literature). Instead, we are restricting our analysis largely to the summaries in Bass (1990), Bryman (1992), Chemers and Ayman (1993), Fulop and Linstead (1999, 2004), Northouse (2001), Wright (1996) and Yukl (1994). They have contributed, in various ways, to that categorisation Foucault talks about, that is, they have imposed an order which dictates what can and cannot be said and what shall be included and what omitted. Their summaries suggest a specific history of thinking about leadership, one which involves a teleological journey, that is, the nirvana of the perfect understanding of leadership will be achieved after striving down a highway pitted with the potholes of imperfect theorising, each failed step offering something that will eventually take us to our journey's end at the Inn of Full Knowledge.

The journey can be summarised thus: leadership theory emerged in the trait theory of leadership which had flaws that were tackled by explorations of leadership behaviours, but the weaknesses in this approach, once identified, led to an understanding of the necessity of gaining better understanding through analysis of leadership situations. Eventually the fruitlessness of such approaches was recognised, and this led to the emergence of theories of transformational and charismatic leadership, to guru theory discourses of leadership and most recently to notions of post-heroic leadership and the leader as servant (albeit that Robert Greenleaf (1997) was writing on this topic in the 1970s). We will now summarise what the literature says about each of these approaches and what came to be regarded as its flaws and weaknesses, necessitating the emergence of a stronger body of theory which, in its turn, has to be put behind us.

The *trait approach*, particularly prevalent in the 1930s and 1940s but still influential, assumed one is born rather than becomes a leader, for the leader was seen to have certain innate personal attributes. This 'Great Man' approach sought to learn from studying such heroic historical figures as Churchill, Gandhi and Wellington. Research focused upon the discovery of a set of traits possessed by all great men. The search proved fruitless (Yukl 1994; Fulop et al., 1999, 2004; Grint 1997, 2000) for there was difficulty both in finding traits common to these great leaders and in comparing them with the traits of organisational leaders, so researchers turned their attention to discovering how leaders *act*, rather than what they *are*. The focus upon leadership *behaviour* sought to isolate essential leadership qualities in those who had achieved positions of power and influence through their behaviours rather than through anything intrinsic within themselves.

Leadership, in this period, became regarded as something that can be cultivated and modified. Early behavioural studies sought answers to questions such as whether autocratic or democratic behavioural styles led to the most effective leadership outcomes. Motivation theory was used in later studies, such as McGregor's work—familiar to generations of management students—to try to establish how a leader's style could influence organisational success. Other studies considered task accomplishment and concern for subordinates, most famously in the Ohio State and Michigan studies (Northouse, 2001). The most recent example of such research is that of 'participative leadership', which is primarily concerned with power sharing and empowerment of followers.

Such behavioural approaches were and are critiqued for analysing the leader in isolation from the context or situation within which s/he works. The assumption that an understanding of context is vital to understanding leadership research led to explorations into the significance of contextual factors such as the environment, the work performed and the characteristics of followers. This *contingency* approach to leadership examines the situational variables that moderate the effectiveness of different types of leadership. In opposing notions of leadership as an essential quality held by certain individuals and not by others, or of leadership as a set of behaviours that can be learned and applied to any situation, the contingency approach superseded these earlier notions of leadership. Contingency approaches to leadership adopt one of two perspectives. In one, managerial behaviour is treated as a dependent variable with managerial/leader activities regarded as influenced by aspects of the situation such as type of organisation or managerial position. The other seeks to pinpoint aspects of the situation that relate leader behaviours to leadership effectiveness, on the assumption that there will be one best style of leadership for a given situation. This differs markedly from those earlier (and many later) approaches which presumed one optimal style irrespective of the situation.

Contingency approaches had intuitive appeal but were critiqued for ignoring power and organisational politics, lack of consistency between studies in the choice of variables or contingency factors, poor justification of the variables chosen for study and inadequate accounting for a range of factors or dimensions. The core assumption within such studies was that in any given situation it is possible to pinpoint a best leadership style and approach (Fulop et al., 1999).

Presumptions of the importance of leadership style within the contingency approach contributed to the next major development in leadership theory, towards transformational leadership, where, for perhaps the first time, the perceptions and attributions of 'followers' are deemed to be significant. The presumption here is that the effectiveness of a leader can be explained in terms of his or her influence on the way followers view themselves and interpret events. Research focuses on how followers regard leaders and what they define as good or poor leadership style, with the unstated assumption that what followers define as good leadership is something which motivates them to work more efficiently and effectively. The transformational leader advocated in this approach appears to have an extreme, almost evangelical and highly charismatic role. S/he 'virtually unaided has the vision to steer the organisation through turbulent changes and crises' (Fulop et al., 2004,p. 340). This approach distinguishes between leadership and management as independent activities, a distinction which can be traced to Zaleznik (1997) and Kotter (1990).

Management, in this perspective, is concerned with the routine running of organisations, and leadership is concerned with strategic issues, including, for example, an organisation's mission, identity and development. The essential difference between leadership and management lies in the orientation to organisational change (Bryman, 1996). This distinction indirectly reaffirms the trait theory of leadership and elevates, again, the 'Great Man' model (Fulop et al., 2004; Tourish and Pinnington, 2002).

Meanwhile, as transformational leadership theories gained in influence in the 1980s and 1990s, 'guru' theories of leadership came to prominence. The 'guru', who may be a hero-manager, an academic or a management consultant but is always regarded as elite (Huczynski, 1993), is often a major attraction on the management conference circuit. Gurus provide comments on management and at the same time attempt to shape and reshape forms and practices of management. Huczynski (1993, p. 38) argues that they do this through offering 'a rag-bag of prescriptions which include the importance of innovation, more teamwork, more empowerment of the individual, more employee participation, fewer levels of hierarchy and less bureaucratization'. Guru theory is predicated upon elaborate claims of being able to transform an organisation, its people and its structures to move it to a different (higher) level of achievement and success through an almost supernatural transformation of the factors that comprise the organisation.

Guru ideas are highly influential among those charged with providing leadership within organisations. Indeed, it has been argued that gurus have provided senior executives with a sense of certainty and direction, by defining the managerial role in terms of the executive's responsibility for managing meaning for their employees, 'for creating employees' moral universe' (Clark and Salaman, 1998, 153). Thus, the gurus' role and their appeal to organisational leaders is the allocation of a central, heroic status to the manager—the focus is very much on the manager as corporate leader, as organisational redeemer. The model is one of an organisational hero, who would endow management with a high-status leadership role in transforming the organisation. The connotations with biblical imagery and prophet-like behaviours are not lost on critiques of the guru industry (see, for example, Clark and Salaman, 1996, 1998; Collins, 2000; Jackson, 1999; Tourish and Pinnington, 2002).

Finally, something called post-heroic leadership grew in popularity during the 1990s, although its origins are to be found in Bradford and Cohen's work in the early 1980s (Fulop et al., 2004). This model of leadership argues that everyone working in an organisation should be regarded as a leader. The focus on styles and contingencies of those who stand out for being remarkable, for having heroic qualities, should give way to this seemingly more democratic approach. The claim is that by giving voice to all people in an organisation, and through harnessing the collective intelligence of the workforce as part of a process of building new relationships within, across and outside the organisation, the organisation's efficiency and effectiveness will improve. The theory is not supported by evidence (Fulop et al., 1999; Fletcher and Kaeufer, 2003; Fletcher, 2004). Indeed, there is some evidence that leaders may be more prone than the general population to suffer from narcissism, which is defined as the most common behavioural condition of the late twentieth century (Downs, 1997; Fineman, 1993; Kets de Vries, 2006; Lasch, 1979). If this is the case then leaders would desire to make their organisation in their own image rather than support an image of themselves as the servants of their followers. (In Chapter 7 we will discuss a new model of leadership which, its proponents claim, will overcome the flaws found in all previous models.)

We have identified six stages on this teleological journey towards identifying the one true theory of leadership. Leadership theory has, it seems, come a long way. It started by focusing upon '*the* Great Man' and now focuses upon everyone within the organisation. These schools of thought can be further categorised into two distinct periods in which the 1980s is the dividing line (Alimo-Metcalfe, 2006, personal communication). In this further example of the urge to categorise, the earlier period is identified as a time when the focus was upon the trait, behavioural and contingency approaches. Here scholars analysed the logistical, communicational and social psychological tasks of leaders. The new leadership approach of the period since the 1980s sees leadership redefined as that which is concerned with the management of meaning (Smircich and Morgan, 1982) and symbolic action (Pfeffer, 1981). This 'new leadership approach' encompasses transformational, guru and post-heroic models and also other emerging models such as 'dispersed leadership' (Manz, and Sims, 1992) which argues that leadership can move between people at differing levels of the organizational hierarchy; 'super-leadership', which aims to develop leadership capacity in all individuals (Sims and Lorenzi, 1992); and 'real teams', where the leader is a group facilitator (Katzenbach and Smith, 1993). In this perspective, leaders have the task of defining organisational realities and persuading followers to believe in that definition. As Bryman notes, the leader (1996, p. 276, quoted by Alimo-Metcalfe, working paper) 'identifies for subordinates a sense of what is important—defining organizational reality for others. The leader gives a sense of direction and of purpose through the articulation of a compelling world-view'.

It is in this latter phase that organisations and governments have become interested in leadership. They have taken actions to improve the quality of leadership available (Alimo-Metcalfe and Lawler, 2002), including sending staff on training courses, as we will discuss in Chapter 4, but also in developing competences, as we will now explore.

Our analysis of competences leads to our offering the theory of leadership that will inform the rest of this book, that is, leadership as an identity or practice of the self.

The response of organisations

Chia (1996) warns that research can actively 'construct the very reality [it] is attempting to investigate' (p. 42). Briefly and somewhat simplistically for now, Chia's argument runs as follows. Organisations are extraordinarily complex things, made up every day through multitudes of interactions between dozens, hundreds, even thousands of employees who, as they construct the organisation simultaneously construct their own sense of themselves 'within' that organisation (Ford and Harding, 2003). Scholars interested in, say, decision making set out to study organisations, but they find this extraordinary confection, this thing called 'organisation', this accumulation of interactions, so complex they cannot describe it. What they have to do therefore is carve out a reality, to separate some of these multitudinous interactions from the rest and categorise and label them. By doing this they create something, in this example, the idea that something called 'decision making' takes place. Universities, notably business schools, then develop this idea and instruct students in how to make decisions. When later generations of researchers go to study organisations they, educated to expect decision making as a routine activity in organisations, seek for it and thus find it. Indeed, they meet people who have been educated into decision making and who will thus claim to be doing that thing, for if they do not do it then they are failing at their managerial tasks. This generation of researchers may then refine their notions of decision making and develop new theories to teach their students.

In other words, there is a dialectical relationship between organisations and academic studies of organisations. Academics study organisations and struggle to make sense of their complexity; organisational members study at universities; and management consultants make accessible the theories generated in academia, so organisations take up ideas generated by academics whose ideas originated in some of those very organisations.

Now, organisations have been faced with huge mountains of literature on leadership; they have hired management consultants or listened to gurus who have brought them the news about leadership; they have been told by the government that leadership is what is needed in the twenty-first century. Their response, as the Alimo-Metcalfe et al. study

(2000) showed, is to place the development of leaders near the top of their list of priorities for organisational development. To achieve their objectives they send managers on leadership training courses which promulgate some of the thinking in leadership theory. Another way in which organisations respond is to develop a list of the behaviours or competences expected of leaders. Aspiring leaders are to be trained in developing the relevant competence, and their success or otherwise can, in theory at least, be measured against the standards that have been set. Alimo-Metcalfe et al. (2000) provide two examples of private sector organisations in the UK which have done this. One had produced a booklet listing seven competences, namely,

- provides clarity about strategic direction,
- focuses on delivery,
- builds relationships,
- ensures commitment,
- develops self-awareness,
- possesses personal convictions and
- develops people.

This list, they point out, contains five competences that are concerned more with inter-personal skills and personal self-awareness, and so it is 'personal qualities' that distinguish leaders from managers in this organisation. The second organisation had developed 'standards of leadership' based on its values and business results, which include:

- people development,
- customers,
- innovation,
- inter-dependent partnership and
- mastery of complex environments.

Within these standards there is a series of competences, that is, an 'operations competency model'.

In the public sector meanwhile, Britain's National Health Service (NHS) has established a common set of NHS leadership qualities designed to 'set the standards for outstanding leadership in the NHS ... which can be used to assess both individual and organisational leadership capacity and capability' (DH, 2002, 1). This set of standards presents 15 qualities arranged within three clusters—*Personal Qualities*, which include such virtues as self-belief, self-awareness and personal integrity; *Setting Direction*, which incorporates political astuteness, drive and intellectual flexibility; and *Delivering the Service*, which comprises leading change and empowerment, holding to account and effective and strategic influencing.

Such responses show that organisations are developing a working theory of leadership which combines aspects of the models summarised above. This theory is that there are certain characteristics of good leadership, and managers may become leaders through taking on these characteristics (which can be acquired through training or other means) and behaving in certain, prescribed ways. Success will be determined, at least in part, by factors intrinsic to the individual leader, but the right person can acquire other necessary, listed traits. There is a recognition that the individual must influence his or her followers so that aspects of the 'new leadership' model are also incorporated; by demonstrating possession of the required competences, leaders will be able to influence followers.

Mangham and Pye (1991, cited in Watson 2001, p. 221) characterise this mechanistic type of competency approach as an assembly process to management development—'so much financial ability added to a bit of marketing and some strategic leadership together with some interpersonal skills and a hint of. . . .' In this, we suggest, they neglect the performative effect of the terms, and how they bring 'the leader' into being. Žižek (1989) has argued that even where people are cynical about a dominant ideology they become caught up in it, or rather it becomes caught up in them. His argument is that Marx's understanding of ideology, that people do not know the ideology but practise it (e.g. in studying for a master's degree they do not realise that they are part of capitalism's imperative to increase profits), has been replaced in late modernism by knowledge of the ideology. Žižek states that the subject may be cynical about the ideology, but does not attempt to break free of it; instead s/he is cynical about it at the same time that s/he practises it. The result, in Žižek's carefully worked theory, is that some notions of belief inhere in the subject before practising leadership; so, even the cynical subject will already have some belief in the 'reality' of leadership. Once engaged in the activities of leadership, the prior beliefs are reinforced.

This leaves open the question of what is this 'leadership' that is believed in prior to practising. We will suggest in Chapter 3 that it is not necessarily leadership as defined in the lists of competences or in the other models referred to in academic studies which is believed in. Rather, it is the leader of the fairy stories of childhood, the leader in

Hollywood films (the pirate captain, the swashbuckler, etc.). Halberstam (1998), indeed, suggests that Satan, 'the original bad guy', continues to inform notions of what she refers to as white masculinity, in which we would include leaders and managers (Lee, Learmonth and Harding, 2008). In James Bond films, for example, 'epic masculinity' reflects and constitutes subordinate forms of masculinity. Epic masculinity (and thus leadership?) 'depends not only absolutely, as any Bond flick demonstrates, on a vast subterranean network of secret government groups, well-funded scientists, the army, and an endless supply of both beautiful bad babes and beautiful good babes, . . . it relies heavily on an immediately recognizable "bad guy". The "bad guy" is a standard generic feature of epic masculinity narratives: think only of *Paradise Lost* and its eschatological separation between God and Devil; Satan, if you like, is the original bad guy' (Halberstam, 1998, p. 4). By this she means that the fight between good and evil found in the Bible informs numerous texts. We would suggest that leadership texts and visions are informed by this battle between 'the good hero' and its binary opposite, the 'dastardly villain'. But that is to anticipate the arguments to come. In other words, the manager who is given a list of competences and told to participate in a training course on leadership may be cynical (or not) about the project, but will already believe in leadership because of its ubiquitous appearance, in various manifestations, throughout recorded history.

Furthermore, the power of the performative works beyond a conscious level of knowing—it penetrates the psyche and allows for the construction of identity or a self. This leads us to our next observation regarding the list of competences. A closer analysis of this list of competences suggests that managers can no longer be charged with the task of *doing* the leadership role and undertaking leadership practices: they must incorporate leadership into the very sense of their selves. This is because the list of competences refers not solely to tasks or traits that a person just happens to possess, but also to the knowledge about the self and a commitment to developing a 'better self', one who is a good leader. Leadership discourses are very much concerned with changing the self so as to become this good leader. In being urged to develop self-awareness, the subject is required to analyse the self as if the self were an object that can be looked at, assessed and then worked on so as to change it. In this way the subject, the self that has subjectivity, must look at itself as a leader, so itself as leader becomes an object for analysis. The subject must stand outside itself and look at its leaderly self as if it were another person. If this object does not possess the relevant 'personal convictions', then they can be practised until, as Žižek observes, they become part of the self. The subject (the leader) regarding the object (the self) and assessing its levels of self-belief, political astuteness, drive, influence on others, etc, must discover ways of developing these personal qualities, qualities that emanate as much from the psyche as from the body or the mind, and practise them until s/he has absorbed them into her/himself.

The manager charged with the task of leadership *therefore has to become a different self.* The manager has to absorb leadership into his/her very identity. Where previously (in the era of 'old paradigm' leadership studies) managers and administrators were subjects who did the tasks of management and administration, now they must become subjects who are leaders. The major task they must undertake is the work on the self: the development of the self as leader. The texts on leadership presume that once they have done this, 'followers' will follow them without demur.

This, then, is our reading of the multitudinous texts on leadership. It is no longer sufficient to be a person who does leadership; now the entire person must become 'the leader'. The person who is the manager must become colonised by 'the leader': the whole self must become the leader through working on the self to develop the relevant characteristics and eliminate anything antithetical to this identity. It is our task throughout the rest of this book to explore how the manager accomplishes the identity of the leader through working on the self so that there is no distinction between self and leader. In this, we are contributing to a body of writing that can be called 'critical leadership studies'. We will now summarise that literature so as to provide the context for what follows. This will lead to an outline of some of the issues which our post-structuralist theory requires that we, and our readers, keep in mind as we explore the construction of the leader in later chapters.

Writers writing critically about leadership

Although notions of leadership are generally treated uncritically, as a 'catch-all and panacea' (Storey, 2004 p. 5), a small proportion of the papers published on leadership attempt to analyse the concept through a more critical lens. There is increasing disquiet among commentators regarding the narrowness of the epistemological perspective in which leadership research is located, in that little research is undertaken that does not have a positivist approach and use quantitative research methods which gather data largely through laboratory—or questionnaire-based studies (Bryman, 2004; Butterfield and Grinnell, 1999). More generally, the claim to a disinterested (objective) pursuit of truth made by positivist research has been fundamentally challenged: indeed, the impossibility of any research being utterly objective or 'untainted' by the subjectivity of the researcher, is widely argued (e.g. Crotty, 1998; Denzin and Lincoln, 1998; Gergen, 1985, 1991, 1999).

The more recent emphasis upon context and interpersonal relationships requires contextually specific, qualitative studies, for laboratory- and questionnaire-based research denies individual difference and ignores context. The valorisation of quantitative methods in leadership research, however, means that research undertaken is inadequate (Alvesson, 2002; Alvesson and Sveningsson, 2003; Fletcher, 2004). As Alvesson (2002) has noted, a cultural understanding of leadership requires an understanding of local meaning. If leadership can be defined, as he argues, as 'about influencing the construction of reality—the ideas, beliefs and interpretations of what and how things can and should be done' (Alvesson, 2002, p. 114), then a socially and contextually specific method of research is required, not methods that ignore the local or subordinate it beneath the general.

A further charge is made that leadership researchers, in attempting to develop theories or generalise from data, mistake or disguise domestic theories as universal theories (Adler, 1999). Most commonly, US-based leadership models and behaviours are generalised to the rest of the world as if the US were culture-free. If it is presumed that the highly individualistic US culture is unique to that country, then so may US management and leadership practices differ from those in most other areas of the world (Adler, 1999). Indeed, UK-based research suggests that the distant heroic model of leadership so favoured in contemporary US writing does not fit the cultural contexts of the UK (Alimo-Metcalfe, 1998; Alimo-Metcalfe and Alban-Metcalfe, 2001).

Furthermore, leadership research has tended to focus upon the director/chief executive role. The result is a leader portrayed as a superior being uninfluenced by subordinates and responsible to no manager or leader. This is seen as a major shortcoming of these studies, as the vast majority of managers are part of a hierarchy and so are themselves subordinates to some at the very same time that they are senior to others (Alvesson, 2002; Fournier and Grey, 2000; Smircich and Morgan, 1982; Watson, 1994, 2001).

Such criticisms, which generally concern the poverty of research methods and inadequate understanding of leadership, may not necessarily be critical in the sense used in this book, that is, one that adopts an emancipatory political stance aiming to eradicate subordination, especially as it occurs in the workplace (Fournier and Grey, 2000).

Rather, much of this type of critique emerges from a frustration about current standards of leadership and the need to undertake better research so as to improve the quality of leaders.

The critics whose works we now turn to argue differently: that high quality research which pays attention to situations, events, institutions, ideas, social practices and processes may, through facilitating more subtle forms of control and assisting managerial abilities of suppression and exploitation, increase managerial power at the expense of employees' freedoms, rights, quality of working life, etc. Those critics who adopt an emancipatory perspective challenge the very existence of leadership (e.g. Alvesson and Sveningsson, 2003; Gemmill and Oakley, 1992; Sinclair, 2005; Halford and Leonard, 2001; Wood, 2005; Wood and Case, 2006; Collinson, 2006; Ford and Lawler, 2007). Such authors, who are very much in the minority, argue that mainstream management writers approach the study of leadership from the unquestioned presupposition that leaders are essential for the effective functioning of an organisation. They maintain that this presupposition is a natural concomitant of the functionalism inherent in the positivist epistemological position of the majority of leadership research.

Leadership, critical writers argue, is reified and appears to take on an objective existence. In other words, notwithstanding the absence of definition, mainstream researchers and practitioners assume that because there is a word 'leader' (or 'leadership'), there must be an independent objective reality described or denoted by such a word. Such assumptions have serious implications, for if there are leaders then there must be followers who are dependent in various ways upon the leaders. In Gemmill and Oakley's words (1992, p. 114), this is 'a serious sign of social pathology, . . . a special case of an iatrogenic social myth that induces massive learned helplessness among members of a social system'. By 'learned helplessness' they mean an inability of people working within organisations to imagine or perceive viable alternatives; this leads to feelings of despair and a resistance to initiating any form of action. As social hopelessness and helplessness deepen, the requirement for a saviour (leader) or miraculous rescue (leadership) becomes more acute.

This childlike dependency basis of the leader myth is supported in Smircich and Morgan's (1982) writing, in which leadership is perceived as a process whereby followers give up their mindfulness to a leader or to leadership. As they state, 'leadership is realized in the process whereby one or more individuals succeeds in attempting to frame and define the reality of others' (p. 258). Here we can see that the positive valorisation placed on the definition of reality by mainstream leadership writers referred to above is seen in a diametrically opposite way by critical organisational theorists. They argue that leadership implies alienation, deskilling and reification of organisational forms and advocate experimentation with new paradigms and behaviours to discover more meaningful and constructive ways of relating and working together.

Our sympathies lie with these critical thinkers, and this book intends not only to contribute to such a critique but also to go beyond it, for we are concerned that too little is yet known about the deleterious impact of this turn to leadership upon those given the task of becoming leaders and those who must therefore be followers.

Our stance commences with a questioning of the ontological status of leadership, that is, what form of existence, if any, does it have? In many ways critics have to presume that leadership exists in order to be critical about it—if it did not exist they could not criticise it, for there would be the ridiculous situation of: this thing does not exist but I am going to argue against it anyway. However, a post-structuralist stance presumes that leadership can 'exist' through the performativity of the term, that is, the naming of something can bring about the very existence of that which is named. This turns the traditional relationship between object and name on its head: rather than a thing existing and being given a name, the word facilitates the coming into being of the object. Eve K. Sedgwick illustrates this well. She has shown, influentially, how the word 'homosexual' entered the lexicon in the last third of the nineteenth century and led to a new form of 'world-mapping'

> by which every given person, just as he or she was necessarily assignable to a male or a female gender, was now considered necessarily assignable as well to a homo- or a hetero-sexuality, a binarized identity that was full of implications, however, confusing, for even the ostensibly least sexual aspects of personal existence.
>
> (Sedgwick, 1991, p. 2)

We follow this perspective as we explore the term 'leadership' and the 'organisation-mapping' it engenders.

A post-structuralist approach does not just presume the performative power of a term but analyses the manner by which interactions between language and subjects produce the social world. For example, Collinson (2006) explores the relationships between leader and follower as a set of dialectical interactions, the results of which will, he claims, allow a better understanding of how leader and follower are co-produced, that is, how each is dependent upon the other for its existence as 'leader' or 'follower'. He identifies three inter-related 'dialectics' for analysis: control and resistance, dissent and consent, and men and women. In each pair, the two terms are not just in opposition to each other but react to and are thus changed by the other; moreover, they depend upon each other for their meaning. Furthermore, there is a dialectical relationship between the three pairs so that, for example, gender interactions influence and are influenced by control/resistance. Collinson brings power into the analysis too. He thus shows that leader and follower are fluid, dynamic identities, always in flux, always in relation to each other, always, in more vernacular terms, feeding off each other. His arguments are thus subtle and we will find echoes of it when we use Hegel's master/slave dialectic, and its development in the works of Judith Butler and Jessica Benjamin, to explore the constructions of leader and follower.

In short, post-structuralist analyses of the body of literature on, and the development of, leadership, are concerned with the following:

(a) *Everything* is a construction, that is, comes into being or is apprehended only through language. A post-structuralist stance thus requires that the terms 'leader' and 'follower' are examined to find out how they are constructed.

(b) Where an 'empty signifier' is in action, a metaphysical presence may haunt writing and thinking about this somewhat imaginary thing. In other words, an idea of what this object is informs thinking and writing. This imaginary object informs the description of that which is discussed, described, analysed and written about: it is thus an imaginary being who is at the centre of the theories about leadership. The writer, in other words, imagines a construct—the leader—and gives it certain characteristics and an identity that make it appear real. This imagined object is the one who is analysed and who informs the writing. By such means, the imaginary object (here, the leader) is given the appearance of subjectivity and thus becomes ever more 'real'. In other words, having taken for granted that such a thing as a 'leader' exists, writers, albeit unknowingly, have an imaginary notion of what this person will be like and it is that person who is analysed and written about. The questions arise, then, of what this imaginary being is like and what texts have influenced its construction.

(c) It follows that there is no homogeneous entity such as 'leader' and 'follower', for what exists are complex human beings, subjects who bring with them to their work a plentiful number of intersecting identities which each inform the other. In the most simple of terms, in large organisations no one is free of a superior, even though that may be the shareholders (in the case of private organisations) or the government (in the case of public sector organisation) who provide some form of leadership. All leaders are therefore also followers. Indeed, a leader cannot be a leader without followers, and vice versa, so each is dependent upon the other for its existence. The distinction between the two is fallacious. The very logic of the dialectic is that there can be no pristine identity, untouched by interactions with others: one's very existence is predicated upon such interactions. Post-structuralism therefore shows how naively simplistic mainstream literature's views on leadership are.

(d) Terms have performative effects and so it is necessary to understand how that which is spoken of, in our case leadership, brings into being that which is discussed. Many texts and organisational practices have merely replaced the term 'manager'with the term 'leader', but post-structuralist perspectives show that this is no 'mere' substitution, no mere sleight of hand or semantic inflation, but one that can bring about the construction of different identities (Burrell, 1992). What these are, that is, what is brought into existence through re-labelling managers as leaders and workers as followers, is the subject of this book. It is sufficient to note here that semantic inflation can bring about, in this case, the demise of entities called managers and their replacement by entities called leaders. A similar example was seen in Britain's National Health Services in the 1980s, when administrators were replaced by managers. Very few actual *people* changed their jobs: administrators became managers through semantic changes which effected the ways in which the NHS was and is organised (Learmonth, 2005).

(e) Finally, any writer who adopts a post-structuralist stance must explore the academic self that informs and is constructed through the writing, that is, how do I (this particular individual writing these words) infect my writing and who do I become as a result of doing this writing? It is not sufficient to be merely reflexive (Probyn, 1993): it is vital to know what has made possible the self who is doing the reflexive thinking. Probyn's (1993) arguments arise from the turn to reflexivity in anthropology in the 1980s, during which time anthropologists realised how much of anthropological writing had been informed by the unthinking presumption of the superiority of the 'great white males' of the British Empire and the inferiority of all other beings. Indeed, as Said (1978) has shown, the superiority of one depends upon the (imagined) inferiority of the other. Probyn looked at how white, male anthropologists attempted to be reflexive and found them wanting, for in their attempts to be reflexive they, as had their predecessors, were using the Other to construct an understanding of themselves as superior. She calls therefore for an understanding of how 'the self as a theoretical movement into the text . . . carries with it the ontological traces of its local origins' (p. 80). Such a self would acknowledge 'the conditions of its possibility, of its very existence'. 'Quite simply', she writes, 'the sound of [the self's] "ontologicality" must be met with an analysis of the positivity of its materiality', that is, 'what had to be in place in order for this self to appear at all' (Probyn, 1993, p. 80). Wray-Bliss's (2002) somewhat similar reflections show how even thinkers committed to a politics of justice and freedom can slide into the appropriating of others' voices, perpetuating those very practices they aim to overturn.

Conclusion: On texts on leadership

Our reading of leadership theory is this. There is a vast body of literature on the subject, although the precise thing that is studied, written about and practised remains elusive. A history of the development of ideas has been carved out, which presents the development of knowledge about leadership in the form of a teleological journey from ignorance (due to inadequate assumptions underpinning research) and oppression (through ignoring followers) to knowledge (through improvements in the presumptions which underpin research) and respect (through taking the subordination out of followership). Research into leadership continues apace. There appears to be a consensus among writers on leadership and organisations as to its importance, its role within organisations. It is taken for granted that leadership exists, that it can be improved and that it has as its aim the maximising of efficiency and effectiveness of the organisation. The tasks the leader is to undertake can be listed, and these tasks now include the development of a self that is so much colonised by the model of leadership that there is no distinction between the self and the leader. Where leadership used to be a series of tasks or characteristics, it is now an *identity*. Our reading of the texts on leadership leads us to define leadership as

'a process of influencing the activities of an organised group in its efforts toward goal setting and goal achievement' (Stogdill, 1950) undertaken by persons known as leaders who have worked on themselves so that their very selves depend upon discourses of leadership, and they become the embodiment of the theory of leadership.

There is a small but growing critical literature on leadership, some of which is critical of how people are led by leaders, others which see leadership as part of the ever more subtle process of achieving control over employees and a small minority of which sees the very term 'leadership', and the writing and talking about it as constitutive of that which is discussed. This last perspective, located within post-structuralist theory, draws on a body of theory that has had a major influence across the arts, humanities and social sciences. In this book we are using this impressive heritage to explore leadership. We have suggested, in articulating our definition of leadership, that all the writing that has been done on leadership, and the ways in which organisations have taken up some of the ideas contained within that writing, has a performative impact, that is, it brings things, leaders, into being. Our argument, already hinted at above, is that the ways in which leadership or the identity of leader is achieved is not a straightforward, mechanistic process whereby a person is persuaded of the need for leadership, goes on courses and through practice becomes a leader. Rather, the subject takes on the identity of leader in ways that work through highways and byways not dreamt of in mainstream theoretical perspectives. As we explore in this book, the becoming of the leader involves the psyche, the memory, interactions between selves and texts, interactions with others, interactions between different aspects of the self, the local context, the geography, the culture. Leadership comes to the subject (who will be a leader) laden with the heroes of millennia of storytelling. It has a history. It is being redescribed in the current epoch.

This book has arisen from several studies we have undertaken, individually and as a team, in the last decade. We have returned to the data we have gathered over the years and explored them anew for this book. The studies have included the following:

- A study of 30 organisations across the public and private sector in Britain, which involved a quantitatively oriented questionnaire and qualitative interviews (Alimo-Metcalfe et al., 2000);
- A study of 18 chief executives in Britain's National Health Service which explored how language worked in the construction of executive's identities. Derridean methods of data analysis were developed and used in analysing the interview transcripts (Learmonth, 2003);

- A longitudinal study of the merger of two large hospital trusts in the north of England involving interviews undertaken while the merger was in progress and 18 months later (Ford and Harding, 2003, 2004);
- An auto-ethnographic study undertaken while delivering leadership training programmes (Ford and Harding, 2008);
- A study of middle and senior managers in local government following an intensive programme of leadership development in that organisation. This study aimed to explore how they took on the identity of leaders (Ford, 2007).

Each of these studies has been rewritten for this book, and in some cases the data have been analysed anew. Details of the research methods used are to be found in the original papers and theses.

We realised when we looked back at the decade of work incorporated in those studies that they contain a cumulative account that is lost as a result of their being distributed over a number of academic texts and across such a time span. In this book we have brought our various studies together into a coherent narrative that is intended to be far more than a collection of papers. Rather, we have re-analysed the data where this helped our current arguments and also rewritten each account so as to develop a thesis that provides ideas and a language for those charged with the task of becoming leaders, to help them think through the impact of that charge upon themselves.

The next part of this book will therefore explore how language works to construct the identity of 'the leader'. It opens, in Chapter 2, with an exploration of how chief executives talk about leadership. The aim of that chapter is to demonstrate the theory we have been outlining in this opening discussion, that is, how language constructs the objects of which it speaks. The approach used follows the theories of Jacques Derrida. Chapter 3 is designed to explore in more depth how language 'constructs that of which it speaks'. Its focus is upon the word 'hero' and how that single word inflects and informs our understanding of leadership and the ways in which we think about ourselves and thus construct our identities. The hero reappears again in Chapter 4, but this time in the context of leadership training programmes. In that chapter we show how various discourses (of 'the hero', of emotions, of the psyche) interact with each other in the construction of the self of the leader. Our aim in that chapter is to show that leadership is not a homogeneous identity, but one that is established through the interaction of numerous discourses.

We summarise the account we have written in those three chapters in 'Closing Notes', which contains the theory we have outlined in this exploration of the construction of the leader. That account shows how leadership contains within it so many positive connotations that its enthusiastic reception is unremarkable. However, that account tells us little of what it is like to be a leader in practice. In Chapter 2 we note that the positive always hides the negative, and it is the task of Part II of this book, consisting of three chapters, to tempt out from their hiding behind the rosy glow of leadership the dark things that make leadership painful and difficult for many people. Chapter 4 had already hinted at some of those, and in Chapter 5 we use queer theory to winkle out some of the norms that leaders must follow but can never attain. Chapter 6 draws on gender theory to explore the ways in which leaders are forced to confine themselves within a narrow range of possibilities of being selves—and we return once more, only in a different guise, to ideas that link leadership to heroism. The impossible demands thus made upon the psyche are discussed in Chapter 7. This section of the book is summarised and concluded in 'Closing Notes', which shows that the leader has an impossible task.

It is not sufficient to leave our readers with a language to help articulate the negative aspects of leadership that have been nagging away at many of them. The majority will not be able to throw away their jobs and start a new career elsewhere. We therefore conclude the book, in Chapter 8, with a discussion of ways of ameliorating the worst effects of the discourse of leadership. Indeed, we suggest that there are positive connotations of leadership that can and should be built upon. Our task in the closing section of this book is to explore the potential for a healthy and ethical leadership, one which acknowledges the humanity of the selves involved as leaders and followers.

2
Leadership as Performative: Or How the Words 'Leader' and 'Leadership' *Do* Things

This chapter's focus is upon how the words 'leader' and 'leadership' are performative, that is, how those two words construct, or make both leaders and leadership thinkable. We are examining chief executives in Britain's National Health Service (NHS) in this chapter, because the history of management and leadership in the NHS lends itself particularly well to this type of study.

The NHS was formed in 1948 through an act of Parliament which brought together the majority of pre-existing medical services into one nationalised organisation. This massive organisation was dominated by hospitals whose governance was largely of doctors, nurses and administrators. There were to be no people officially known as 'managers' for almost 40 years. In the 1980s the then Conservative government, anxious to reduce the ever-increasing costs of providing a national health service, brought in a businessman, Sir Roy Griffiths, to advise on ways of improving efficiency and effectiveness. The subsequent NHS Management Inquiry (1984) expressed consternation at the absence of management in the NHS. Administration, it seemed, was inadequate to the job and managers were duly brought in. By the turn of the millennium, the Labour government's 'discourse of modernization' (Newman, 2000, p. 45) included much reference to leadership as the way to achieving its social goals (Currie, Boyett and Suhomlinova, 2005), for management was deemed to have failed in its duty.

In many cases, the people who had been administrators took on the managerial roles, and the ex-administrators turned managers were, in turn, charged with becoming leaders.

As noted in Chapter 1, these sorts of changes in language are generally assumed to be merely an *expression* of the revolutionary transformation of organisations. Terms like leadership, management and administration appear, in that view, to be simply the names of different things in the world. However, what we will discuss in this chapter is how these words, *in themselves*, can be understood as discursive resources that have fuelled organisational change and, in so doing, have offered different possibilities for identities or selves. As Grey has observed:

> The ascription of the term 'management' to various kinds of activities is not a mere convenience but rather something which has certain effects. The use of words is not innocent, and in the case of management its use carries irrevocable implications and resonances which are associated with industrialism and modern Western forms of rationality and control.
>
> (1999, p. 577)

To emphasise, language in this perspective does not merely reflect reality but is actively engaged in the very constitution of reality. So this chapter will bring to attention the kind of things we *do* (with reality and to reality) when we deploy the words 'leader' and 'leadership'. When language makes certain things possible, it also makes other things impossible. In this case, language prevents our thinking of any other ways of organising how work is undertaken other than in a hierarchy governed by managers and, more latterly, leaders (Learmonth and Harding, 2004).

This chapter therefore follows work in the linguistic turn in organisational studies (Alvesson and Kärreman, 2000; Deetz, 2003), especially that which looks to Jacques Derrida for its principal theoretical inspiration (for examples of Derridean research in the organisation of health care see, Fox (1997); Wood, Ferlie and Fitzgerald (1998); Learmonth (1999; 2004); Peterson and Albrecht (1999) or Traynor (1999).)

Analyses following Derrida understand language not merely as central to organising, but more radically, as Currie and Brown have put it, assume that language 'in all its forms . . . are simultaneously the grounds, the objects, and the means by which struggles for power are engaged in' (2003, p. 565). In this chapter, therefore, we nurture our critical reflection on leadership through exploring how the dominant language used renders leadership both intelligible (something we can understand) and contestable (something we can debate) in particular ways. In doing this, we will achieve Willmott's aim of 'expos[ing] and disrupt[ing] habitual patterns of thought by inducing greater self-consciousness about the presence, operation and partiality' (1998a, p. 89) of such language. In other

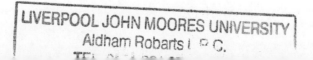

words, we ask the reader to reflect upon how they understand the words 'leader' and 'leadership' and to be prepared to think about them in a variety of different ways.

The study

The empirical work we draw on here is interviews of NHS hospital chief executives conducted in 1998/1999. At this time, shortly after the Labour government had replaced a Conservative government that had been in power for almost two decades, management had been strongly established in the NHS as the successor to administration. Where, just a generation earlier, people working in the NHS known as administrators had generally held relatively prestigious jobs (and were mostly men), by this period NHS administrators were typically relatively poorly paid (and female). This change in designation of jobs in a short period of time lends itself superbly to a study of how the use of different words brings about different possibilities of being a self, or having an identity. Furthermore, a discourse of leadership was clearly available to chief executives in the NHS in the sense that the word was regularly mentioned—in fact, it occurs in most of the excerpts used. However, whereas management had been made intelligible by opposing it to administration (the manager (strong, in charge) was not the administrator [weak, did doctor's bidding]), at this stage, leadership was not generally constructed through sharp distinctions with management—the two terms seemed to be used more or less as synonyms. Within a few years this situation was to change for, as Parker points out, under 'New Labour . . . management itself . . . [is] beginning to go out of fashion (now being discursively articulated as something rather like administration) and leadership . . . [is] the new panacea' (2004, p. 175).

That is the context for the discussion in this chapter.

Some historical background: Managers, not administrators

Let us return to the history we outlined briefly at the start of this chapter. In 1983, at the request of the Secretary of State for Health and Social Security, a group of businessmen headed by Roy Griffiths produced the *NHS Management Inquiry*—a document that was widely read as recommending the adoption of 'a clearly defined general management function throughout the NHS' (DHSS 1983, p. 11). Such proposals had been made before with no effect (Wistow and Harrison, 1998) but this time, within two years, the Thatcher government announced that managers had been appointed at all levels of the NHS (Klein, 1995), albeit in the teeth of bitter opposition from many healthcare professions (Timmins, 1998).

Though at the time some commentators were less than enthusiastic (for example, Day and Klein, 1983; Hunter, 1984, 1988; Davies, 1987; or Pollitt, 1993), many of the individuals who came to be called managers were themselves deeply committed to what they believed were the new ideals of general management (Strong and Robinson, 1990) even though most had previously been known as administrators (Petchey, 1986). The officially sanctioned rhetoric by the late 1980s had come to be that the NHS had been 'transformed from a classic example of an administered public sector bureaucracy into one that is increasingly exhibiting qualities that reflect positive, purposeful management' (Best, 1987; cited in Flynn, 1992, p. 66; see Harrison, 1988; 1994 for the detailed policy background).

These events are all some years ago now but two of the authors of this book lived through them as, firstly, administrators, and later as managers. They have some vivid memories of the heady period after the release of the *NHS Management Inquiry*. Traces of similar experiences are apparent in the discussions with the chief executives. Each one was invited to describe his/her professional background: of the 16 interviewees, one was a clinician, two were accountants and one had come in to the NHS from another sector in the last ten years. In the case of the other 12, an exchange such as the following was typical of the very beginning of the interviews:

Q: If I could just ask you what your professional background is

A: Well administration, health service administration.

Q: Right right, good good. OK first question then, I'd like to ask you to describe the heart of your job

A: Leadership.

Q: Right right fine ha ha. Tell me about leadership

A: Well we, er I, am personally accountable for the managerial performance of the organization, the organization consists of three thousand people and to achieve my objectives I physically can't do it myself; when I was an administrator I had tasks to do which I did myself but as a leader you inspire, lead, manage others to do the work.

Or:

> [m]y professional background? I mean I came into the health service as, at that stage, a career administrator, straight from university; on to the administrators' training scheme and if you like moved into management, as management developed in the NHS, from an administrative background

This sort of opposition was not something that occurred merely at the start of the interviews, though its striking regularity here was what prompted a search of the transcripts for other examples. In the course of the interviews, the radical differences claimed to exist between administrators from the past and those holding current top leadership posts were sometimes elaborated at length:

> [j]ust as a caricature I would make the observation that many administrators in the 70s and 80s the top ones were employed mainly, well mainly, for their brain power *per se* as I say a lot of them were intellectuals Oxbridge graduates and so on; and the current generation of chief executives are also very clever people but they have their skills are now rooted in common sense and people skills. So it's not just about administering legal or financial affairs which require a certain set of administrative skills and brain power it's more to do with empowering people and leading people and having those skills. And I've many a time come across in my career people whose intellect has got in the way of their common sense, people skills. So it is they're now different animals

There are a number of ways in which these sorts of statements could be interpreted.

> Firstly, the most common way of interpreting such statements would be to regard them as straightforward reflections of reality: this is the history, this is how it all happened, what is said can be tested to show that it is accurate. Indeed, there is a long tradition of research which adopts this approach, research that seeks to answer the question '[h]as public management replaced public administration?'
>
> (Boyne, 1996, p. 680)

However, to assume that what interviewees say is a direct and straightforward reflection of the reality they have lived through is one of the weakest, most undertheorised and ill-developed forms of social research

(Knights and Willmott, 1992). For example, this kind of empiricism (or descriptiveness) downplays the ways in which such work may have a double hermeneutic effect (Giddens, 1984), in other words, that interviewees will already have carefully selected the kinds of things researchers wish to know (the first stage of interpretation), and the researcher then analyses those carefully selected statements (the second, or doubled, stage of interpretation). Further, in making their careful selection, the interviewees will have chosen terms that are already informed by academic analyses—so the interviewer will be analyzing transcripts informed by previous generations of analysis (Willmott, 1998b)! It is interesting to note in this respect, how excerpts of the interview resonate with definitions of management and administration like the one provided by Hughes:

> Public administration focuses on *process*, on procedures and propriety, while public management involves much more. Instead of merely following instructions, a public manager focuses on achieving *results* and taking responsibility for doing so [italics in original].
>
> (1994, pp. 3–4)

So, the chief executives interviewed seemingly presented administration and management as more or less unproblematic terms representing different things in the world. However, they, like many academic accounts, saw management as superior to administration, and thus they located the terms in such a way that they were hierarchically dichotomous. In other words, for Hughes (1994) as well as for these chief executives, management involves *much more* than administration. Calling certain practices administration and others management is thus not simply to name them, it *does* things to them, most obviously perhaps, in the sense that it values them in different ways.

To illustrate the point, let us take another excerpt from the interviews, where a chief executive is talking of the top management team immediately before her appointment (including the former chief executive). According to her, they had been unable to cope with the new demands of partnership working:

> there [had been] no radical or strategic thinking enough to do that sort of work; em [name of hospital] used to be peopled by a bunch of administrators basically

Of course, this statement could be read as an empirical claim, but whether or not we want to read it in that way, it *does things* that amount to more than setting out a state of affairs. For example, it is pretty clear-ly a denigration. Indeed, the addition of 'basically' suggests that the term administrator is widely understood pejoratively in the NHS, conjuring up images of what Parker and Dent have called the 'reactive functionary' (1996, p. 349). But note also how the denigration of administrators also allows the speaker to *do* something else with her words—to construct a sense of her own self. *She* is (emphatically) *not* an administrator, she is radical and strategic and she thus describes herself as possessing some of the defining characteristics of people leading excellent organisations (Peters and Waterman, 1982).

Furthermore, these sorts of statements can be read as making one's identity as a manager reliant upon administration. This is because what a manager is and does is made intelligible by being opposed to administration—managers are *not* administrators.

Indeed, if we read these transcripts merely as potentially true or false claims about the changing nature of workplace duties, then we miss how the language used by interviewees constructs a certain sense of self for the speakers (Giddens, 1991; Halford and Leonard, 1999; Brown, 2001). Understanding oneself as a manager (not an administrator) provides positive cultural valences that enable one to construct an affir-mative reflexive understanding of self. It is good to be able to think of oneself as a radical and strategic manager or an empowering leader—not as (merely) administering paperwork (Clarke and Newman, 1993; Alvesson and Willmott, 2002). Furthermore, and relatedly, being known as a manager (not an administrator) is more likely to construct the sort of public image that others may see as legitimate—and to which they will therefore defer. As Clarke and Newman have pointed out, the 'discourse of managerialism . . . is part of the process through which "administra-tors", "public servants" and "practitioners" come to see themselves as "business managers" . . . "strategists", "leaders" and so on' (1997, p. 92).

Performativity

In order to explore further what the words 'management' or 'administra-tion' (and in due course 'leadership') might do, let us turn to some of the work of Jacques Derrida, a thinker whose ideas are of particular value in analyses concerned with the relationship between language and the world to which (we might assume) language refers. The corpus of Derrida's work is large by any standards, both in terms of the range of issues with which it engages and its sheer volume, so it should be empha-sised that the strand of his work that examined language as performative far from exhausts the potential of his ideas to inform political science (Beardsworth, 1996) and organisational theory (see Cooper, 1989 and Jones, 2004 for reviews). But as far as performativity is concerned, for Derrida (1979), in a radicalisation of John Austin's (1962) *How to Do Things with Words*, language never only states the way things are, it is also always performative. Performative language, following Royle, is language that 'does something, in actuality, in reality, with reality' (2000, p. 9; italics omitted). It is Derrida's radicalised version of Austin's speech acts theory that we will use to understand how words are performative.

Austin called *constative* those speech acts he considered merely to set out a state of affairs; but his interest was in speech that, in and of itself, *does* things—using the term *performative* for such utterances. Austin's concern, as he put it, was with the 'performance of an act *in* saying something as opposed to [the] performance of an act *of* saying something' (1962, p. 99; italics in original). Instead of considering a statement such as 'there is a bull in the field' (Austin, 1962, p. 32) primarily as a constative statement—in terms of what it describes about the scenery—Austin showed the importance of looking at what the statement does: Is it a warning, a request, a complaint, and so forth?

Derrida's thought has a number of affinities with Austin's in that they both unsettle the traditional image of communication as the straightforward transportation of meaning from one speaker to another (Potter, 1996). Derrida welcomed Austin's move as an antidote to ideas that underpin, among other things, traditional understandings of empirical inquiry:

> Austin was obliged to free the analysis of the performative from the authority of the truth *value*, from the true/false opposition . . . The performative is a "communication" which is not limited strictly to the transference of a semantic content that is already constituted and dominated by an orientation toward truth [italics in original].
>
> (Derrida, 1979, p. 187)

However, their ideas diverged when theorising *how* words do what they do. Austin argued that the 'force' (1962, p. 100) of a performative is provided primarily by the authentic intentions of the speaker, usually allied to the context in which speech is uttered and the lack of ambiguity in the formulation used. So, for Austin a priest in a wedding ceremony who says, 'I pronounce you husband and wife' would be uttering a speech act which would be successful in doing something (marrying the couple) because of the intentions of the priest and the couple involved—along with the context and the unambiguity of the formulation. In opposition to Austin however, Derrida made clear that for him the force of a performative is not intention, but citation. The notion of iterability or citation is what for Derrida underlies any 'successful' performative:

> Could a performative utterance succeed if its formulation did not repeat a 'coded' or iterable utterance, or in other words, if the formula I pronounce in order to open a meeting, launch a ship or a marriage were not identifiable as *conforming* with an iterable model, if it were not then identifiable in some sort of way as a 'citation' [italics in original].
>
> (1979, pp. 191–2)

To continue the example of marriage, Derrida is pointing out that a priest can only marry someone because the words spoken are recognisably part of a marriage ceremony: "I pronounce you husband and wife" must be a *citation* for it to marry a couple. Citation, Derrida argued, is prior to intention; indeed it is a condition of possibility for intention to operate. This is not to deny intention and context have a role in speech acts, but as Derrida argued, intention and context 'will no longer be able to govern the entire scene and system of utterance' (1979, p. 192). Put at its simplest, the words have to exist and their meaning understood in order to allow the action to take place.

Following Derrida then, if terms like leadership, management or administration do things in the world, they operate, not primarily because the intention of the speaker successfully governs the action of speech, but because these words, in some sort of way, are citations. By their repeated use they bring into being that of which they speak. Indeed it is surely uncontroversial to claim that both management and administration (and leadership more latterly) have become conventional categories to use in representing the ways in which things are done in organisations such that it is now hardly possible to make intelligible statements about organisations without recourse to these terms. Derrida's point (perhaps not too distant from Giddens's double hermeneutic) is that the effects on the world of these terms rely upon the accumulation of academic research, official reports, routine talk and so on in which these terms are deployed. Part of the value of his work, therefore, is that it enables us to see something of what language does—the first step, it is submitted, in making it do different things.

Derrida revisited these ideas and the controversies they spawned, and developed the general theme (1988; 1992a; 1992b; 1996; 1998 and

2000). Others have used ideas about performativity explicitly influenced by Derrida's radicalisation of Austin; see for example, Butler (1995 and 1997); Sedgwick and Parker (1995); or Sedgwick (2003). We will draw upon these writers in later chapters in this book.

Management and administration doing things

Let us take some more excerpts from the interviews to illustrate in more detail what talking about leadership, management and administration might do and how the effects might work. The excerpts all come from talk about the chief executives' conflicts with doctors (for the general background see Harrison et al., 1992; Harrison and Pollitt, 1994; Hunter, 1994; Harrison, 1999 or Llewellyn, 2001) and are used here to theorise some of the consequences and implications of the discursive change from administration to management—and thence to leadership—that have generally been marginalised in the raging debate about managers versus doctors. Following Cooper (1990, p. 194), it is important to emphasise that because it is words that do things, it is the actual words *themselves* that have become 'the very object of the conflict. It is necessary to understand that, viewed in this way, language and speech are not merely the vehicles for the expression of conflict but become the objects to be appropriated'. This alerts us to examining how individuals adopt aspects of language to stake their claims about how things are (or should be).

So first:

> . . . when consultants actually want to diminish what I do they call me an administrator.

> **Q:** Yes, I remember that from the early eighties.

> Still do, still do, because that's about your job is to support what we do; accepting that I'm actually a chief executive gives me a leadership position. . . .

Here, consultants are said to do something with words, for the respondent feels diminished simply by being called an administrator, while what gives him a leadership position is being called a chief executive. The words 'administrator' or 'chief executive' in the mouth of a consultant have a force that works in a way that is not dissimilar to the wedding pronouncement of a priest. Following Derrida, we understand that this speech act can *do* the things it does because it has accumulated cultural intelligibility given constant authoritative use—its citation in particular ways. Indeed, in this excerpt, the interviewee felt able, as it were, to cite the accumulated cultural intelligibility associated with the terms: *administrator*—'that's about your job is to support what we do'; *chief executive*—'gives me a leadership position'. Of course, the speaker does not have to be a consultant to achieve these effects; as we saw earlier, chief executives calling one another administrators have a very similar sort of impact.

It follows then, that viewed in this way, one of the performative effects of saying 'I am a manager/leader' (and *ipso facto* not an administrator) is that it is a legitimatory device—a legitimatory device hidden by understanding it merely as a (constative) statement of fact. What the excerpt also illustrates is Cooper's point cited above—how the words 'leadership', 'management' and 'administration' have in themselves become objects to be appropriated in the conflict over what they do. Words associated with management and leadership construct and legitimate an organiszational world in which the speaker felt he had supremacy; 'administrator' on the other hand, does things that undermine the prestige and authority he would like.

Such insights are reinforced and further explained by the next excerpt in which some of the history of the power relations between doctors and managers (or should we say administrators?) are represented in more detail:

> [e]arlier on in my career where the successful administrators in the sixties and seventies were those which were actually able to facilitate what the doctors wanted to do that's how you were judged.
>
> **Q:** Right, not influence it at all?
>
> Well you might influence it provided you didn't tell people you were influencing it; it was actually quite a clever game—you let the doctors think that it was their idea but actually your skills were in terms of making it happen and using the process or whatever. Of course the real skill was that you didn't make happen those things that you didn't want to make happen, but if you made nothing happen then you were not a good administrator and you would alienate the doctors and then you would be unsuccessful.

Prior to the *NHS Management Inquiry*, administrators were widely seen (by themselves and by the medical staff) as doctors' support workers

(Harding and Learmonth, 2000). Any prestige they might have had arose from their success in fulfilling doctors' wishes rather than from the activities they chose independently (Harrison, 1988). This much is relatively uncontroversial.

But one way of reading this excerpt is to see it as an implicit statement that the re-labelling from administrator to manager that was licensed by the *NHS Management Inquiry* was not one that necessarily altered the substance of administrators'/managers' activities. Senior administrators of the past and contemporary health care leaders can be represented as carrying out much the same activities: according to this excerpt, making things happen, more or less as they feel appropriate. However, individuals called administrators had to make sure that what they did appeared to be done in the service of others. Their self-identity was therefore continuously defined as subservient and secondary—the need to be able to subvert the apparent relationship by playing 'quite a clever game' no doubt merely reinforced this identity. However, the implicit corollary to the status of the administrator is that what being called a manager (and perhaps even more being called a leader) *does* is it legitimates the so-called manager acting in a way that is independent of 'what the doctors want'—thereby radically changing the nature of their respective senses of self.

What both these last excerpts illustrate therefore, is that the discursive change from administration to management can be understood as a *resource* to be called upon in struggles for power and legitimacy. But interpreting Derrida, Butler has pointed out that 'a performative "works" to the extent that it *draws on and covers over* the constitutive conventions by which it is mobilized' (1995, p. 157; italics in original). All the talk we have examined so far clearly draws on the conventions about leadership, management and administration in the NHS; these terms work as a performative however because the associations that now surround them have come to be naturalised. Constant citation has covered over the constitutive conventions by which the effects are mobilised, so much so that it has been forgotten that leadership, management and administration are conventions: the cultural intelligibility associated with the terms have become 'truths' through frequent repetition (Lawler, 2002). Paradoxically enough, administration and management can do things as words because people who use the terms generally assume that they do *nothing*; they are thought to be merely the labels for distinct 'things' out there in the world.

Simultaneously drawing on and covering over the constitutive conventions of management seems to have been something that the respondents generally achieved by deploying the term management as an apparently uncontroversial and routine way of talking about all sorts of activities. For example:

> One of the things that I learnt was that we often expect too much of doctors—in terms of their ability to manage and also their capacity to manage and their commitment to do the things that managers have to do because their livelihoods depend on it—doctors don't [have to do these things]. And I felt that, [and] the medical director he felt, that the emergence of clinical governance was an opportunity to refocus the doctors' role on clinical management, leadership and the management increasingly of clinical practice informed by evidence, rather than on the management of service delivery and staffing budgets and so on

In this excerpt the speaker deploys the term management in at least two senses. There is the more or less conventional sense of management—the distinctive occupational functions of certain people identified as professional managers by their job titles. Management in this sense is represented as 'the management of service delivery and staffing budgets and so on'—which the speaker believes doctors need not do. However, in juxtaposition to this, he also uses the same term—'management'—to represent rather different functions, functions he considers to be legitimate medical duties: 'clinical management, leadership and the management increasingly of clinical practice informed by evidence'. But it is not implausible to believe that what he is talking about here could equally have been represented in more traditional language, as part of the ordinary, routine duties that senior medical staff have done for many years; that is without recourse to the terms leadership and management.

Deploying management and leadership in this context does things then by *re*-presenting medical work as managerial. And if managerial language successfully colonises doctors' routine talk and thinking, they are likely to come to understand their own identities as managerial, at least in part (Halford and Leonard, 1999; Grey, 1999). Of course, the logic of such an understanding tends to imply that they should be accountable to the professional expert in the field—the chief executive—and furthermore, that more traditional considerations for the NHS, especially ones based on welfarism, caring and compassion can plausibly be played down and rendered subservient to the tough job of ensuring good economic management (Parker, 2000). As Grey has argued, 'it is the insinuation of management into a huge range of human activities and actors previously thought of as lying outside the specialist domain of management which constitutes one of the key "achievements" of managerialism' (1999, p. 572).

Management, like any other term, can of course have a number of shades of meaning that potentially allow distinctions to be constructed between say the *'management* of clinical practice' and the *'management* of service delivery and staffing budgets'. But for Derrida these distinctions are always precarious because these shades of meaning are not discrete ideas that might in some way exist without the term and can therefore be separately signified by it. Derrida suggests not that terms allow or include multiple meanings but that all a word's meanings are always present when the term is used, regardless of context or intention. Words such as management always simultaneously 'refer to a *same* that is not identical, to the common element or medium of any possible dissociation' (Derrida, 1981, p. 127; italics in original).

The final excerpt is intended to illustrate further how 'management' can refer to a same that is not identical and the effects of its doing so. Again it comes from another chief executive's account of interactions with medical staff and is taken from the point at which the respondent was asked to explain what seemed an intriguing use of the term consultant-managers:

Q: Do you mean all consultants are managers or do you mean that there are certain consultants who are managers like clinical directors or whatever?

Okay, I mean both. All consultants are managers em; not all consultants would recognize that or recognize the implications of that as readily as others do but they all manage resources, they all manage their time, manage junior medical staff and have therefore particular accountability for them.

Her statement about what she means by manager—'I mean both'— coincidentally happens to be a fair summary of part of what Derrida is getting at in his understanding of language—the ability of language to refer to the same that is not identical. And furthermore, it also illustrates how her striking repetition of 'manage' can be understood to function simultaneously as both a constative and performative speech act.

On the one hand, the accumulated cultural intelligibility of management means these statements can be seen simply as constative; that is, as setting out the facts about management as a more or less universal activity that is as desirable and inevitable for doctors to do as for everyone else. Read in this way, she is simply saying that senior medical staff manage resources, manage their time, manage junior staff and so on. At the same time, other cultural associations that also surround call to manage (for example, industrial and economic ones) give these statements a performative dimension—implying that economic prerogatives should be the supreme consideration over all others. Indeed such statements can be read to suggest a desire for a managerialist rationality to colonise the way medical staff regard their time and their relationships with colleagues—each being constructed as 'resources' susceptible to instrumental calculation for which they have 'accountability'.

Martin Heidegger once observed that 'language is the house of Being' (cited in Rapaport, 2003, p. 29). What the deployment of the language of management and leadership does is it shapes the kind of 'house of being' that people in the NHS inhabit. In as much as this language acts in ways that are unexamined, management (and administration) *impose* versions of social reality on those involved—the dominant language limiting what can be spoken, thought and known (Westwood and Linstead 2001). This imposition can be understood as what Catley and Jones (2002) call structural symbolic violence. The resulting domination they say 'is something you absorb like air, something you don't feel pressured by; it is everywhere and nowhere and to escape from that is very difficult' (ibid, p. 28).

The inseparability of management and administration

In spite of the difficulties involved, Derrida consistently tried to find ways of lessening (if not escaping from) this symbolic violence—what he himself called 'violence and the letter' (1976, pp. 101–40). In some of his later work that developed Heidegger's insight, Derrida introduced a paradox that he called a rule of language:

We only ever speak one language . . .
(yes, but)
We never speak only one language

(1998, p. 10)

It is true that all speakers of English, for example, speak the same language in the sense that all competent English speakers can talk intelligibly to one another about, let us say, management. But the respondents, especially perhaps in the last two excerpts, who seemingly talk of 'management' as the *single* appropriate term for a range of activities, might be interpreted after Derrida as insisting that we only ever speak one language; that is, *my* language, the language of managerialism. This attitude, a sort of cultural imperialism that claims its own interpretation of a language is the one, true, correct interpretation, is what Derrida (1998) has called monolingualism.

In his essay monograph, *Monolingualism of the Other*, Derrida (1998) argues that an illusion of monolingualism allows cultures, traditions and nations to become thinkable; not merely in the sense that they would otherwise be unimaginable, but that without this illusion of monolingualism thinking as a collective simply cannot take place. The deployment of 'manage' and 'management' in these excerpts then might be interpreted as ways of incorporating others into the language practices of managerialism. In other words, the signifying environment of management constructs and identifies all subjects as particular social beings with an identity that is, in part, marked by the (managerial) language that is spoken. Others then become judged in terms of managerial language.

Nevertheless, for Derrida there is always an insistent 'yes but' in response to the appearance of monolingualism. Derrida argued (1998) that we never speak about organising practices (or anything else) in just one language, because even within an apparent state of monolingualism, and even when there are powerful voices that argue the contrary, other languages are always present. Following Derrida we might therefore understand that what management might be and do is not an established, positive given. Indeed, as we have seen, the language of management works together with what it opposes—the language of administration— according to a complex interplay of implicative differences. What makes management management, and administration administration, takes place in a constituting process in which management calls upon administration as an Other so as to be able to demarcate itself, and be what it is, in difference from administration (Derrida, 1978; Gasché, 1995). Indeed much of the talk we have examined can be read as attempts to maintain definite demarcation lines—boundaries between management and administration that secure the purity of management and therefore secure for the speaker a settled sense of self as a manager, *not* an administrator.

But the paradox of boundaries is that they don't just separate—they also connect (Derrida, 1987). Thus, in spite of (or better, because of) attempts to separate them, anything called management in the NHS necessarily has a connection with administration. Such connections mean that what management is—and what it does—is intrinsically precarious: the apparent monolingualism of management is always at risk of being contaminated with an other language—the language of administration. As the chief executives themselves implicitly acknowledged at the start of their interviews and as those (both consultants and chief executives) who call chief executives administrators make explicit, claims to be a manager are ineluctably connected to administration.

It is likely, therefore, that these connections limit what the language of management can do in any organisation, for administration preceded management not only in the NHS but in all organisations. For individual chief executives, even those who have never been administrators themselves, the discursive history of the term manager in the NHS always has the denigrated shadow of the administrator behind it: people called managers are intrinsically vulnerable to being cast as 'mere' administrators.

The turn to leadership

Perhaps it is the negative associations accumulated by management and administration that underlie the popular and officially sanctioned turn to leadership that has occurred in the last few years across the public and private sectors (Ford, 2004). In terms of the NHS, this was exemplified in 2002 with a government minister saying, on the National Nursing Leadership's Project website:

Good clinical leadership is central to the delivery of the NHS plan. We need leaders who are willing to embrace and drive through the radical transformation in services that the NHS requires. Leaders are people who make things happen in ways that command the confidence of local staff. They are people who lead clinical teams, people who lead service networks, people who lead partnerships and people who lead organisations (2002).

Such statements about 'clinical leadership' bear comparison with the respondents' talk of 'clinical management' cited earlier. Both sorts of statements can, of course, be seen as constative claims—both no doubt intended to represent the world *as it is*: nurse 'leaders are people who make things happen'; consultants 'manage resources, they all manage their time, manage junior medical staff'. But again, understanding either statement as *only* constative overlooks (and thereby reinforces) what such words do. Deploying leadership, as we have argued in respect of management, can also be seen as a speech act that does things—in the above extract, it seems more or less calculated to have the effect of 'regulating employees' "insides"—their self-image, their feelings and identifications' (Alvesson and Willmott 2002, p. 622). Indeed an official endorsement of leadership to represent organisational practices can be interpreted, in part, as a growing recognition that calling activities 'leadership' does more than calling them 'management' (and, it goes without saying, more than 'administration') in terms of encouraging individuals to identify with policy or organisational aims.

In a further radicalisation of Austin, Derrida argues all words always have a performative element fundamentally because representational practices cannot simply represent things *themselves*: 'in the first place because there is no thing itself' (1976, p. 292). This statement is not a denial of the materiality of the universe; the point he is making is that our representational practices are *always* irredeemably implicated in the constitution of how we think of a 'thing' 'itself'. More simply, things have a physical existence, but we can only understand them, talk about them, think about them, approach them, through language. Words for Derrida do things most fundamentally by making reality intelligible in particular ways.

So in the context of our current debate, Derrida might remind us that apparently static concepts and categories like leadership, management and administration do not reflect entities in an external world separate from our understanding of them. While commonsensically we may conceive of a particular happening as say 'doing administration', another as 'doing management' and yet another as 'leadership', such happenings are best understood to be *intrinsically* amorphous, fluxing and undifferentiated. It is our efforts at organising happenings into categories that give them meaning—that constitute them as administration, management or whatever. It is submitted then that leadership, management and administration are performative at root because they represent methods of engaging with organisational practices that make such practices intelligible in particular ways. Their taken-for-grantedness makes them *appear* to be only ways of communicating different empirical realities. Read in this way, leadership, management or administration become merely provisional, subjectively significant and hence contestable heuristics to make the world comprehensible.

It follows then that many activities carried out by staff 'are' management or leadership in the sense that they are currently given these names; however, these same activities are always potentially *not* management or *not* leadership in the sense that they can always be called by other names—and as we have seen, they have been given different names in times past. What a particular activity 'is' does not rely on some essence within it—things like leadership, management or administration, indeed all categories through which we experience the world, are human creations, a reflection of conventional ways of apprehending the world and not a reflection of what the world is 'really like' (Frug, 1984; Cooper and Law, 1995). What leadership, management and administration have come to represent therefore has been made to appear self-evident through an inescapably arbitrary process of inclusion and exclusion of significance, a process held together only by convention and power (Willmott, 1998a).

Conclusion

In this chapter we have drawn on the work of Jacques Derrida, applied to reading interviews with chief executives, to show how the words 'management' and 'leadership' are performative, that is, they do not function to describe what people called 'managers' and 'leaders' do, but they carve out the space and allow the identity of the manager or the leader. Furthermore, we have shown that language is at one and the same time shared by a people and also contested by them—we can only understand what is meant by leadership through the language that is available to us to think about it, but one person's understanding may be very different from another's. This gives the first hints of why some readers may feel a discomfort about taking on the role of leader but do not know why they feel uncomfortable—they only have a limited language through which to think about leadership.

We mentioned above that Derrida shows that words have many meanings. Although it appears that we only use one meaning of a word at one time for if we don't then misunderstanding follows, Derrida argues that all possible meanings are always present, influencing each other, in every instance of use of the word. We will now turn to exploring how leadership is imbued with more than one meaning.

3
The Leader as Hero

One of the principal aims of this book is to unsettle the dominant identity of organisational leaders as disinterested, rational figures who lead others for the good of their organisations. That is an identity that, we argue, is not only unachievable but also highly controlling of those charged with the task of leadership. We showed in Chapter 2 how the very words 'leader' and 'leadership' construct the very people and tasks that we are discussing, and we showed how the words may have numerous meanings and are open to contestation over how they are defined. The result of reading that chapter should be that readers now realise that they have a theory and definition of leadership that may be at odds with those we are using as we write these pages. Indeed, no two readers should share precisely the same definitions—every time someone offers one it is open to debate, discussion and rewriting.

In this chapter we are taking those arguments forward by developing further understanding of what the words 'leader' and 'leadership' can do (which is to say: not what they can mean). The interpretation we will develop in this chapter is that inherent in the 'rational' language of leadership is an 'other' identity that supplants the dominant one. This is an 'other' identity of the leader which has to be ignored or marginalised because it threatens the hegemony of the dominant leadership identity. (By 'hegemony' we mean the dominant, unchallenged way of thinking, one that is so powerful that it prevents our thinking in any other way.) However, this other image is bound up with the comprehensibility of what is often assumed to be the common sense and obvious identity of organisational leadership—the 'common sense' understanding could not make sense without this marginalised perspective.

We will continue to use the interviews of 17 chief executives of NHS hospitals. This reading shows that the more orthodox representations of leaders—in this case hospital leaders—is contaminated by the (emotionally charged, self-interested) identity of the fictional hero. This is a theme to which we will return throughout this book. Heroism means that the 'true' identity of the leader is radically open to question, being ultimately undecidable. The reading is not intended to say 'they are one or the other, you have to choose', nor does it claim 'they are a bit of both'. Rather our use of the 'hero' term is an attempt to demonstrate the *necessity* of what the Chief Executives do see of their identity being *systematically* related to what they do not see (Johnson, 1981).

The hero is an articulation of some-'thing' that is excluded by the talk of leaders rather than an exploration of what it affirms; and yet this is a something that is necessary to its very constitution. Thus we suggest, following Derrida, that our term hero is best placed under erasure—*sous rature* (Derrida, 1976). In Derridean terms, 'hero' is therefore a mark on the page *sous rature* which constructs a play of differences between itself and more orthodox representations of leaders. This is a play of differences which the reader can apprehend, yet which must be subject to erasure because Derrida uses words with the understanding that they are representations of the play of differences between ideas, not essentialist representations of reality. In other words, by crossing out the word 'hero' but leaving it on the page, he shows that the word and its many definitions, all present despite their seeming absence, all work at the same time to construct what we regard as our reality. We are unaware of all the different meanings, but they are there, having an effect, all the same. In this case, 'hero' is a signifier that haunts the terms 'leader' and 'leadership'—whenever we think about these terms the idea of the hero, in its many manifestations, informs our thinking. Hero is an(other) attempt to paint the figure of the leader, but as Derrida (1976) puts it (as we noted in Chapter 2) "[t]here is never a painting of the thing itself and first of all because there is no thing itself ' (p. 292)—which is to say that the thing itself cannot be separated from our representational practices.

Heroism and leadership

The (more or less conscious) genesis of our use of the term hero to inform the discussion of leadership arises from the first analysis of the interviews with the chief executives. What struck most forcibly during the exercise was that the transcripts were full of accounts of successes—usually against the odds—and what is more, only successes. Like conventional fictional heroes, the subjects always triumphed in the end. But, again like fictional heroes, their versions of 'success' often hid what might be open to be seen as other people's failures, humiliations or even tragedies. In the same way as, for example, from the point of view of Polyphemus the Cyclops, Odysseus' triumph over him meant his humiliation and blindness (Homer, 1980 pp. 99–112); so, when 'unco-operative' members of staff were 'dealt with'—from their perspective it might have meant humiliation among colleagues or even the end of their career. But this was never acknowledged; indeed there was often a triumphalism over such successes (in which it was assumed the inter-viewer would share) which had the effect of obscuring any other read-ing than a triumphalist one.

Furthermore, and rather paradoxically, all the interviewees regularly implied that they were thought well of by the people who worked in 'their' organisations. In a sense they believed they were their staff's heroes (it is only possible to be a hero if other people see you as their hero). This was especially apparent as they talked explicitly about leadership—a dis-course used by all the interviewees—and linked to 'heroism' by numer-ous authors (see, for example, Pfeffer, 1977; Clark and Salaman, 1998; Gabriel, 1999). These kinds of readings then, led to the further investiga-tion of the possibility that much of the material was open to being read as drawing upon hero stories. An appeal to heroism might be seen par-ticularly easily in the excerpt below, from near the beginning of one of the interviews where the 'captain of the ship' gives us glimpses into something like the world of Odysseus. We use it to introduce, in one brief extract, some of the themes that we develop in this chapter.

Okay so the first proper question, can you tell me about what you see as the heart of your job . . .

Oh gosh yes well yes of course I can. I suppose the three the three main elements to it, and I may add to this as I go along, but I think the first element is the kind of captain of the ship role, which is I suppose ultimately about trying to co-ordinate what is going on in this organisation at the top level giving it a sense of direction and and making sure that we are moving in that direction and it seems to me that's a role that nobody else can play. I don't see it as my role to necessarily determine the direction because I do think in an organization like this it's very much a team matter but there are occasions when when I will stamp my view on what we should do and particularly where there isn't a great deal of room within the [obscured three words] so that's the first thing captain of the ship. The second is managing the Board mainly the Chairman of the

Board and what I mean by that is that in the same way that I think I'm responsible for making sure that the organization has a sense of direction with and is moving in that direction then I have to try and make sure that the Chairman of the Board contributes to the same direction but don't but don't blow us off course; and that is quite a tricky role making sure that they are involved constructively and feel involved and feel that they are shaping and influencing things and again there is nobody else but the chief executive who can do that. The third thing which I think is important in my role is—em I know this sounds arrogant but I don't feel like that—it is protecting the organization and the people within it from this torrent of non-sense that pours out of Whitehall into Quarry House through Regional office and so on.

How might this sort of text be interpreted? The orthodox way would be to assume that the Chief Executive is simply telling us about his world 'as it is'; the language employed (if noticed in itself at all) understood simply as a more or less unproblematic tool for the logical representation of the essential or real (Chia, 1996b). But this is to forget that, as Gergen (1992) says,

> our theories of organization are, first and foremost, forms of language. They are guided by existing rules of grammar, and constructed out of the pool of nouns and verbs, the metaphors, the narrative plots and the like found within the linguistic context.
>
> (p. 207)

So 'heroes' in the title of this chapter is intended to draw particular attention to a narrative plot highlighted because much of the interviews can indeed be seen to have striking parallels with classic 'hero' stories in literature. According to the literary scholar Hourihan (1997), all hero stories take the same basic form:

- [o]f a journey [as shown in the above excerpt. All the interviewees quite explicitly used this metaphor of a journey to make sense of their job] and follows an invariable pattern.
- The hero is white male, British, American or European and usually young. He may be accompanied by a single male companion or he may be the leader of a group of adventurers [all the chief executives represented themselves as leader of a team—or as in the above excerpt particularly strikingly as 'captain of the ship'; 11 of the 16 subjects

are (biologically) men—feminine characters in the plot, like nurses and secretaries, always being treated as marginal].

- He leaves the civilized order of home [Trust HQ?] to venture into the wilderness in pursuit of his goal.

- The wilderness may be a forest, a fantasy land, another planet, Africa or some other non-European part of the world, the mean streets of London or New York, a tropical island etc. etc. It lacks the order and safety of home. Dangerous and magical things happen there. [The hospital is typically seen as a dangerous threatening place always on the verge of chaos—in the above extract, like being aboard a ship in danger of being blown off course. This dangerous environment is, incidentally, said by some to have claimed many less able managers as victims.]

- The hero encounters a series of difficulties and is threatened by dangerous opponents. These may include dragons or other fantastic creatures, wild animals, witches, giants, savages, pirates, criminals, spies, aliens [the stories focus on these 'difficulties' and I understand the 'fantastic creatures' to be most often doctors; though might also be—as above—Chairmen of the Board with powers to blow a ship off course and government civil servants able to produce, demagogue-like, a 'torrent of nonsense'].

- The hero overcomes these opponents because he is strong, brave, resourceful, rational and determined to succeed. [All the interviewees *always* said they have succeeded—not one had failed]. He may receive assistance from wise and benevolent beings who recognise him for what he is. [Mentors, sympathetic academics and others from whom they have received advice feature in the interviews.]

- He achieves his goal which may be golden riches, a treasure with spiritual significance like the Holy Grail, the rescue of a virtuous (usually female) prisoner, or the destruction of the enemies which threaten the safety of home [the interviewees do not seem to have reached this stage—they are still engaged in battles in the wilderness].

- He returns home, perhaps overcoming other threats on the way, and is gratefully welcomed.

- He is rewarded. Sometimes this reward is a virtuous and beautiful woman. (pp. 9–10)

It is through this lens that we reread the transcripts as stories told by the heroes themselves as they are on their dangerous journeys—on what Bowles (1997) describes as "the quest for the corporate grail" (p. 795). In other words they have not got to the stage of the last 3 points above, though one or two are getting near. (For an account providing variants on Hourihan's hero storyline see, for example, Campbell, 1949; Brower, 1971; Hillman, 1980; Jackson, 1982.)

Heroes and the problematics of representation

But why read the transcripts as hero stories? The term 'leadership' is generally accepted as unproblematic at least as a topic for research whereas in this context heroism is unorthodox, to say the least. Further, this interpretation might be read to imply a challenge to the received wisdom underlying the identity of leadership, for if leaders were to be read as representing themselves as heroes then they would be less likely to be seen as rational and disinterested 'strategists' or as 'servant leaders', who put the interests of others before their own.

Thus, the deployment of the term 'hero' is a way of shocking the reader into being reflexive about the operation of language. Indeed, there are numerous criticisms of orthodox representations of leaders for implying (in the sub-text of the claims) that leader = hero. However, most are made 'in passing' and the ideas surrounding heroism are not developed. For example, Burrell (1992) comments:

> The rise of 'management' from the aristocratic kitchen and stable . . . into the corridors of power has allowed some to talk of managers as if they were heroic figures. In the United Kingdom, for example, the growth in management education, the Thatcherite emphasis on the enterprise culture, the variety of reports calling for improved training for managers given their presumed importance to the economy, and the huge number of biographical and autobiographical accounts of 'successful' corporate executives . . . has produced a climate in which managers have high status—supposedly.
>
> (p. 68)

In the context of the leadership of the NHS, Strong and Robinson (1990) attempt to evoke the feelings about general management among the leaders themselves. They say it was

> not just a quest for greater economy . . . [rather the leaders themselves believed it to be] a far better way of running health services; a way in which higher quality care would be delivered from co-ordinated frontline workers. Down the tatty corridors of the NHS, new and dedicated *heroes* would stride—the general managers. Inspired by their

leadership a new sort of staff would arise. Armed with better information and new techniques from the private sector, much more closely monitored yet working as a team they would at last take collective pride in their work—and responsibility for it.

(p. 3; emphasis added)

Or as Hunter (1996a) puts it, also in relation to leaders in the NHS, 'the cult of heroic leadership persists in many quarters so that the solution to any problem lies in the myth of the professional manager being at hand' (p. 21).

However, for these authors, what heroism signifies seems to be assumed as straightforward and the idea *per se* is not developed. Indeed, where it is developed, its deployment is often one that is far from intentionally critical or ironic. For example, Sculley and Byrne (1987) in their autobiographical book, *Odyssey: From Pepsi to Apple*, self-consciously compare Sculley's activities as the leader of the Pepsi organisation to the literary character who is arguably the prototype for all future heroes: Odysseus. Other authors have used an analogy between the 'hero' and leaders in order to suggest their ability to rise (heroically) above difficulties and adversity to secure better services for the population (Couto, 1991). So, for example, Bellavita (1991) in the context of the US public sector claims that 'the hero metaphor can be used descriptively by administrators to interpret what happens to them in public organisations. The metaphor can also be used prescriptively to suggest how an individual can improve public service' (pp. 158–9). Bowles (1997) similarly argues that the hero applied to managers and leaders can manifest positively: 'the manager as hero can, for example, provide a vital new direction and impetus for change. Rightly or wrongly, Richard Branson is often cast as such a hero' (p. 796).

In this chapter, as already stated, 'hero' is used as a way of drawing attention to an explicit and regularly mentioned assumption in the transcripts—that respondents believed that they were thought well of by the people who worked in 'their' organisations. Thus, drawing attention to leaders as heroes is open to be read as complimentary. However, Bowles also points out that in idealising 'the hero . . . others can miss the fact that their own interests are not only not served, but in fact undermined' (p. 796). So, for example, the masculinity inherent in the term 'hero' is (we think) hard to miss. But masculinity as a source of oppression in leadership practices is often missed (Acker, 1990; Calás and Smirmich, 1992; Wilson, 1996). What is more, in some psychoanalytically informed literature, the 'hero' can be understood as an *adolescent* masculine image (see Campbell, 1949); linked in Freudian theory to the phallic stage. So for Gabriel (1999) it is a form of individualism found in organisations 'that acknowledges neither pain nor suffering, neither compromise nor cost; it revolves entirely around victory and defeat, noble deeds and villainy' (p. 70). Gabriel goes on to assert that the heroic individualist

> constructs organizations . . . as an arena for heroic exploits where distinction and excellence may be achieved . . . critical readers will not fail to notice [however that] . . . these images of organizations are thinly veiled phantasies which act as wish fulfilments . . . the heroic individualist [envisions the organization] as something that will express his or her desire for epic achievement . . . invest[ing] organizations with meanings and symbolism, imbuing them with ideals and their close relatives, illusions.
>
> (pp. 75–6)

In the specific context of the NHS this interpretation is also open to be read as ironic, suggesting perhaps that we may be poking fun at these Chief Executives. Who would ever think of NHS bureaucrats as heroes? Stereotypically, they are the antithesis of the heroic—men in grey suits (Ham, 1995; Learmonth, 1997), rather than knights in shining armour. So, we proceed by using the elements of the hero narrative outlined in Hourihan's (1997) framework (cited above) to show how heroism is present in its absence within the interview transcripts.

The civilised order of home

Here we argue that the 'civilized order of home' (where, according to Hourihan, hero stories typically start) can be understood to be represented by the Trust Headquarters, where the Chief Executives' offices are located. In order to illustrate the point, we proceed by documenting the observations made during the visits to these places to carry out the interviews. Most headquarters have been created in their current, relatively luxuriant form, since the establishment of Trusts in the early 1990s.

In all our research into the management of hospital trusts, appointments always required navigation through large unfamiliar hospitals. The wrong turn down an ill-signed corridor could lead, as it often did, to somewhere like an outpatients department full of anxious patients queuing up for their appointments and being dealt with by hassled-looking staff; or in an unsightly service corridor cluttered with trolleys containing half-eaten meals. The contrast with Trust Headquarters when we found it, generally located on the hospital site but in a separate building or at least clearly delineated from the rest of the hospital, was immediate. Here calm and order reigned. Admittedly, the contrast just presented may be overdrawn in some cases but is not entirely unfair as it captures the feel of the headquarters and the rest of the hospital. (Compare our account with Fournier's (1998) description of the contrasting physical appearances of the offices in the 'core' and at the 'margins' of a large British service sector organisation.) Typically there was a reception occupied by a woman in a conventionally 'corporate' environment. Unlike the people queuing in outpatients, we, the respectable researchers, did not have to queue, and indeed the interviewer was often the only person in the waiting area. The procedure rarely varied from the following. A greeting by a receptionist, who asked for details of our names and our appointments, was followed by a telephone call which led to a subsequent statement along the lines of 'the Chief Executive's secretary will collect you in five minutes' and 'would you like a coffee?'. The hush of the place strikes anyone waiting. The only punctuation in the stillness is perhaps an occasional ringing telephone at reception or the passage of a small group of people with tidy haircuts, wearing well-pressed suits and polished shoes, possibly chatting about a meeting to which they had just been. The air of calm continued as we were escorted by a well-presented (always female) personal assistant to the Chief Executive's office.

These offices always had a feeling of spaciousness, generally accompanied by what can best be described as a restrained sort of opulence. The furniture and fittings apparently were chosen to suggest that the office belonged to someone who was 'important'—nothing was ever tatty or worn—but without giving an impression of overt extravagance. Hardly anyone had a cluttered desk; on the contrary, in many cases, the desks were noticeably almost totally free of anything at all, except perhaps a copy of the letter requesting the interview, a phone and (not always) a PC. Like their colleagues noticed earlier in the reception area, all interviewees conformed to the conventional Western executive dress code; indeed, almost all were exceptionally 'smart' in this sense (Harding, 2003). They were all gracious and helpful. It seemed therefore that the chief executives themselves along with the general appearance of the HQs (especially when considered in comparison with the other parts of the hospital) were giving the impression of being profoundly 'ordered' and 'civilized' (to use Hourihan's terms).

Why? One reason for this contrast, we suggest, is that it helps to create and sustain the existence of the civilised ideal necessary in order for the arena of the heroic deeds—the wilderness—to be represented plausibly as such. This is because the representation of another place as an uncivilised wilderness can only be made comprehensible and credible by positing first its opposite—the primary, favoured civilisation. Following Derrida (1981), once the ideal of order is established it allows that which is different from it to become definable as chaos and disorder. As Cooper (1990) has argued, organisation and disorganisation are mutually constitutive. Once defined against order, disorder is then seen, not as an entity in itself, but as a negative, corrupt and undesirable version of the order exemplified in the Trust HQ. The disordered 'other' is something, therefore, that can plausibly be said to need 'leadership'.

The wilderness

To illustrate the wilderness in which the heroic acts of leadership take place, let us look at the following excerpt where one of the interviewees is explaining her expectations about what medical consultants should tell her about planned or unplanned changes in their practice. She does not want every detail, but

> I need to know where there is an acute problem that is likely to blow up; or if someone is going to do something that might be particularly risky or slightly off the wall I would expect them to bounce that around with me first—I wouldn't stop them but I would want to know and be part of that so that if it does go pear-shaped we can do something about it. I don't want to read things in the newspaper; I don't want the first I know of things to be when I get a phone call from the Regional Office saying 'what the hell is going on in [name of Trust]?'—that kind of thing I can't live with

Here we have a representation of an environment suitable for a hero— on the edge of chaos—with things that are 'risky' as they are so dangerous they might 'blow up'. Here indeed, or so it appears, is the wilderness where, as Hourihan says, 'dangerous and magical things happen'. Looking at this excerpt, this wilderness is represented as an environment outside her own—she needs people to come and tell her about what might be happening—but also an environment in which, like superman, her leadership can save the organisation against any threat. Reading this extract privileging an understanding of leaders as heroes, she can become the hero others need to get themselves out of trouble—her job can legitimately become to 'do something about it'—to (un) pear-shape the problem; we might say, to civilise it. This heroic reading also makes more apparent how her account can be understood as a (self-serving) interpretation of a situation which could easily appear (misleadingly) as though it is the natural way of things, the only possible representation. It gives the appearance that these 'risks' are inherent risks and, as a corollary, that her doing something about them becomes the obvious and taken for granted way things are. So in this excerpt there is an example of what can be understood, following Kerfoot and Knights (1993), as an attempt 'to display attributes of control over the definition of the reality of events, and to secure the compliance of others with regard to that definition' (pp. 671/2).

It would of course, be plausible to see these sorts of situations in quite different ways. An event that a Chief Executive might interpret as dangerous (for example, the local press getting a story about staff shortages in the hospital) might, from (say) the perspective of a clinician be welcomed, perhaps as a source of pressure for the 'shortages' to be remedied (see Thorne, 1997, for a discussion about differences in perspective between clinicians and NHS leaders in this context). Perhaps then, the reason that she 'can't live with' not being told about things that she interprets as risky can be understood as an assertion that her version of events must have primacy. The excerpt can be read to suggest that in making these omissions people are simply being unacceptably incompetent—lack of prior knowledge about these 'risks' would embarrass her in front of others and deny her the opportunity for heroic deeds. However, we suggest there is something more fundamentally at issue here, which is this thing she 'can't live with'. Is it not the case that these omissions suggest others may not accept the pre-eminence of her representations, for her representations (re-presentations) define certain things as risky and dangerous? Having defined them as risky and dangerous, it follows that a leader is needed who will do something about them.

Journeying through the wilderness, overcoming difficulties

The scene is set for heroic battles:

> You know, in a way it almost feels like we're driving a tank; and I'm up at look out saying what's ahead and they're down below saying how the engine's performing.

The heroes telling the story were always successful. Others who had gone before them in similar threatening circumstances had, like soldiers, fallen:

> Well I have huge respect for the administrators the senior administrators after all. But I now recognise that their skills, unless they were able to convert, I mean many did convert but many didn't, many fell by the wayside, because they couldn't convert to the philosophy of general management

Or 'floundered hopelessly':

> What happened was the organizations which couldn't function like that, which actually didn't have the management talents to actually work their way through and do things well and manage things appropriately and didn't have a vision about where they were going, they floundered hopelessly

The success of the heroes is often said to come after taking on and heroically overcoming obstacles of various kinds. These were not merely ordinary obstacles: they were regularly described, following the tradition of hero tales, in terms open to be read as suggesting more than usual difficulty. Hence, as we see in the excerpts above, the descriptions of obstacles as having the ability to defeat (those implicitly understood as) lesser men and the need for the hero to have the protection of something like a tank. At the same time, however, part of the tradition of the hero story is that there is no ambiguity about whether or not the hero would be successful—one can be assured that he would always triumph in the end. This means that the hero narrator can imply that while these 'difficulties' might be extremely arduous for ordinary people, *for him,*— and we use a gendered term advisedly—they represent no significant problem. Take this excerpt from a relatively new Chief Executive:

> I'd an issue here where we had no leadership in the [particular treatment unit]. We had no clinical leadership in the [unit], we had people just doing sessions and nobody was going to agree about who could be the clinical leader. And I was told when I first arrived that this was unmanageable and untouchable. I just took the view that it was unacceptable not to have a clinical leader in such an important area, so I actually got a clinician from elsewhere who I know—to come in have a look and make some recommendations. And that

stirred everybody up because they didn't like what he said, and also made the people who refused to make the decision rather embarrassed because other clinicians from outside the anaesthetic fraternity were beginning to point the finger. And suddenly they all wanted a leader

Here is an example, we are to assume, of an obstacle to success—'no leadership in the [unit]', one said to be described by others (as in numerous hero stories, with hints of the supernatural) as 'unmanageable and untouchable'. However, like heroes before him, in spite of no one believing that he could ever achieve the feat he had set himself, he triumphed—apparently with unambiguous success—at the end, as 'they all wanted a leader'. What is more, he might even be seen as being dismissive of the difficulties about which he was warned. In explaining how he started to deal with the matter, he opens with the words, 'I just . . . '— implying, perhaps, that for him (in spite of the strong expectations to the contrary) it was not at all difficult.

Below is another somewhat similar 'success story':

I know that if I've got over 12 month waiters[1] I am [in] the spotlight and the consultants know that so you get into some sort of negotiation with the consultants. [The consultants say] 'we think these other cases are all clinically more urgent that's why [we have over 12 month waiters] and we think these can wait' [he replies'] 'well just a minute; well all right; well we'd better refer them to somewhere else then'. I mean I've sat in this room within the last six months saying to a particular consultant who's got a large number of over 12 month waiters 'I think I'm going to have to write out to the GPs and say you are obviously so popular that you are getting so many referrals, that actually you're getting more work than you can do, and as a direct result of that people are having to wait over 12 months and that's not in anybody's interest including the patients that are waiting over 12 months so for the next three months will you please send no more new referrals to this particular consultant.' Now he really really doesn't want that. He

[1] Patients waiting for admission to hospital for treatment. Twelve-month waiters are people waiting for a year or longer. Government policy at the time was to drive down waiting times for treatment. The NHS is funded from taxation and delivers its services free at the point of delivery. There has therefore in the past been rationing by waiting list. However, the political sensitivity of the NHS means that governments do not allow it to be run without strict guidelines from themselves.

really really doesn't want that and well [the consultant says] 'you can't do that'; 'well yes I can'; 'but you've never ever done it before'; 'but I don't know how else to tackle this problem of your over 12 month waiters because it's a real problem for me and you tell me that you're not prepared to compromise your clinical priorities and I understand that—I wouldn't want you to have to do that—so come up with another solution'. Well, it just so happens that the next month his number of over 12 months waiters had gone down

Here again, there is the expectation established that the Chief Executive is facing a major obstacle: 'I've got over 12 month waiters I am [in] the spotlight'; 'it's a real problem for me' and to compound his situation, the most powerful group in the hospital—the consultants (and one in particular) have different priorities. It is the sort of problem over which he could lose his job. But he gets his success (as we knew he would) in a manner, incidentally, that echoes what is made more explicit in the earlier excerpt—by a threat to embarrass the consultant concerned. Further, the implication might be (especially with the repetition of the phrase, 'He really really doesn't want that', along with the apparent helplessness of the consultant in the face of pressure who is forced to say, 'but you've never ever done it before'; and the Chief Executive's own confidence) that the consultant has not merely been stalled in his attempts to retain control over his waiting list; rather that he has been subjected to a final defeat—from which there is no return.

So here we are given a picture of a leader who, we are invited to believe, succeeds. He succeeds apparently because (returning to Hourihan's frame-work) he is strong and brave in the face of challenging opposition; resourceful and rational in his use of sophisticated tactics to 'encourage' compliance; determined to succeed in spite of the odds stacked against him. But this apparently unambiguously positive picture is able to appear plausible as such because the representation does not invite us to wonder whether the actions and motives of the hero are questionable. This process is similar to that which allows, for example, James Bond to be portrayed as shooting an individual in cold blood, making a humorous quip immediately afterwards and still be regarded entirely favourably (rather than being seen as having a psychopathic personality disorder).

The hero is male

We have left Hourihan's first point until the end of this analysis because we believe that masculinity is implicated intimately in all that has gone before. As in most other hero stories, the interview transcripts are populated by conventionally masculine characters—whether enemies or as allies. Kerfoot and Knights (1993) argue for an understanding of what they call 'competitive masculinity' to explain behaviour in the organizations they studied. This phenomenon they say, in parallel to our arguments here and, incidentally, echoing themselves the language of the hero epic 'is caught in ceaseless striving for material and symbolic success, and where conquest and domination become exalted as ways of relating to the world' (p. 672).

Perhaps what has 'caught' people in our current study—the term allows a reading that those 'caught' may be victims rather than complicit in the process—is the dominance of the hero myth itself; which, perhaps because of its invisibility, is not open to challenge. Five of the sixteen interviewees were women. It appeared to us that at least one of them was making a more or less conscious attempt (albeit an apparently uncomfortable and limited one) to make a compromise between the conventionally masculine and feminine. It is possible that in doing so in such a masculine world she was indirectly quoting elements of the Greek Amazon myth in which women were able successfully to compete with men on their own terms, but at the cost of having to renounce elements of their femininity. According to Malamud (1980) their

> burning out the right breast [a practice of the mythical Amazons] plays the role symbolically of a renunciation of the *purely* feminine and the integration of a masculine component. This integration is concretely expressed in their learning 'male' crafts and engaging in typically masculine activities.
>
> (p. 55 italics in original)

As an illustration of this idea, below is an excerpt from her transcript—it seems to us that she might be understood here to be 'caught' by the masculinity that becomes apparent when leadership is seen as heroism—enduring the burning out her right breast as it were—and compromising to an overwhelming masculine world:

> I think as managers we are not good at making clear either our own personal values or organizational values and we don't live them. And I suppose it comes back to some of the HR issues: you know people talk about 'we are a learning organization' you know 'we value our people', 'we invest in development'. Where's the evidence of that

within the organization, you know does the chief exec demonstrate
it by sharing their learning? You know, do they show people that it
is all right to go off and do different things and their own behaviour?
You know, do they look at a payback for the organization from training and development? You know, how are all these things integrated?
I think there are other things around family friendly policies—you
know, what is the point in having a family friendly policy which says
to people you can work sensible hours when you have got a chief
exec who insists on working twenty hours a day and insists that
everybody else works the same around them? Again it is around what
is important. I suppose there is an issue about demonstrating your
own personal behaviours. It is as much about how you treat people
how you talk to them; you know the faceless chief executive—are
you visible within the organization? Are you seen to people? Do people understand your values? Are you explicit about them? Are you
prepared to stand by them? I have young children and a husband.
I don't want to spend twenty hours a day in [name of place]. If I did
I would be spending most of that time working at 50% capacity cos I'd
be knackered you know. I would rather spend a sensible amount of
time at work have some valuable quality time at home and come
back to work feeling rejuvenated and enjoy that. When I came [to
name of Trust] there was a macho culture which was about kind of
what presenteeism as people call it; it is about being there; it's not
doing anything it is about being there. I had to quash all of those
things I go around telling people to go home. If the ladies in the
office are still here at 6.00 pm I am the one who goes: 'what are you
doing—get yourselves home?'; 'have you taken time off in lieu?' and
just making sure. But a friend of mine is a secretary to a chief executive in another Trust and because he works you know endless hours
he expects her to be there. He is paid £100,000 a year and she is prob-
ably paid about £20,000. Unfair you know. If he wants to do it fine
but you know don't put that kind of pressure on to other people. So
I would be the first to acknowledge that the job is a bloody hard one;
it is an incredible complex agenda.

Her claim to have a friend who is a secretary; her stated desire to go
home at a reasonable hour; her 'two young children and husband' all
explicitly link her to the conventionally feminine. Similarly, her attempts
to distance herself, both from 'a [male] chief executive in another Trust'
and from the 'faceless chief executive' make that same sort of link
implicitly. Yet, notice how assertions that might suggest femininity are

'corrected' immediately as she returns to quotations from the masculine and heroic. Talk of values and valuing our people are juxtaposed with the harshly functional: 'Where's the evidence?'; 'do they look at a payback for the organization?'. Similarly, mention of spending time with family is justified on functionalist grounds—she says that she can 'come back to work feeling rejuvenated and enjoy that'. Criticisms of a macho culture are rendered paradoxical by representing herself as having 'to quash all of those things'—an action described in terms which suggest a macho culture. Possibly most tellingly, however, her claim to have a friend who is secretary is undermined by having just patronisingly distinguished herself from 'the ladies in the office'. A phrase implying that, as leader, this is a group of which she is emphatically *not* a member.

Read through the lens of heroism, this excerpt might be understood, therefore, as an illustration of how masculinity comes to be defined as the normal desired state through the construction of femininity as the undesirable corruption of it. Leaders cannot freely adopt the discourses of femininity without, in doing so, threatening their credibility in a masculine hero's world (Hearn, 1993). On this note, we close this first rereading.

Conclusion

In the previous chapter we showed how language constructs that of which it speaks, that words always have many meanings and that the meanings are open to contestation. So, when language constructs that of which it speaks, there is no straightforward and direct relationship between a word (a sign) and that which is constructed. The many meanings of a single sign are always there, always *sous rature*, so out of sight and out of consciousness but still influencing that which is brought into being. In this chapter we have shown something of the complexity of meaning of a single word, here the word 'leader'. A reading of interview transcripts shows that when those who are called organisational leaders talk about themselves and their jobs, they incorporate notions of heroism and of the hero into their definition of the term.

We will turn now to leadership training programmes and to another study. Here we will continue to bedevil the straightforward presumptions of the achievability of a definition of leadership by showing further examples of what is *sous rature* when the words 'leader' or 'leadership' are used, what is always hidden but haunts and thus influences meaning.

4
Learning to be a Leader—Training Courses

In Chapters 2 and 3 we discussed how the terms 'leader' and 'leadership' have a performative impact, in that they serve to construct the very things they describe. In this chapter we turn to an arena more overtly concerned with the production of leaders and leadership: training courses.

In this chapter we draw on two interrelated studies to explore what goes on in leadership training rooms so as to gain a better understanding of what happens when people are called to be leaders. The first study is a survey, involving questionnaires and interviews, of leadership development in UK organisations we carried out with Beverly Alimo-Metcalfe and John Lawler in 2000. This shows that most large organisations, across the public and private sectors, now send managers on these programmes. The second study is based upon the autoethnographic opportunity allowed to us in our role as trainers in some of these courses. We critically interrogate accounts of the experiences of participants from the standpoint of our selves as academically informed, reflexive participants. Lest the academic voice overly dominate, we use quotations from participants in the first study to illustrate experiences of participants. We thus develop a critical account of the constituting of the identity of leader through leadership training courses.

We suggest that the courses work in three ways: upon the identity or practices of the self of participants, on their psyches and upon their emotions. Such courses fit into a broader agenda of changing the definition and thus identity of 'manager' or 'leader' in the twenty-first century. We conclude by suggesting that such courses, as part of this change of identity, may serve on the one hand to increase control over managers and leaders. On the other hand, given powers of resistance and, indeed, the encouragement of raised expectations of how organisations should treat their staff that are implicit in the training programme, the move towards leadership may offer potential for change towards, at the least, more emancipatory work environments.

The chapter is laid out as follows. We firstly summarise the results of the above-mentioned survey so as to provide the context for the paper. We then outline the contents of a typical leadership development programme, using various stages in the programme to identify three ways in which these programmes work upon participants. In our conclusion we point to the unpredictability of outcomes from these programmes.

Leadership development in the UK

The first study we report on here found that organisations in the UK, much like academics, still cannot agree on a definition of leadership and use a multitude of definitions. Despite this, the practice of sending staff on leadership development courses is widespread; so numerous managers are being trained in practising something highly nebulous, a 'floating signifier'. With colleagues (Alimo-Metcalfe et al., 2000) we sent postal questionnaires to 44 private and public sector organisations; 30 completed forms were returned. Representatives from six major organisations from both the public and private sectors were interviewed to augment those data.

As indicated above, this study showed that the term 'leader' is widely used but is so ill defined that it becomes a nebulous concept. The following table (Table 4.1) summarises the definitions of leadership given by staff interviewed in just six organisations. The term was often used rhetorically and without any significant meaning.

Definitions of leadership within six organisations

Respondents reported a shortage of leadership skills (whatever these may be), with only one of the 29 organisations stating that it has the leadership skills considered necessary for success. Leadership development was thus a top priority in 21 per cent of responding organisations and an important priority in 57 per cent. Only one-fifth of organisations stated that it was of moderate or lesser priority. Organisational appraisal schemes emphasised very strongly the role of leadership development in one-fifth of organisations, 46 per cent (13 organisations) place 'some emphasis' upon it and 25 per cent (seven organisations) a 'little emphasis'. Only two organisations, that is, eight per cent of the total, do not include leadership in their appraisal schemes. Leadership

Table 4.1   Definitions of Leadership

Definitions of Leadership

- The 'trinity' of 'example, persuasion and coercion'. This last, coercion, has to be the 'last of the "golf clubs" brought out of the bag', for the more it is resorted to, the worse is the leader;
- Empowering others so as to achieve the goals;
- Providing resources;
- Taking responsibility for the outcomes;
- Being a role model;
- It's a complex range of 'different skill sets', many of which can be learned;
- Is similar across all organisations;
- It differs not only between organisations but within various departments or work groups within organisations;
- Leadership is based on charisma;
- It's got nothing to do with charisma;
- It's based on organisational 'values' that include setting clear targets, demanding results, 'leading', motivating, acting with integrity, openness, honesty, avoiding politics and refusing to use people for their own ends, getting results;
- It's based on individual characteristics involving passion, belief in a vision, ability to communicate and excite people, courage, determination not to give up, conviction, integrity, creativity;
- It has negative connotations, for it implies it is something that can be left to the senior executives, so in one organisation the term 'leadership' is replaced by the phrase 'empowering values system';
- It is distrusted by some who think 'it is all a bit "namby-pamby"—and it gets a bit too psycho and some people get afraid of that'.
- Consideration of the different leadership styles is something that should be left to the Chief Executive;
- Consideration of the different leadership styles is something that should be undertaken throughout the organisation;
- It's not something that can be learned, as it's part of the individual's character;
- It's about, for those who have recently been on training courses, 'new paradigm' leadership, that is, 'true transformational leadership' not transactional leadership;
- It's distinct from management;
- Anyone in a senior management position has made it on merit and thus is a leader;
- It varies between national cultures (from a British organisation);
- It does not vary between national cultures (from a multinational company);
- It is 'in the soul'; it involves getting 'under the skin of your people, and when you talk about teams you mean it';
- It involves practising what you preach, leading by example, and totally embracing the organisation's values;
- It involves 'having a vision for where you are going, being able to articulate that vision back into practical steps that are going to take you there. And being able to manage, support and develop people so that they actually go with you'.

(Continued)

Table 4.1   (*Continued*)

- It involves being able to enthuse people so that everyone goes 'into battle together';
- It's part of an individual's personality, and you've either got it or you haven't;
- It 'is just the projection of your personality', so anyone who passes certain tests can demonstrate it.

development initiatives were common, with 82 per cent (23) of organisations in this study stating that they have them. Around 60 per cent of these initiatives had been started within the two years prior to the study, showing how recent the concept of leadership development is. Eleven per cent of organisations sent only top executives on these programmes, 30 per cent sent members of the top three management tiers, 30 per cent sent participants from all management tiers and 15 per cent from all levels of the organisation. Fifteen per cent did not send staff on such programmes.

The major form of development of leadership skills was through short courses, with only one-fifth of organisations sending staff on courses which ran for more than two weeks. The impact of these courses was not known, with 60 per cent of respondents to the postal survey reporting that no formal evaluation had been undertaken. Little support was provided to participants either while they were on programmes or upon their return to the organisation. Where support was available it tended to be informal, contingent upon the social relationships and belief systems operating in various sections of organisations, and psychological rather than physical.

This study, therefore, showed that organisations reflect academic literature in their inability to define leadership. The term is something of a floating signifier, requiring a certain 'nodal point' to stop its sliding and fix its meaning (Žižek, 1989, p. 87). However, organisations still think it vitally important that this nebulous thing is developed, and invest time, money and effort in ensuring their managers are trained in it.

So we are left with a conundrum, or rather a research question. There is this 'thing' which no one can define, but large numbers of managers are being trained in it. What then is effected by the training? To use another definition of performative, that of Judith Butler (1990; 1993), what subject positions, subjectivities or identities are brought into being as a result of these programmes? There has been little evaluation of these courses, and those evaluations which have been published tend to be descriptive and do not question the assumptions upon which the courses are built (Edmonstone and Western, 2002). The more informed evaluations, such as Blackler and Kennedy (2004), show that participants are enabled to cope better with the demands of their stressful jobs, but the managerialist perspective of such evaluations focuses only upon what goes in (the contents of the programme) and what comes out (whether or not participants become better skilled at their work). Ignored are the performative outcomes, that is, what managerial identities are constructed through immersion in leadership courses.

To answer this question, we report upon a form of autoethnographic 'fieldwork' (Ronai, 1999; Ellis and Bochner, 2000; Denzin and Lincoln, 2002) in which the researcher becomes part of the researched. Leadership training is offered by private sector training companies and also by UK universities as part of their 'third arm' or consultancy services. We have ourselves participated in such courses, and we have also been employed in their delivery. In this chapter we use those experiences to offer a theory of what goes on within the space of the training room. For some years we have turned upon ourselves, in our role as trainers, our internalised academic gaze, for these excursions into the world of industry offer an ideal research opportunity. We have explored our own experiences as trainers and the physical, emotional and intellectual experience of stepping into this very different world, and we have observed the processes through which we and the participants progress through the course of a programme. We offer below a theory of the performativity of leadership training programmes, based upon this 'fieldwork'. However, there is a danger in autoethnography that other voices, those of other participants in the social world studied, are silenced. To avoid this, we include in the discussion quotes from participants involved in the empirical study reported above. Their voices are given in italics.

The trainer's voice

The exasperation among authors regarding the impossibility of defining leadership is not reflected in training courses, for they commence with very precise definitions of the term. For example, the 32,050 'front-line nurse leaders and managers from primary and secondary care' participating in a three-day course known as LEO or 'Leading an Empowered Organisation' are told that the British government's current 'modernisation agenda' for the NHS will need people who can lead the change with respect and dignity using both personal and position power' (course handbook). The course handbook does not define leadership, but on p. 13 it does define the role of the leader, drawing upon literature from the American organisation which developed the programme:

Role of the leader

Leaders

- are key to the quality of service or care rendered in the organisation and need to see themselves as valued in that role.
- choose their results (are proactive).
- create the vision.
- understand that empowerment as a person and as a leader requires an understanding of power, the choice to take it and the skills to build it.
- take risks and encourage risk taking in others.
- use a problem-solving approach that focuses on results.
- create an environment for success.
- develop rather than control others.
- respect others.
- understand that élitist attitudes are unethical.
- model rather than mould.
- trust their experiences.

Participants are introduced to the process of becoming a leader both through such definitions (typical in such courses) and through a 'talk and chalk' exercise which asks participants to give their definitions of leadership. The programmes thus commence with an appearance of certainty which disguises the lack of definition of the concept. Typically, participants are then introduced to a variety of research evidence which shows the history of leadership thought, current research into leadership, the effects of poor leadership upon organisations, the inter-relationships between good leadership and various measures of organisational performance. Participants, in our experience, will be very willing to ask questions about the research which has been undertaken, seek clarification of statistical methods, etc.

Having been inducted into the history of leadership, research participants then begin a process of self-analysis accomplished through the measurements provided by a range of psychometric measures. These typically involve participants in one-to-one discussions with qualified users of such instruments. The most popular of these instruments at the time of writing are 360-degree leadership profiles and Myers-Briggs Type Indicator (MBTI).

The '360-degree' profiles, of which there are several, require participants to request that their boss, two or more of their organisational peers, and two or more of their subordinates (often called 'direct reports') complete anonymised questionnaires in which they rate the putative leader on a range of dimensions. These include such aspects as leadership and influence, performance management, communication skills, personal skills, professional knowledge, decision making and administrative or managerial skills. These headings are divided into various dimensions including, under leadership, such things as 'sensitivity', ability to collaborate, persuasiveness, and capacity in empowering others, etc. People are rated on their delegation, coaching and appraisal skills, their tolerance for stress, ability to learn, and so on and to show how important the various skills within the organisation are. Participants complete a similar questionnaire, rating themselves upon each dimension. The completed questionnaires are analysed by a computer programme, and the feedback given verbally. The feedback emphasises that any major discrepancy between how the individual has rated themselves and how others rate them should, firstly, be tested by going back to the raters and asking them to explain the shortfall in performance, and secondly, by treating it as a 'learning opportunity', with opportunities for development highlighted. One participant in the above study describes the power of such an instrument:

> *The basis of it was we had a 360-degree system that had obviously been prepared beforehand . . . it draws out a profile of you. And then you are allowed another five people, or they should be made up from the boss and people that work with you and people that work for you. So the basis of it was discussing that profile. And it was very much about sharing, I mean the whole thing was to try and make us all more open and to share both our strengths and weaknesses in terms of our leadership skills and how other people perceive us. And it was bloody eye opening stuff you know really.*

The MBTI meanwhile is based upon a questionnaire completed by participants, which asks them to show their preferred response to a variety of questions. The answers allow the rater to identify into which of the 16 personality types, based on Jungian theory, the participant falls. Feedback takes about an hour, and it is emphasised that the participant is an expert about themselves, and that the choice of which personality type they belong to is ultimately theirs. Having identified the personality type, the individual is given a single sheet which explains that type according to:

- How they appear at their best;
- Their characteristics;
- How others may see them;

- Potential areas for growth; and
- How they may respond when under great stress.

The descriptions are remorselessly optimistic—any shortcomings are a result of either not having developed sufficiently an aspect of their personality (such as their intuition, thinking skills, sensing skills, etc.), or being in an organisation or role which suppresses their natural talents. Difficulties with other people are explained through the notion of conflicting personality types. Participants remember clearly, and uncritically, the aims of such discussions:

> *The aim of the feedback discussion is that by its end the individual should have greater understanding about themselves, the ways they function within their organisation, how others see them, and areas for growth and development required for them to become good leaders.*

There is huge intuitive appeal to these instruments. The MBTI type that is most common in management, for example, is the Sensing, Thinking, Judging Types (STJ), that is, people obsessed with order, clarity, logic, rationality, deadlines and so on. The majority of academics tend to be NTs or intuitive thinkers; they have 'original minds' and are ingenious, resourceful in solving new and challenging problems, well read, theoretical and abstract, interested more in ideas than in social interaction and so on (Briggs Myers, McCaulley et al. 1998). It is this intuitive appeal, possibly arising from the tautologous nature of the research which arrived at these constructs, that perhaps has made these instruments so popular. In many ways they are similar to horoscopes, but their claim to scientific integrity allows them to tap into the power/knowledge veins of the current epoch (Case and Phillipson, 2004).

At the end of the training course the participants disperse back to the workplace, where they will perhaps continue to meet as a group a few more times before being absorbed back into the day-to-day environment. They may be involved in action learning groups, in which case the programme will continue for a few more months, with regular feedback and discussion sessions being organised.

What goes on in the training room?

We have given a bald description of typical leadership development courses. We move now beyond the descriptive to explore what goes on while the above activities are going on.

The courses are about 'personal development':

> *But it is just good to know that the Chief Exec is fully behind the course and recognises that you need time out for personal development . . . that is recognised as my time and is helping me to develop, but also, helping the organisation to develop.*

But what is 'personal development'? The answer to this question is that personal development is concerned with developing the 'I' as a person who will contribute to the organisation. This causes us to ask: what is this emergent 'I', the 'I' who emerges from the training, and is it colonised by the organisation? These questions lead us into our analysis of what goes on in these courses, beyond the superficial level which can be observed and recounted in evaluation forms.

Our intention in this section is to theorise the processes which could lead one interviewee to describe his experience as 'eye opening':

> *[We had to identify] what is actually important about our jobs, what are the really important things we do, rather than the crap that we get stuck into. It highlighted very much the importance of our jobs being very, very much about leading people. And [the course helped] us understand what are the key things that we have got to do in terms of leading people. And what struck me the most about it, I think the most lasting thing for me is the need to appeal to people's hearts in terms of leaders of the future, and people that are going to be able to appeal to their people's hearts and get the most out of people from that point of view. Be open and honest with people, be very good in terms of giving them coaching. We had this grid where we talked about the loving, challenging culture, which is the combination of being challenging and positive in your feedback. We compared that to our current situation and how we felt about our boss. I have been in the situation where I had a boss whose style was just completely about bashing me around the head. So it was all about challenge, there was no positive feedback.*

This participant is describing an experience that involves

(a) entering a place which is physically removed from the organisation and which, because of the process of change that occurs, is a liminal space (Gennep, 1960; Turner, 1974);

(b) looking inward into themselves, a process of looking inward designed to be performative, i.e. to bring about changes in the self, and

(c) encouragement to develop new and different aspects of themselves, i.e. new emotional selves, which they will take with them back into the everyday world of the organisation. We will now analyse each of these to suggest a theory of the leadership training course.

The Liminal Space

In this space, forms of ritualised, theatrical practices are invoked which involve trainers wearing the relevant costume (smart suit, rehearsed smile, tense body), who lead participants through processes whose ostensible aim is identity (re)formation. These ritual, scripted and cere-monial behaviours within the training programme have a performative dimension, in which what Parker and Sedgwick (1995, p. 2) call the extroversion of the actor and the introversion of the signifier work to develop a presumably straightforward conversion of the participants from 'manager' to 'leader'. By this they mean the acting out of the pro-gramme by participants and their internalisation of the terms used in the programme. Two things are therefore going on at the same time—acting and becoming. The actor stops mimicking when s/he has absorbed the meaning of the words used into their psyches. The train-ing room is thus a complex place in which much more happens than the gathering of information and ideas.

Furthermore, the individuals who arrive at the venue are not *tabula rasa* or clean sheets waiting to be written on. They are mature individ-uals who have grown up in a culture which has shaped and influenced them. They have been educated and trained, have been taught to read and write and will have read numerous books, papers, magazines and articles. They will no doubt have watched many films and television programmes, if not have visited theatrical performances and art gal-leries. Leadership is something not restricted to organisations: it features in all the many art forms of Western cultures. Participants in leadership development courses do not arrive, therefore, totally naïve and untu-tored in concepts of leadership, for having grown up in a culture in which leadership is venerated they will have read and heard many sto-ries involving great leaders. The word 'leadership' carries with it trace memories of our earlier encounters with leaders and leadership—heroic tales of Hercules and Ulysses, of Obi Wan Kanobi, or William Brown, Meg, Jo, Beth and Amy, the 'Little Women' who appealed to a past gen-eration, Buffy the Vampire Slayer who has taken their place in the early twenty-first century, Harry Potter, Lara Croft, and so on.

No matter how hard the gurus of leadership strive to distinguish new concepts of leadership, to carve out a new space for organisational leadership, the cultural transmission mechanisms of history and of social memory and social forgetting (Roach, 1995), of intertextuality (in which texts each inform others and is informed by them) and notably in this case the systems of myths which tell a culture about itself (Barthes, 1972), will work within the imaginings of participants in leadership training courses. The free-floating syntax, or difficulty of defining leadership, allows the subject to grasp at both images and the 'surviving fragments of authentic myth and delusion' (Jameson, 2000, p. 105). As we discussed in Chapter 2, it is impossible for someone to hear the word 'leader' and dissociate it from the numerous meanings they have encountered throughout their lives. The term thus has great libidinal energy: when the word 'leader' is heard earlier encounters with the term will be remembered and the excitement of those earlier encounters will make it exciting in the present. So earlier codes of leadership will suffuse any other possible meanings (Žižek, 1989; Jameson, 1991) and give them power. We saw in Chapter 3 how a single term always has present numerous meanings, and how the term 'hero' informs leaders' talk about leadership—the hero is just one of the characters that will suffuse the word 'leader'.

When the trainer stands up and attempts to interpellate participants— turning them into leaders through this single act of calling them leaders— she thus offers a performative term, one which brings into being that which it describes, freighted with so much meaning that the 'reiterative and citational practice by which discourse produces the effects that it names' (Butler, 1993, p. 2) produces something other than that aspired to in the formal aims of the training programme. The signifier 'leadership' with its numerous possible meanings is not one 'pregnant object' but many, into which participants may project themselves, or imagine themselves as being, and so their own interpretations of leadership will be absorbed into how they think of themselves as leaders. Participants may draw upon a host of cultural references when imagining themselves as leaders. In dreaming themselves as leaders they will project themselves backwards into the heroic age of myths of knights in shining armour, and forward into future selves undertaking heroic deeds within the organisation. They are seduced (Calás and Smircich, 1991).

The turn to leadership can therefore be seen as an invitation to seduce oneself through the dream of heroic leader. It lures managers into thinking of themselves as leaders.

The performativity of looking inward

Again, I think there is a little bit emerging of 'is all this time on personal leadership styles and action learning and individual so on a little bit wishy-washy, a little bit detached from the business?' But at the moment I think it has been received pretty well. And a number of people who have been on it perhaps the slightly less hardened chestnuts see it as a positive experience.

The 'slightly less hardened chestnuts' are those who can be broken open to allow an impact of another to have an effect. In other words, their meaning (of the self, of the organisation) is to be managed, for 'leadership is realized in the process whereby one or more individuals succeeds in attempting to frame and define the reality of others' (Smircich and Morgan 1982, p. 258). Participants are encouraged to see as important a mechanistic list of 'competencies', such as 'so much financial ability added to a bit of marketing and some strategic leadership together with some interpersonal skills and a hint of' (Mangham and Pye, 1991, cited in Watson 2001, p. 221 and referred to in Chapter 1) delivered by a person who is now amenable to the feelings of others ('a little bit wishy-washy').

These endeavours can be seen as a means of controlling or seeking to regulate an individual's identities within the organisation, wishing from them conformity to specific traits and competencies. Thus the powerful voices of the organisational leaders strive to persuade the rest of the workforce to conform to organisational norms and behaviours (Knights and Willmott 1992; Alvesson and Willmott 2002). In response, participants on these programmes may (or may not) collaborate by adopting the very behaviours and skills that are being promulgated. Having taken up a particular position as one's own, a person sees the world from the vantage point of that position and in terms of the particular images, metaphors, beliefs and concepts offered within that particular perspective. Management consultants, trainers and educators who run these programmes on the organisation's behalf collude in the presentation of a core identity, that of 'the leader', and seek to promote this identity among course participants. This traditional view of the self presumes a central, unitary identity, a coherent view of the self against which it is possible to gauge whether an individual's actions are true or false, genuine or spurious, good or bad. So, when participants enter the training room, they bring with them limitless possibilities of what it can be to be a leader. Those possibilities are then whittled down and down and down.

Specific inventories such as MBTI profiles and 360 degree feedback instruments serve in the restricting of the potential selves a leader could be. They provide the portfolio of evidence that supports the production of just one central, unitary identity, an identity that the individual can 'manufacture' or 'adopt' to fit the profile created by the dominant discourse of leadership. It is a label the person-turned-leader should wear on his/her lapel.

In post-structuralist, interactionist and constructionist accounts these assumptions of a core and single identity are thrown open to challenge. Gergen (1994), for example, asks why we should compare an individual's actions with some core and solo image. Identities are constructed in a multiplicity of ways, and the constructions we call the 'I' or the 'me' are put together within available discursive resources and can be highly fluid (Antaki and Widdicombe, 1998). As a consequence, who we are is always an open question, with the answer changing from moment to moment, according to the positions made available in any moment and through the stories by which we make sense of our own and other's lives (Davies and Harre, 2001). Identity is very much a relational and comparative concept, constructed through interactions with others (Mouffe, 1995). In Schnapp's (cited in Wetherell, Taylor et al. 2001) terms, each of us is knitted into the historical constructions of other's identities just as they are into ours.

The possibilities opened up by such an interpretation are reduced by psychometric and other personality profile inventories. They constrain the possibilities of identity to a narrow band or range of types of behaviours. Told 'this is you', people are called into being that type, that characteristic—it becomes a part of the performance of their identities. Here we have not the iron cage of bureaucracy but the iron cage of personality profiles. Further, in the context of the leadership programme, the facilitators provide the participants with a model of how a leader should *be*, providing an order that promotes the dominant model of 'the leader' used in Western organisations. The person may become 'the leader' rather than 'the manager' or 'the administrator', but the possibilities of becoming are restricted to one narrow construct.

So leadership training courses invite participants to seduce themselves into the concept of leadership, and then limit the range of possibilities of being within that identity of leader. The libidinal energy roused in seduction remains alive, ready to be transferred to a less romantic model of self-as-leader. Something else is going on alongside this: a change in the emotions that managers may experience and display is encouraged. In what follows we show that the presumption that emotions are fixed and unchanging over time and between cultures is wrong, and suggest that leadership training courses are attempting to encourage managers to express the range of emotions that has evolved in Western cultures in the late twentieth century, rendering those previously deemed publicly acceptable as archaic, even dangerous, in their elevation of the rational over the emotional (Rumens, 2005).

New emotional selves

The thing that assists it is a willingness to change. There are a lot of people with the willingness to change at the senior level. Having said that there is an awful lot of people . . . who have not been used to that kind of environment. It is actually quite hard to move culturally from an environment which has been very much about command and control to suddenly say to people 'we want you to be open, I want you to challenge me now—I want ideas to come from you. I don't know it all—I am the boss but I don't know it all'. And I don't know, it is a bit of a cultural thing you know, it can't change overnight. And people are either sceptical or scared, or can't understand it or don't want to take part or whatever. So that's a problem. I actually think there are just some specific people who are blockages to this as well in terms of their attitude. And I think we should, we should get rid of some people.

This openness to others, to be achieved through the leadership courses, encourages managers to be *nice*. To be nice means that a limited range of emotions are all that can be expressed, but certain practices are to be encouraged. Happiness is encouraged while depression is not; calmness is valued, anger criticised. Leaders are expected to talk openly about themselves to colleagues, to ask them to tell them openly and honestly about their strengths and shortcomings (the follow-up to 360-degree feedback), for understanding of both oneself and other people is expected to minimise interpersonal conflicts arising out of clashes of personalities (MBTI). Reasons for the display of negative emotions are revealed (MBTI) and can thus be anticipated, explained and avoided, and positive relationships with people, in the form of empowerment, coaching, support, and so on (360-degree) are encouraged actively. This suggests, at first sight, that leadership is nothing but a development within the human relations school of management thought, where 'nice' managers encourage more output from workers. Read through the lens of Foucauldian labour process theory (Wray-Bliss, 2002), such leadership courses could be read as attempts to develop managers' ability to control staff through colonisation of the psyche (Alvesson and Willmott, 2002).

We concur with this interpretation but also suggest it is too limited and that something else is occurring, which is that in the late-modern or postmodern world this turn to 'niceness' contributes to the control of leaders through the attempt to constitute a managerial identity that is malleable and unquestioning.

This turn to niceness is, we suggest, part of the changing understanding of emotions in organisations. There is an emerging narrative of a history of emotions in organisations. This sees a progression from Taylorism and Weberian bureaucracies, when modernist management attempted to suppress emotions, to late-modernist organisations where the potential for using emotions as a managerial tool was indicated, notably in the work of critical researchers such as Hochschild (1983), and on to postmodernist theories of organisations which are seen to seek to celebrate the liberation of emotions from modernist rigidity (Fineman, 2000; Hancock and Tyler, 2001). There is in this history an assumption of an essentialist body of emotions which has been at various times suppressed, manipulated or feted. We suggest rather that available emotional repertoires (Hughes, 1999), and the resultant range of emotions which can or cannot be expressed, change over the course of different stages of capitalism. Rather than emotions having been liberated from modernist rigidity in the postmodern, it would be more correct to say that in the postmodern the range of emotions that can be articulated differs from that of modernism.

Literature, history and philosophy do indeed demonstrate how definitions of feelings and emotions, or recommended norms which govern the shaping of and reaction to emotional expressions (Stearns, 1994), change over time. In the eighteenth century, for example, feelings were characterised as transpersonal, autonomous entities that seemed to 'wander extravagantly from one person to another' (Pinch, 1996, p.3); Hume saw them as ignorant of the boundaries of individuals, visiting people from without (ibid). A private realm of feeling emerged in Britain between the sixteenth and nineteenth centuries, a period which saw the appearance of a new sensibility, alongside the conditions of possibility for thinking about the new concept of a mode of production (Jameson, 1998). Feelings in this era became gendered, that is, the province of women, and 'sentimentality' became something to be despised due to its relationship with 'untrue' feelings.

The 'feeling rules' of the twenty-first century are shifting. The British version of 'cool', the stiff upper lip, has been declared dead (Cameron, 2000). Read through Jameson's perspective, the fundamental ideological task in twenty-first-century capitalism remains that of co-ordinating new forms of economic production with new forms of practice and social and mental forms (Jameson, 1991, p. xiv), where the 'new forms' include a new 'structure of feeling' (p. xviii) or a 'whole new type of emotional ground tone' (p. 6) exhibited by 'new people' who evolve out of a 'continuous reciprocal interaction and feedback loop' between culture and the economic (pp. xiv–xv). The various preconditions for this new 'structure of feeling' pre-exist their moment of 'combination and crystallization into a relatively hegemonic style' (pp. xviii–xix).

In management and business studies these changes have been anticipated in the huge popularity of 'emotional intelligence' (Goleman, 1996, 2002). Goleman's is a modernist view of emotions—they are something, he argues, that can and should be taught and, through the concept of the emotional IQ, measured and thus rationalised. In this, he apparently contradicts the 'conventional approach' that emotion is, in the modernist era, the opposite of reason (Barbalet, 2001) and takes us towards a more critical approach in which emotion supports rationality (ibid.), but Goleman's book says something more. Emotional repertoires changed in the eighteenth century before there was a language to express such changes. Jameson (1998, p. 18) notes that 'radical breaks between periods do not generally involve complete changes of content but rather the restructuring of a certain number of elements already given: features that in an earlier period or system were subordinate now become dominant, and features that had been dominant again become secondary'. This helps situate Goleman's book between the modern and postmodern eras: between a dominant style (which is used to legitimate the new) now becoming subordinate and the striving for a language in which to articulate the new. We thus go further than Rumens (2005), who suggests Goleman's claim that emotional intelligence can be cultivated among employees is simply wrong. We suggest Goleman has anticipated, but misinterpreted, major cultural changes.

Now this has occurred alongside a loosening of the gender system's heteronormative regime (Hennessy, 1995) (that is, a period in which heterosexuality is compulsory, with anyone who is not heterosexual regarded as debased and corrupt), for there has been a disturbance in the assumption of 'typical' gender behaviours to one biological sex. With the destabilising of gender identities rigid definitions of what it means to be 'a man', 'a woman', 'gay' or 'straight', and the concomitant psychosocial apparel attached to each, are shaken. We referred in Chapter 3 to a female leader who appeared to move between masculine and feminine positions and shall discuss this in more depth in Chapter 6. Where previously 'emotions' were seen as weak, polluting and feminine, and thus one reason for restricting women's access to public realms, as many feminists have argued (Benn and Gaus, 1983; Pateman, 1983; Hearn, 1992), in the postmodern world emotions become de-gendered expressions to be appropriated when constituting fluid, postmodern identities. The new structure of feeling of which Jameson speaks is therefore, we suggest, not so much 'new' as a generalisation across all spheres and all genders of an expression of emotions that have been only since the eighteenth century regarded as female, demeaning and polluting. Alongside this has been a diminution in the status of other emotions (rationality, logic, calmness, anger) which had governed the male, public realm (Hearn, 1992; Seidler, 1994).

Therefore, during feedback about their (supposed) leadership styles and personality types, a new discourse is inserted into participants' free-floating imagination of themselves as leaders. This interruption of the daydream does not replace its heroic verities, but rather superimposes another layer upon and within it. The new leader is, or should be, heroic, but also a very nice, approachable person who is open and able to emote.

Conclusion

Many managers have already participated in, or soon will register for, leadership training courses. They will at the start be perhaps perplexed as to what this notion of organisational leadership is, for it remains something that is open to individual interpretation. However, they do not enter the training room naked of assumptions, for Western culture is saturated with concepts of leadership. Leadership training programmes draw upon the libidinal energies thus aroused to persuade participants to open themselves to a new way of being, to a new identity. The subjectivity that shall be experienced is limited to a range in which openness and forms of emotionality are to be praised and practised. The new leader must be willing to analyse himself—or herself—and to discuss the self-analysis with strangers and with colleagues. The process of self-analysis may indeed serve to bring into construction a new self, but one constrained within the taxonomies of personality profiles.

Instigated by organisations, leadership training programmes are, of course, a form of control over managers. In encouraging managers to be nice, the courses may be effecting subtle managerial controls over other employees.

However, there may be more emancipatory aspects to these programmes. Participants are encouraged to think about themselves and the organisations in which they work in new and different ways. In the process of self-examination they look also at how they have been treated by their managers. Receiving feedback about how their staff regard them, they are given an opportunity to see themselves as others see them. Participants are therefore facilitated to explore the negative and controlling aspects of the work they undertake as managers and the ways in which the organisation controls and dominates them.

There is a possibility therefore that leadership training programmes may instigate in some participants a form of rebellion against or resistance towards the organisation. Rather than return to their daily work determined to lead employees to greater productivity and higher conformity, they may do the opposite, and return determined to bring about changes of a different kind. What those are we cannot predict. We can conclude only that there are possibilities that the leadership style evoked may just as likely be that of a quiet revolutionary as that of the more effective manager.

Closing Notes to Part I

The four chapters of Part I have shown that there is a huge body of literature on leadership. Most of this is uncritical and tends to be descriptive rather than analytical.

We have shown that such literature cannot achieve only the outcomes it is seeking. Where it may be desired that leaders will use the literature to develop their own practices, we have shown how passive that presumption is. Just by picking up a leaflet with the word 'leader' outlined in bold type on the cover means that something is happening in the reader. The word itself will engage with the reader, enter into his/her psyche. It will stir memories of the past, and there will be anticipations of the self as leader in the future.

But there is no such thing as a word in itself, for each word will have several possible meanings which will all interact with each other. One of the words that informs understanding of leadership is 'hero'. This brings with it notions of romance and of danger, of challenges and of threats overcome. Such a meaning will bring with it libidinal energy that will inform the interpretation, in the imagination of the reader, listener or speaker, and what they will imagine the word 'leader' to mean.

Furthermore, there is now seemingly common agreement that the words 'leader' and 'leadership' bring with them a requirement for a new form of person: an individual who can emote openly, who has a great deal of self-knowledge and who can therefore engage actively with people. Leadership is about interpersonal interactions.

All this seems in many ways laudable. The multiple possible meanings of the terms 'leader' and 'leadership' mean there is little danger of homogeneity, of too many people turning out like peas from the same pod. Who can object to the idea that people can talk openly about themselves, and thus improve communication?

But there are other interpretations that suggest such a rosy and uncritical reading will do a disservice to leaders and the people they work with.

Part I has shown that the words 'leader' and 'leadership' construct the very things of which they speak. Part II will explore in more depth the things that are constructed.

Part II Deconstructions

Opening Notes

In Chapters 2, 3 and 4 we showed that the words 'leader' and 'leadership' do not merely describe but actively *create* identities or subject positions (i.e. a position in which one becomes a subject). When people call themselves leaders, or are told they must become leaders and/or are sent on training courses to learn the arts of leadership, they are required to do something with those much-freighted terms. They are required to change themselves, to take on a new form of the self. Although we have shown something of the complexity of such constructions, that there is no such thing as a simplistic transmission mechanism by which someone becomes a leader after being told they are to be a leader, our arguments to date have been analytical without being critical. We now turn to a more critical analysis in which we explore the dark side of the performativity of the terms 'leader' and 'leadership' and their effects on individuals.

In the first two chapters in this section we will focus on theories arising from gender studies to articulate our concerns. Chapter 5 opens the discussion with an exploration of leadership development. It thus in some ways continues the discussion from Chapter 4, but largely from the perspective of those who commission leadership development programmes. Through analysing interview data from a study of leadership development and analysing those data through a queer theory lens, Chapter 5 will show that the 'Great Man' thesis is still alive and well and informing leadership in organisations. The discussion will go on to argue that the very vagueness of definitions of leadership, discussed in Chapter 1, is itself part of the performativity of the words 'leader' and 'leadership'. It is shown that some understanding of the term exists, but this understanding sets the definition of leadership so high that it is impossible for leaders ever to achieve it. Leaders are therefore doomed to a perpetual round of trying to achieve an unachievable norm. At the same time, followers are constructed as inferior, lacking, insignificant. Leadership thus can be seen as far distant from the somewhat romantic ideal envisaged in mainstream leadership studies.

Chapter 6 takes the analysis further by exploring leadership using perspectives from feminism and men and masculinities. That chapter draws on a study of an organisation which had invested in a major leadership development programme. The interviews showed that the longstanding organisational culture was and remains one that is macho and domineering. The managers who work within that culture now have to be leaders working within a gentler, more 'feminine' culture. We argue that this means they occupy an impossible position, required at one and the same time to be the opposite things of macho managers and gentle leaders.

The post-structuralist stance adopted in this book uses psychoanalytical theory in much of its theory development. In Chapter 7 we draw on one branch of psychoanalytical theory, objects relations theory, to analyse the claims of the newest theory of leadership, Authentic Leadership. Authentic Leadership has many claims made in its support. Our reading suggests that it contains the seeds of its own destruction, for in its requirement that the leader be 'authentic' or full of self-knowledge, open and honest, it turns that leader into someone who is not human, and therefore not authentic. Our reading prophesises that authentic leadership would cause trauma and suffering if introduced into organisations.

This section therefore paints a gloomy picture of leadership. It argues that leadership is a norm the leader must strive and always fail to achieve. In that striving, the leader will have to occupy contradictory and self-defeating subject positions. Academia is responsible in many ways for constructing such an uncomfortable position that will leave real people suffering. These conclusions lead to our positing a different way of conceptualising leadership, which we set out in the concluding chapter of the book.

5
Queer(y)ing Leadership

Turning now to a more critical analysis of leadership, in the first two chapters in this section we will focus on theories arising from gender studies to articulate our concerns. Chapter 6 will explore leadership using perspectives from feminism and men and masculinities. In that chapter we will explore how leaders have to take on feminine characteristics, while management requires that they take on masculine characteristics. We will suggest that leadership creates huge anxieties for managers as it puts them in the contradictory position of having to be both masculine and feminine at one and the same time, so whatever they do is unacceptable. In this chapter we will establish the setting for that argument by using queer theory to show that leadership is normative in that it provides a vision of 'the normal', which leaders have to attain. We will show that attaining the norm of leadership is impossible.

Queer theory emerged as a result of the footwork and hard slog made by feminist theorists in showing how women are discriminated against. However, a critique made against feminism in particular, but one that applied equally to men and masculinities (which had turned a feminist eye upon men), was that these perspectives presumed all women were similar just because they were women, and all men were similarly united by the single fact of their being men. Although feminism in particular claimed to be anti-essentialist in that it rejected whole-heartedly the idea that there is anything 'given' that makes a person into a woman, it still presumed there was something about being a woman which united all women. Black women, working-class women, women from ex-colonial powers and lesbian women argued forcefully that, in assuming this 'universal' woman, theorists ignored the wide variety of ways of being a woman. Theorists were therefore charged with having been supportive of a privileged form of womanhood—white, heterosexual, middle-class women from developed economies (Alsop et al., 2002).

Meanwhile, stimulated in part by the liberatory potential of the work of the French academic Michel Foucault, a highly political gay liberation movement emerged in the 1980s in both the United States and Western Europe where feminism has radically changed women's lives so that few women expect to spend their lives 'chained to the kitchen sink'; gay rights is bringing about remarkable changes in the lives of people who do not conform to what is known as 'the heterosexual matrix'.

Readers may be wondering what the relevance of political movements in favour of women's and homosexual rights may have for leadership theory, or for themselves as leaders. Our perspective in this and the following chapters is that feminist and queer theories are the clearest examples of how academic theory and political practice can each inform the other. Queer theorists have done this firstly through identifying how people are subordinated and suppressed by things so taken for granted and so familiar we hardly know they are governing us. Then they show that there is nothing 'natural' about the norms, practices, ways of thinking and ways of being that suppress 'minorities'. Through illustrating the constructed nature of the norms through which we are governed and controlled, it becomes possible to change those norms and the institutions which support them. Knowledge, therefore, is the vital step to bringing about changes.

This way of thinking, of 'queering' the taken for granted, that is, of looking at something that appears normal and seeing how queer, or odd, it is, can be applied not only to gender and sexuality but to numerous other areas of our lives. One example is food: Elspeth Probyn (1993, 1999) has done sterling work in queering the ways in which food is understood and consumed in the Western world in the twenty-first century. With regard to the workplace, Parker (2002) has argued the merits of using queer theory in organisation studies, and a number of authors are experimenting with its use in the understanding of organisation and management (Brewis, Hampton and Linstead, 1997; Harding, 2003; Bowring, 2004) and in public administration (Lee, Learmonth and Harding, 2008).

Our intention in this chapter is, in a nutshell, to 'queer' leadership, or to look at this thing called leadership as if it were odd or queer. As soon as we start thinking about what we regard as normal we find how peculiar the 'normal' is, leading us to ask: Why are things this way? So 'queer' here does not refer to sexuality, but to ways of recognising and exploring (queer(y)ing) the things we take for granted as 'normal' in our working and non-working lives. Our aims in this chapter are therefore to look at how leadership theory and practices have constructed new norms or rules that govern how leaders should live. We will show that these norms are unattainable, and so suggest that leadership (a) controls leaders and (b) makes workplaces worst for leaders and followers.

We will achieve these aims through re-analysing data from the study into leadership development we carried out with Beverly Alimo-Metcalfe and John Lawler in 2000. In that study we surveyed the leadership development plans of 29 organisations across the public and private sectors, based nationally and internationally, and carried out interviews in six of those organisations. Our plan here is to identify the norms that inform the thinking about leadership development, that is, to 'queer' it. The chapter interweaves data, analysis and explanation of the theory in its pursuit of an understanding of 'leadership' and 'leader' as normative terms which dictate the standards people should attain, but which make those standards so refined that they are impossible to achieve.

Queering leadership

Although much current leadership theory argues that leadership should feature at every level of an organisation and, indeed, that all people in organisations should be able to discover their leadership potential (see Chapter 1), organisational practice is much different. As noted in Chapter 1, the numerous writers on leadership have been unable to arrive at a coherent definition of leadership. Our study of leadership development found that in only two per cent of organisations was there found to be a seemingly robust definition of leadership shared across the organisation.

Both the mailed questionnaire and the interviews carried out for that study showed that the language used to describe leadership varied from one organisation to another. For the armed forces, developing leadership was defined as 'inspiring our people to reach their potential'. This spokesperson identified a 'trinity' at work in leadership, consisting of 'example, persuasion and coercion'. The last, coercion, has to be the 'last of the "golf clubs" brought out of the bag' for, it was stated, the more it is resorted to the worst is the leader. In speaking as a member of the armed forces, this interviewee noted that leadership involves not telling people how to do things, but telling them what to do and then empowering them to achieve the goals and providing them with the necessary resources. This involves 'transparent accountability' in the leader, for the leader is responsible for the actions of those s/he leads and must be willing to accept that responsibility.

Some respondents understood the British model of leadership to differ from those of other cultures. For example, the spokesperson for the armed forces quoted above felt that the British approach to leadership is 'in the soul'; it involves getting 'under the skin of your people, and when you talk about teams you mean it'. There is nothing superficial about it, for the British leader 'really has to live his style', that is, to 'practise what they preach'. It involves leading from the front, leading by example and totally embracing the organisation's values.

In contrast, some multinational organisations studied were determined to discover, as one director of human resource management stated 'what the strategic leadership competencies are internationally'. Definitions of leadership in these multinational companies, just as in the national organisations and across the public and private sectors, were woolly (Alimo-Metcalfe et al., 2000). As one respondent from a multinational company said, 'you can't be specific about what leadership is'. Some respondents defined leadership by its opposite. A multinational pharmaceutical company, for instance, had until the late 1990s given preference, the Director of Human Resource Management (HRM) said, to 'strategic thinkers' rather than 'leaders'. This was by 2000 seen as a mistake, for the former are 'not deliverers and not people that carried people with them, that take people's hearts and minds and you go into battle together'. Some respondents, in a postmodernist frame of mind, were satisfied that leadership is whatever individuals define it as. For example, the last speaker said 'we all . . . have very different ideas about what leadership is'.

There is, therefore, replicated within organisations that inability of academic researchers to define leadership, despite decades of trying, as noted in Chapter 1. In earlier chapters we showed that language brings into being that which is spoken about, so we would expect all this talk of leadership to construct the identity of 'leader', an identity which can be taken up and absorbed into the concepts of the self of those charged with becoming leaders. However, this difficulty in definition suggests something awry. If leadership cannot be defined, then what is the shape of the subject position that is to be occupied and absorbed into the self? What sort of self is it that will practise the arts of leadership? We will here introduce queer theory (QT), as it will provide some answers to these questions.

Queering the absence of definition of leadership

Queer theory (QT), as we use it, is regarded as a set of political or politicised practices and positions which explore and are critical of normative (how things should be) knowledge and identities (Lee, Learmonth and

Harding, 2008). This means that QT has potential both to explain and to bring about changes.

The first thing to say is that QT has been developing for about 20 years as a theoretical perspective having important explanatory power in the arts, humanities and social sciences (Doty, 1993; Seidman, 1997). It offers two major advantages: firstly, it helps cast new light on behaviours and activities formerly seen as unproblematic and well understood and secondly it can contribute towards political and emancipatory projects. It complements the work of theorists who link post-structuralism explicitly to political action, such as Derrida (1994), Laclau and Mouffe (2001) and Young (2004) and thus to emancipation. QT exhorts us to interrogate taken-for-granted assumptions about what is 'normal'. We rarely think about 'normality'—we are surrounded by it, like fish are surrounded by water, and its omnipresence means we do not even notice it is there. However, QT argues that for there to be normality there must be that which is abnormal or queer; people who are regarded as abnormal or queer are unequal, and their oppression or exploitation is either unnoticed or regarded as acceptable. Our particular example is, of course, leadership which, our argument will show, does not have the emancipatory potential claimed by its supporters. In fact, it may have just the opposite effect as it brings into effect norms which govern identities and practices and which subordinate some while controlling the dominant identity.

QT is a post-structuralist perspective, so it encourages what Hall (2003, p. 10) refers to as 'diverse reading strategies and multiple interpretative stances'. By this is meant that we should 'queer' how we read so that we see beyond the 'straightforward', get a better understanding of how texts and practices work and thus learn how to resist 'regimes of the normal' (Warner, 1994, p. xxvi). By 'regimes of the normal' is meant those notions of normality which govern and manage people's activities and expressions of selfhood. These include, importantly, 'normal business in the academy' (Warner, 1994, p. xxvi), so QT can be used to explore how academic understanding serves, albeit unknowingly, in the constitution and maintenance of oppressive practices. (Chapter 7 provides an illustration of this.) Queer theory (or indeed queer theories) seeks to trouble what we regard as normal and helps us understand how we oppress ourselves, unconsciously or unknowingly, even as we participate (again unconsciously or unknowingly) in the oppression of others.

As noted above, QT evolved in part out of feminist and gender studies (Petersen 1998). Feminism challenged institutions and knowledges initially through 'adding in' the study of women and followed this by offering a fundamental rethinking of every category of analysis within the social and political sciences, arts and humanities. Gender studies 'added in' lesbian and gay studies, alongside the study of heterosexual men in 'men and masculinities'. Queer theory, however, does more than 'add in' the study of lesbians and gay men to political and social analysis: it firstly aims to make analyses queerer through exploring 'all those whose lives transgress heteronormative assumptions . . . and then theorizing from their lives' (Budgeon and Roseneil, 2004, p. 129). It then goes on to challenge *all* categories of 'the normal'.

QT requires that we recognise and then challenge norms, discourses and practices that serve to subjugate some to the benefit of others. QT now theorizes from the lives of any categories of people whose lives are in various ways unliveable (Butler, 2004) in that it puts into question *any* activities regarded as 'normal' and examines how the maintenance of 'the normal' makes many people feel 'abnormal'. What is defined as 'normal' is seen to exclude those who do not or cannot conform, who are thus 'abnormal', for the normal cannot exist unless it has an abnormal by which it knows itself. In terms of leadership, the 'abnormal' would include those who are questioning or cynical about what leadership might mean, those who refuse to take on a leadership role, those who do not possess whatever it takes to become a leader, those who have failed as leaders and, finally, followers. As the majority of leaders also have to be followers of those more senior to them, the vast majority of people in an organisation will be included in the category of 'followers'. It is obvious that there cannot be leaders without followers, but what is not obvious is how being defined as inferior (not having what it takes to be a leader) affects a person. A QT perspective argues that now that leadership is regarded as being vital at every level of the organisation, anyone who is not regarded as a leader is 'abnormal', second rate and inferior. The majority of leaders will themselves be led by others, so leaders are both leaders and followers, both normal and abnormal, suggesting a peculiarly painful identity problem, for how can one cope with being both normal and abnormal?

Queer(y)ing leadership development

Our study shows that people are identified as potential leaders, rendering those not thus identified as 'not leaders' and therefore as inferior to the superior leader. The manner by which people are identified as 'leaders' and 'not leaders' is somewhat surprising; for though words may fail the attempts to define leadership, the senses do not.

As the following quote from an interview with a director of personnel at a large multinational pharmaceutical company shows, those deemed to have the potential for leadership are identified and separated, like wheat from chaff, from those with lesser potential. Asked about training policies and practices in the organisation, s/he replied that the majority of more junior managers participated in 'off the shelf' courses, but the 'bright young things' were treated differently. They were deemed to need

a little bit of something special and also a little bit of a pat on the back. And what we would do would effectively through senior management discussions [is] select a group of people and maybe out of a population of several hundreds choose twenty. Bright young people to go on an event which would open their eyes much more to broader issues in the organisation.

At an early stage in their careers in this organisation managers are categorised as successful or otherwise. Young people who will not have worked in the organisation for long will be told that (i) leadership potential is vital for a successful career while (ii) only a small proportion of people have that elusive factor, that *je ne sais quoi*, which marks them out as potential leaders. The vast majority are deemed not to have what it takes, to not be a 'bright young thing'.

But what is it that marks the minority of people out as potential leaders? We are not told what the identifying marks are and, indeed, the characteristics seem elusive, but there is an emphasis throughout the interviews that leadership is *visible*, that it can be seen.

For example, the Director of Human Resource Management, whose quote opened this section, went on to say that at the courses attended by the 'bright young things'

the presence would be seen of senior finance people, heads of department or towards executive level. And possibly executives from across the business to really make them feel loved and wanted and wow that's something to go on. Encourages a little bit of a competitive spirit 'why aren't I on this?'—which has its own negative consequences. But for those who go on it very much 'opened my eyes and gave me a sense of confidence, strong sense of attachment to the organisation'.

Note the phrases here that refer to seeing and being seen: 'the presence would be seen' and 'opened my eyes'. This senior manager is espousing the belief that nothing more than the opportunity to *look upon* the

senior managers, to see them there in front of them, is needed to motivate the company's future leaders. Implicit here is an assumption that
leaders possess something that we cannot describe in words but we know
it when we see it. This is seen in the following quote from the Director
of Human Resource Management of another multinational company,
who observed that

> [O]ur Chief Executive Officer is seen to be a very good leader, he is
> very inspiring. Anybody that sort of has a presentation from him says
> 'wow, I really bought that'. And a number of Senior Managers when
> they come into contact with people are seen to be 'wow'. However,
> unfortunately there is still a large group of senior management that
> talks the talk but doesn't translate into practice.

The Chief Executive *is seen* to be a very good leader, and others who possess this inarticulable leadership 'thing' are 'seen' to be 'wow'. Those who
can talk about leadership ('talks the talk') but do not possess this indefinable, but highly visible, something are not regarded as good leaders.

This is seen articulated most precisely by a manager working in a public sector organisation who was discussing the leadership course he'd
attended a month before the interview. He observed that

> I know from the XXXX course I have got some of the concepts in
> with mine now, and I can look at people perhaps in that way now
> and sort of think 'that person has and that person hasn't'.

Just by looking at people he can divide them into those who have and
those who have not got whatever it is that good leaders can be seen to
possess.

What we can therefore conclude is that the leader is someone who
emanates something, some quality or qualities, that can be seen by others. This thing that is emanated pertains to the individual and is related to
the ways in which they relate to other people. This leads us to the second
point to note, which is that it is this 'certain something' that distinguishes
the leader from the manager. The Director of Personnel in another multinational organisation pointed out that the company had developed

> seven leadership capabilities [which] provide clarity about strate-
> gic direction, focuses on delivery, builds relationships, ensures
> commitment—and develops self-awareness, personal convictions—
> and develops people. So there is only two which you could sort of

immediately see as businessey. The five of them are all about inter-personal skill—about personal self-awareness—about development of people. . . .It is much more about personal qualities and competencies that distinguish leaders from managers.

If it is 'personal qualities' that distinguish leaders from managers, it is these same personal qualities which distinguish 'true' from 'false' leadership, as exemplified in a quote from a HR Manager in a Europe-based multinational company:

There is something about I suppose in the company now of late appreciating that maybe we have been missing some tricks in terms of leadership training. And I think maybe we have not identified that as such a key competency in the past, or maybe we had identified it as a key competency but we didn't really understand what true trans-formational leadership was. And we were training leaders, but at a very transactional level.

This speaker later expanded upon the distinction between 'genuine' and 'not genuine' leadership, for

I think a lot of people are only beginning to appreciate in the last six months what genuine leadership is. And that it goes further than making sure everybody in your team has got objectives or smart objectives, and they get an annual appraisal and the occasional bit of coaching. . . .And I don't think people have really appreciated what true leadership is, what we have been trained in and what we have been doing is managing rather than leading.

Here we have the distinction, often mooted by leadership theorists, that leadership differs from management. Leadership is transformational while management is transactional. Managing involves the assignment of tasks and checking how they have been carried out; leadership involves interpersonal relationships between the persons responsible for ensuring that aims and objectives are met (leaders) and the persons responsible for undertaking the tasks that will achieve those aims and objectives (followers). The 'true' leader is someone, it seems, who will emanate a certain something, a *je ne sais quoi*, that will make the other person feel motivated just by being in their presence. The manager may give out the tasks but her/his physical presence does not contain that certain, motivational something.

In Butler's much-cited analysis of the drag artist, she shows that drag artists demonstrate that all gender identities are a kind of impersonation and approximation. There is no original or primary gender that drag imitates, for gender is a kind of imitation for which there is no original; in fact, it is a form of imitation which produces the very notion of the original as an *effect* and consequence of the imitation itself. In other words, what appears 'natural', in this case, sex and gender, are produced through imitative strategies, through miming; what they imitate is a phantasmatic ideal or imagined idea of heterosexual identity. But it is the imitation that produces the effect. In this sense, the 'reality' of heterosexual identities is performatively constituted through a 'masculinity' or 'femininity' that are actually imitations, for there is no original thing that is being imitated—they are copies of something for which there is no master copy. So, the imitation gives the impression that it is based on something that exists, but it is the imitation itself that brings the thing into existence. In other words, every morning that a woman gets up, puts on women's clothes, does her make-up and arranges her hair and the way she walks and holds herself, she is imitating what it is to be a woman and is thus creating 'the woman'. Heterosexuality, Butler argues, is always in the process of imitating and approximating its own phantasmatic idealisation (that is, a fantasy located in the unconscious) of itself—*and failing*. This allows the exploration of how all identities are based upon a phantasmatic idealisation, or the translation into the physical world of an idea located in the (unconscious) imagination. As the idea is in the imagination it is an ideal, a fantasy, and it is so perfect it is impossible to ever attain those imaginary standards. The result is anxiety and trauma (Harding, 2003; Lee, 2007).

This takes us back to the 'Great Man' theories of leadership, theories which dominated earlier studies but are now regarded as not only outdated but based upon an overly narrow definition that limits leadership to a very few, exceptional individuals. The 'Great Man' theories suggested that certain rare individuals possessed characteristics that attracted others to them in huge numbers. Chief among these characteristics was charisma, something that is indefinable but we know it when we see it. The charismatic qualities are also present in many so-called transformational leadership theories, that we explored in Chapter 1, most notably in those distant and heroic theories promulgated by some US writers on transformational leadership, such as Bernie Bass and Bruce Avolio. This charismatic characteristic, of course, is how the above managers talked about the people who are or would be leaders: they possess something indefinable that yet can be 'seen'.

What these data, therefore, suggest is that 'Great Man' and charismatic theories continue to inform understandings of leadership in organisations. Research showed it was impossible to define what it was that made the 'Great Man', or indeed anyone else, 'charismatic': these interviews demonstrate that the charismatic, 'Great Man' echoes through current beliefs about leadership. But there are so few examples of the 'Great Man', and these are referred to over and over again in books about leadership (Churchill, Gandhi, Mandela, Hitler, Napoleon, etc.). QT tells us that these are not mere examples, but phantasised ideals. We can understand them only in our imaginations, and we are encouraged to see these Great Men as special—in our fantasy they take on superhuman characteristics, and it is those superhuman characteristics that become the measure of organisational leaders.

Queer emanations—the 'Great Man' lives

Queer theory argues that for some to be regarded as 'normal' others must be regarded as 'abnormal'. The 'abnormal' may have unliveable lives, that is, lives in which they are always made aware of their 'abnormality' and so cannot live a 'normal' life (Butler, 2004). The data from this study show that managers are divided into two groups—the leaders and those who do not have what it takes to be leaders. What it takes is indefinable, but it is something that can be seen and recognised for what it is when it is seen.

Much discussion has shown that the 'Great Man' was someone who became great due to the circumstances in which he (it was rarely 'she') found himself (for example, Grint, 2000) In other words, the 'Great Man' was created by circumstances and often the recognition of greatness was granted in retrospect. We can therefore paraphrase Butler to the effect that there is no 'Great Man' prior to the performance of the 'Great Man'. The 'Great Man' is, in effect, a phantasmatic idealisation—an imaginary idea of what leadership is about. Some people have certain qualities that make them appear somewhat different from their fellow employees, and so they are deemed to possess the characteristics that mark them out as leaders. But there is no 'leader' behind this set of characteristics: there are beliefs and ideas, but no 'reality'. We think we see 'leadership' but what we see is an individual upon whom we have projected, as if s/he were a cinema screen, our understanding of what leadership is about. Individuals then have to live up to that ideal.

So, rather than the 'Great Man' and charismatic theories disappearing from leadership studies, following the proof of the inadequacy of their analyses, it seems that the theories continue to have huge influence. This sits badly in a meritocracy, where those with the best potential are supposed to rise to the top. Rather than potential, what is valued is something that appears to be some form of inner glow which can be generated outwards. We will discover more about this by introducing some more of both the theory and the data.

Queer(y)ing the performance of leadership

Queer theory's roots are to be found in the work of Michel Foucault (1979, 1986, 1992) and to a lesser extent perhaps that of Jacques Derrida (1976). Their ideas have been developed notably by Eve Kosovsky Sedgwick (1991) and Judith Butler (1990, 1993, 1996). Sedgwick and Butler question the essentialist, given nature of categorisations such as straight/gay, heterosexual/homosexual and, indeed, male/female. These are binary opposites, pairs which permeate how we think about and construct our social worlds. In such pairs, one is superior, the other inferior. The superior relies upon the inferior half of the coupling for its existence. (For example, how could we know there was such a thing as daylight if there were no such thing as darkness?) The inferior part of the pair is suppressed and subordinated by the dominant term's struggle for survival (Petersen, 1998; Roseneil and Seymour, 1999; Jagose, 1996). Thus women have been regarded as inferior to men, homosexuality to heterosexuality and, in our case, followership to leadership.

QT's initial focus, as noted, was upon gender and sexuality (Jagose, 1996; Butler, 1990, 1993, 1996; Sedgwick, 1991). We will, therefore, now provide an overview of how the grounding categories (i.e. what are regarded as essential to existence) of gender and sexuality have been queered and use that overview to continue our queering of leadership.

Gender and sexuality are conventionally regarded as fixed, stable categories determined largely by biology. Feminism argued that gender is a social construction (Oakley, 1972), that is, gender is something that is *learnt*, with biology determining the behaviours that are achieved. QT goes further, in that it argues that biology, too, is socially constructed (Butler, 1993). The *materiality* of the body, that is, its physical status, is not denied, but QT argues that the ways in which we understand our bodies is through our social worlds. Here we echo some of the Derridean arguments outlined in Chapters 2 and 3. In different epochs and different cultures, bodies are understood (and therefore experienced) very differently. QT therefore goes beyond social constructionism for it shows that what are constructed are *regulatory fictions*, or stories we tell ourselves as a culture and which regulate how people within that culture behave. Regulatory fictions both establish order and provide the rules through which we organise ourselves to ensure order is maintained. They make such ordering and organising appear natural and right. What is important here is QT's argument that these regulatory fictions are just that—fictional. They have no authenticity. QT, like most post-structuralist theories, turns accepted ways of thinking on their heads. Where we traditionally think that something exists and that it can be described using language, post-structuralism argues that it is language that brings into being those things that exist. QT's use of these insights leads to the argument that there is no 'core' (such as biology) that produces gender, rather there is this language, biology, which provides a language through which we can understand our bodies and which thus allows gender to be constructed.

This makes comprehensible Judith Butler's famous theory that 'there is no gender behind the expressions of gender' (see the discussion above) for identity is performatively constituted by the very 'expressions' that are said to be its 'results' (Butler, 1990). By this she means that it is not gender that dictates how people should behave (for example, women should sit with their legs neatly together while men should sit in ways that take up lots of space). This seemingly trivial observation is one that illustrates how the banal, everyday, utterly taken-for-granted ways of doing things are implicated in, and indeed vital to, the practising of gender as an identity. Rather it is the very *doing* of these gendered behaviours, behaviours that accord with the norms of how a person with the relevant genitalia should behave, which construct gender. We will soon see that it may be the performance of this thing called leadership, by those given the title of 'leader' who emanate that certain something, which constitutes this thing called leadership.

Thus, when Butler (1993) argues that discourse always precedes and enables the 'I' she means that in order to exist as a person, as an 'I', subjects must conform to the norms of the society into which they are born, norms which pre-exist them. So, in Western culture we have to be either 'male' or 'female' and anyone who cannot conform (such as those born as hermaphrodites) cannot have a livable existence. To refuse or to be unable to conform means that the only 'I' which can exist is one that is unrecognisable, and is therefore strange, subordinate, inferior, 'queer'. It follows that recognition, without which it is impossible to exist as human, is not conferred upon but *forms* a subject. For example, by being called a girl the child comes to be that girl, and to refuse to be a girl means she fits into no category, is unrecognisable and 'queer'. In Butler's words (1993, p. 225) the 'I' is a 'historically revisable possibility of a name that precedes and exceeds me, but without which I cannot speak'.

In organisations, the names which precede us are those of the manager, the professional employee or the worker and now the leader—we have to be categorised into, and known by, one of these names. These titles will have changed their meaning over the course of the nineteenth and twentieth centuries, as they will undoubtedly do over the course of the next century, so they are 'historically revisable' (ibid.).

A discourse therefore *constitutes* the subject, or facilitates the formation of an identity, as we have seen in Chapters 2 and 3. QT shows that discourse does this in such a way that some people are regarded as 'normal' and others as 'abnormal', but there is nothing intrinsic to individuals in their being regarded as normal or otherwise. Rather, it is a culture which imposes abnormality upon some. To be abnormal is to be abject, and to have an unliveable life. When we discuss leadership, therefore, we must explore whether or how leadership depends for its viability on rendering some people abject at the same time as it grants a superior position to others.

Let us now apply these arguments to the data.

With the exception of the person who had been on a leadership course, the speakers whose words we have been quoting here are all people who commission leadership development courses. We have suggested that they define leadership as very much concerned with interpersonal relationships in which one party emanates particular, indefinable qualities that are recognisable when seen but cannot be precisely articulated. Further, the analysis of the interview transcripts shows a clear presumption that, firstly, these qualities come from self-knowing and, secondly, self-knowledge is something which can be developed. For example, the speaker whose words we used to open this analysis had developed a leadership development programme that consisted of three sessions spread over eight days which

> started off with individuals reflecting on their own leadership style and their own personality. A Myers Briggs type indicator was used extensively, and at that point the support and challenge [action learning] groups were set up. In the second of the modules of [the] Programme there was more of an intention to look at how groups were functioning—the individual groups. So there was the focus on the individual and building the action learning group, then there was a little bit more about the group dynamics. And also, starting to think about issues in the business. And the third module . . . was

more taking these action learning groups and support and challenge groups effectively into the business and keeping them going post the [programme].

The structure was designed so that

> maybe a group of twenty-four on an individual programme met for three days and would break into action learning groups of six. So this idea of a broad group to get you familiar with a number of people, but then breaking down into a smaller group who you could talk about your personal development needs to and so on.

The 'personal development' was important because of the 'need' to

> make them reflect on their personality. Need to make them think about the whole issue of what is it to be a manager or a leader and to break the probably quite strongly held paradigm in their head about order and about logic. And introduce this whole issue of the connection between them as persons and them as managers and leaders.

The distinction between management and leadership undergoes further refinement here. The manager is equated with order and logic and the leader with 'personality' and 'being'. This speaker thus articulates very clearly a trajectory that is clear within the history of thinking about leadership: the move from disembodied rationality and objectivity required of managers towards an embodied, emoting presence required of leaders. Where managers would all be interchangeable identikit parts, leaders are unique personalities, as the above speaker goes on to note. It was important, s/he said, that the programme encouraged

> [A] realization of the connection between you and your personality and a needing to understand that Myers Briggs personal feedback and so on, and you as a leader. This leadership thing isn't simply about skills you gain on a course; *it is about you as a person.* (emphasis added).

We have been exploring in this chapter how leadership cannot be defined in words but is known aesthetically, through the senses. The difficulty of definition appears to lie in an absence of words that can capture something which can be recognised when it is seen for it emanates visibly from persons. There is a strong presumption that it can be developed, hence the huge investment in leadership training courses (Alimo-Metcalfe et al., 2000). These courses, as this speaker demonstrates, are presumed to help develop leadership by encouraging those who would be leaders to think deeply about themselves, develop self-understanding, realise the effect they have on other people, and work on improving that effect. Leadership is very much a two-way relationship, regarded as inherently *motivational*, with the motivational aspect arising from the personal qualities of self-knowledge possessed by the leader.

Following the more recent trends in leadership thinking, some organisations now agree that leadership should be operative at all levels of the organisation. The manager quoted above noted that

> I would like to put it down to the fact that we have now appreciated that you don't have to be the managing director or on the board of directors to be a highly motivational leader. You need motivational leadership qualities at just about all levels of the organisation, and maybe in the past well 'we have got a leader you know it is our MD' that kind of thing 'we follow him'. But now I think we are starting to realise that in this new culture of we are being encouraged to take more risks and be a bit more entrepreneurial in spirit that with that comes the requirement to lead from all levels of the organisation to lead and to challenge.

The result is that, following a project undertaken with a major firm of management consultants, leadership has been identified as one of the competencies for the organisation, so that

> everybody is regularly appraised on leadership across the standard developed and highly developed criteria for that competence.

In line with what we have noted above, about leadership being something that emanates from 'within' an individual, people are appraised for the amount of self-work, or work on the self, they do:

> People that have looked at the new competency and thought about themselves hard in that context and tried to identify behaviours within themselves that meet the highly developed thing.

That this did in fact occur is encapsulated in the following quote from a manager who a month before the interview had attended a leadership development course which left him/her convinced that leadership is concerned with

> appealing to peoples' hearts and souls rather than to their minds and their wallets kind of thing. And the way to peoples' hearts and souls was a difficult one, but things like a clear shared vision of where the company and the department that you lead is going in support of the company. And a lot more emotional humanistic kind of approach with your team. I don't know? To motivate them towards this vision in a less tangible way than just 'look here is your objective go away and deliver that' kind of thing.

The distinction between the public and private selves had to disappear, for 'personal development' included

> we were charged with going away and thinking about our vision, and as our vision for life or our vision for work—both if you could marry them together.

Similarly, what officer cadets from the armed forces remembered from the lectures they had received on leadership was that 'leadership is just the projection of your personality', and the projection of the personality was something that could be learnt.

The leader who emerges from these discussions is someone who has developed knowledge of themselves to such an extent that they understand their impact upon other people. They are people who show their awareness of their own emotions and understand what motivates them. They have been selected for development on the basis of their already possessing a certain something, a *je ne sais quoi*, which cannot be described but can be recognised when it is seen. Through developing excellent self-knowledge they can hone those indefinable qualities and become able to relate to others with ease and aplomb. This will be to the benefit of the company.

Queer conclusions

We saw above that the 'Great Man' and charismatic theories continue to inform organisational practices of leadership. We have now shown that those identified as leaders must look inwards and develop intense self-knowledge. It is presumed that the very fact of having in-depth knowledge of the self is sufficient to ensure that a person who has been identified as a potential leader will become that very thing, a leader.

However, QT, as we noted above, shows that it is the very act of doing something that creates the identity that is claimed, and that there is no identity behind the doing. This leads us to conclude not that there is anything intrinsic to self-knowledge that creates a leader, but that the person identified as a leader must go through the actions deemed necessary to become a leader, and those very actions create that person as a leader. There is no known causal link between self-knowledge and an individual's capacities for this elusive thing called leadership, but there is a causal link between being called a leader, doing the things that are deemed necessary to turn one into a leader, and creating one's self as the identity that is now enforced upon one. In other words, HR directors presume that certain managers have something intrinsic to themselves that gives them the potential to develop leadership qualities. QT suggests that it is the very fact of being singled out as a potential future leader that endows the individual with (the illusion of possession of) the elusive characteristics.

Creating the normative leader

We started this chapter with an exploration of the 'woolliness' of definitions of leadership. We will return to that topic, having made something of a long detour, by returning to the work of Eve K. Sedgwick who, as we showed in the above discussion, in *Epistemology of the Closet* (1991) shows what a conundrum such woolliness causes. Sedgwick demonstrates how the appearance of a new word in the lexicon can govern identity. The word 'homosexual', she argues, did not enter Euro-American discourse until the last third of the nineteenth century, leading to a new form of 'world-mapping'

> by which every given person, just as he or she was necessarily assignable to a male or a female gender, was now considered necessarily assignable as well to a homo- or a hetero-sexuality, a binarized identity that was full of implications, however confusing, for even the ostensibly least sexual aspects of personal existence.
>
> (Sedgwick, 1991, p. 2)

Before the appearance of this one word, there were people who participated in certain sexual practices. After its appearance new identities were made possible and the acts that governed the imposition of those identities came to govern whole lives. Using theories that should now be familiar to readers, Sedgwick argues that this happened because words have a performative impact. In other words, language brings things into existence. Ideas, notions, possibilities for being and other social 'structures' are constructed through discourse, and the physical world can only be interpreted and understood through discourse.

This implies that the terms 'leader' and 'leadership' should offer quite distinct definitions whereby people can be categorised into two groups: leaders and followers. For queer theorists, people are categorised very distinctly through their object of sexual choice, and once categorised they will performatively enact and thus become the subject of the label that applies to them. If leaders and leadership can be similarly categorically defined, then leaders should easily fit into the subject position of leadership and achieve the identity of leader. The position should be similarly definable for followers. However, what happens when a subject position is indefinable?

The answer to this question lies in the idea of 'the norm'. QT, following Foucault (1979, 1986, 1992), shows that norms are never achievable. They are held out as the ideal, as that which we should attain, but such perfection is always out of reach. For example, many women work hard to attain the types of female identities that are culturally validated, and many men do likewise with regard to masculinity. However, no matter how hard we strive (and goodness but do we strive to achieve the perfection of the norm), it always remains out of reach. This is because the norm eradicates difference—it requires that all should be alike. Such absence of difference is impossible.

This queer reading therefore leads us to suggest that leadership has developed as a norm which governs the behaviours and identities of managers and many other people working in organisations. The very vagueness about leadership means that no matter how hard anyone strives, they will never feel secure in their achievement of the identity of leader. They will have no templates against which to judge themselves, no criteria against which to measure themselves. They will always doubt how good they are as leaders. And therefore they will always have to keep on working to improve themselves.

This is because norms are always accompanied by *normalizing strategies*, whereby a model of the ideal citizen exists to which all citizens feel compelled, more or less strongly, to approximate (or indeed to rebel against). We suggest that the development of self knowledge as part of leadership development is a normalising strategy, and thus a method of control over leaders.

Think firstly about the 360-degree models of leadership used on training courses, and how these define what the ideal leader is. The individuals who participate in a 360-degree questionnaire are, it seems, discovering how they are regarded by those with whom they work. They are encouraged to learn to see themselves as others see them, and to eradicate any aspects of the self that are deemed to be less than ideal. The MBTI and other psychological measures encourage individuals to reflect upon the self, and so better to know the self. In these reflections there is an implicit and unspoken ideal against which individuals must measure themselves. They are encouraged to know the ways in which the self fails to achieve this ideal, and to work on the self so as to eradicate shortcomings and develop strengths. The aim is to become flawless—but the flaws that must be identified and then eradicated are those dictated by organisations.

Butler writes that the ideal is 'the symbolic ought to be rethought as a series of normative injunctions that secure the borders of sex through the threat of psychosis, abjection, psychic unlivability' (1993, pp. 14–15). In other words, we have an idea of how we 'ought to be', even if we are not consciously aware of it. We try to approximate that ideal, and if we fail to live up to it we feel chastened, and worse. What 'ought to be' governs what we aim to be. In organisations what 'ought to be' is what assists the firm achieve its aims. The requirement that leaders look within and identify ways in which they fall short of the organisational ideal is thus a normalising strategy designed to ensure that managers conform to a very narrowly defined managerial self. This self is utterly charismatic, knows and understands its impact on other people and is utterly devoted to the organisation.

Our conclusions in this queering of leadership are that, organisations identify some people who have the potential for leadership. They send them on training courses. Those not deemed to possess the elusive characteristics of leaders, we have conjectured, may therefore feel as if they are failures. Those sent on the courses have to achieve the norms of leadership, and we have shown that this requires that they become charismatic. Whatever charisma is, it is indefinable, but it is a norm and one whose achievement must be extraordinarily difficult. So leaders have to strive to live up to an impossible norm. They have to stand out from the crowd, to be 'Great Men'. By definition only a tiny minority can be 'great'.

Two for the price of one: Creating the follower

QT demonstrates how dominant regimes depend upon their subjugated opposites, their other, to know and sustain themselves. In other words, a privileged 'inside' could not exist without a demeaned 'outside' (Fuss, 2001). For example, if the world was peopled only by men they would not know themselves as men, they would not be an intelligible category; for there would be no opposite, no women, against whose difference men could define themselves. In QT 'heterosexual' can only be an intelligible category when there is also the linked category 'homosexual'; in leadership theory the 'leader' can be intelligible only through the linked category of 'follower'. The hierarchy of dominant/subordinate terms is maintained by repressive means that historically have involved exclusion (for example, of women, homosexuals and people of colour) from public life. They are denied civil rights, disenfranchised and suffer other forms of exclusion and abuse. The subjugated other is 'symbolically degraded' (Fuss, 2001, p. 353) in contrast to the symbolic purity of the dominant construct, and so the subjugated other is defiled and dominated. The follower is someone who is bidden to follow, and to have no voice, no choice, no influence: their only role is to do the bidding of the leader. The manager who is a leader to some and a follower to others is therefore in a very peculiar position that requires both voice and silence.

Practices ascribed to the inferior part of the binary are regarded as polluting, those of the superior part as pure: it is this ascription that allows the superior to know itself as superior, as unpolluted. Homosexuals, for example, are 'individuals for whom shame and guilt are at the core of their sense of self' (Fuss, 2001). The leader is someone who is intelligent, caring, resourceful—the list of descriptors is always positive. The follower must therefore lack these qualities, or if s/he possesses them they are only brought to the surface through the auspices of the leader, whose own qualities are always superior.

However, those in the dominant, unpolluted category are also controlled, restricted, compelled to live by norms. As Seidman (2001) writes, 'regimes of heteronormativity not only regulate the homosexual but control heterosexual practices by creating a moral hierarchy of good and bad sexual citizens' (Seidman, 2001, p. 354). We can paraphrase this and write 'leadership is a regime that not only requires that followers are regulated, but also controls leadership practices through creating a moral hierarchy of good and bad organisational members.'

Meanwhile, the follower is the subordinated other by which the leader knows itself, so the leader will see his/her failure reflected in the eyes of those they must subordinate. To buttress themselves in the identity of leader requires that the individuals who occupy that subject position regard the follower as inferior and subordinate. But leaders are also followers and so they must battle with the impossibility of their ever being ideal leaders at the same time as they must be aware of their own inferiority in their position as follower.

There is very little known about followers—they are often the absent-presence in theories of leadership. QT suggests they have to be second-rate, inferior and subordinate, so that leaders may know themselves as the superior beings theory assumes them to be. It is followers who provide the yardstick against which leaders can measure their superiority. Against the shining brightness of the leader, the follower has a dull uniformity, so dull s/he remains hidden from view behind the leader who dominates the discussions of organisations.

Discussion

This queer reading of leadership shows that leadership is a fantastical and highly restricted identity, located within presumptions that, rather than describing leadership, *create and govern* the very thing that is described. To be a leader is to enter into a subject position governed by non-achievable norms of perfection. The leader must work on eradicating any shortcomings with the aim of achieving flawlessness, but such perfection is normative and not achievable. The leader, this reading suggests, must conform to a performance of the self that is based on a fantasy. It is a fantasy of 'the Great Man', the rare individual who rises above all other human beings.

In other words, queering leadership shows that the theory tells people: 'this is how you should be as a leader, these are the norms that must be attained, and if you fail to attain them, that is if those around you judge you to have failed in any of those norms, then you will have failed as a person as well as a leader.' The result can be traumatic: psychosis, abjection and ontological insecurity (or problems in knowing who one is) as we will show in Chapter 6. Ford (2007) has shown the anxieties experienced by leaders.

Furthermore, QT argues that norms are ideals which have no existence in the material world and so are, by definition, unattainable. Applied to leadership, the person charged with the task of becoming a leader will strive to become something which is beyond reach—it is impossible for any living, breathing human being to be as perfect, as flawless, as leadership theory requires the leader to be. The leader will constantly strive to become the ideal leader, but failure is built in and so no one can become that thing they are striving to be.

So, where we said above that QT shows how there is no choice but to adopt a recognisable identity and to perform that identity according to

the name that one is called (or called to), QT also shows how tentative, how preliminary, how insecure, is that identity. *To be a leader is to constantly strive and repetitively fail to be a leader.*
Secondly, QT has helped us identify the norms that govern leaders' identities. To be a leader is to emanate something indefinable but special, something that is generated as a result of self-knowledge and that can be seen by, and has an impact upon, others. To be a leader is thus to be extraordinary, to stand out from the norm. At the same time, this is the norm, so everyone must aspire to achieve this norm and difference must be eradicated and all must approximate as closely as they can to this norm. This leads to the question of how it is possible for everyone to be extraordinary, for a practice that requires everyone to be extraordinary means that the extraordinary becomes ordinary.

What would result if leadership courses had the intended effect is, it would seem, a charismatic herd (the unbearable heaviness of having to be charismatic?), where everyone who has the title of leader has that indefinable something which marks them out from others, but at the same time makes them the same as all other leaders. To be ordinary is not allowed. To be grumpy, angry, less than attractive, less than perfect, none of these are allowed when performing one's self as leader.

There is, furthermore, a breakdown of the boundary between the public and the private self—the leader must show to the outside world what s/he sees when looking inwards, at the self. Privacy is something that is not allowable within the norms of leadership. This leads us to ask a question that we will repeat in Chapter 7—what happens if the self that is identified and generated to others is unattractive? The possibility of such a thing is not deemed possible in this theory, which assumes that looking at one's self, gaining greater understanding of one's self, leads to the discovery of an extraordinary person. Can there be any person who is such a flawless paragon? Indeed, would we be able to trust anyone who projected the identity of a flawless paragon?

So what is unspeakable here is the possibility of being human, in that being less than perfect, of being a character (Bollas, 1993) is denied to those who would be leaders. The leader becomes a leader through the performance of leadership, but the performance is impossible.

And what is further unspeakable is the position of the follower. A presumption in all theories of leadership is that followers are enthused to work harder, motivated to give their all, through being in the presence of the leader. The mechanisms by which they are so motivated are unclear. There appears to be nothing more than a simple Pavlovian response at work, by which the mere presence of a leader results in their changing their actions.

It follows that followers must be imagined as lacking in any intelligence or decision-making powers of their own. They are presumed to be like well-trained dogs who respond enthusiastically to the tones of the voice of the master.

Further, followers must, by definition, lack the attributes possessed by the leader. The question is never asked of how this must affect followers— it is presumed that any effects will be positive, but that is as far as analysis goes. We suggest that to be a follower is to be told that one is inferior, and to be told that one is inferior has negative consequences on self-understanding. The follower is, in Judith Butler's (2005) terms, rendered abject.

Indeed, we suggest that leadership is predicated upon the debasement, the rendering abject, of followers, so that leadership contains the seeds of its own impossibility. It seeks to exhort followers to be motivated to work productively through the example set by leaders, but what the leader actually does is relay to followers the fact of their own lowly status, their own inferiority.

This queering of leadership theory is therefore leading us to positing the idea that just as the leader is someone who looks inside and finds a paragon of virtue, the follower who looks inside must find someone deviant, in need of being led, unintelligent, passive and second-rate.

Conclusion

Leadership theory, our reading suggests, if put fully into practice could have deleterious effects for both leaders and followers. Those who would be leaders would be doomed to failure, for they would have to constantly strive to reach an unreachable and indefinable ideal. Followers would suffer the slings and arrows of outrageous inferiority.

Thankfully, the 'real world' of organisations is so complex that leadership theory cannot be fully enacted. Rather, leaders try to practise aspects of leadership but are prevented from doing so by numerous demands on their times and their psyches (Ford, 2007). Leadership, in Ford's reading, is something that managers find attractive and to which they aspire, but in finding it unattainable they suffer disappointment and become demotivated. Leadership theory is perhaps problematic because it *exaggerates* what can be achieved through a focus on the interpersonal and intrapersonal, that is, on relationships between managers and staff and on self-understanding. If our aim is to have organisations in which there is equity, job satisfaction, pride in delivery of excellent services or products, no exploitation or oppression, then the theories we seek to translate into practice must be challenged to ensure they do not bring about that which they are trying to remove. QT, we contend, is a useful way of anticipating the potential effect of our proposed actions. It acknowledges that we cannot escape from the norms that govern our existence, but insists we ensure that those norms do not render some, or indeed all, abject.

6
Gendering Leadership

Our explorations have shown that the words 'leader' and 'leadership' bring those very things into being in that they provide an identity, or a way of being a self, for the people charged with the tasks of leadership. In Chapter 5 we queered those terms to show that the 'Great Man' and charismatic theories live on, and therefore becoming a leader is a task that is impossible to achieve, so out-of-reach are the norms of leadership. We also posed the problem of how leadership relies on the subordination of followers. In this chapter, we draw on a study of leadership in a local authority, a council we call Woolbury, to show the impact of the norms of leadership on leaders. The research on which this chapter is based found that managers in the organisation suffered from a great deal of anxiety (Ford, 2007). In this chapter we discuss some of the causes of this anxiety, notably how a 'macho' management culture battles with aspirations towards a 'gentler' post-heroic, or transformational, leadership culture, with the battle played out in the psyches of the leaders involved. The outcome is that leadership is a function fraught with anxiety.

We draw on gender theories, notably feminism and men and masculinities, to analyse the data discussed in this chapter. Gender theory has been largely ignored by writers on leadership. This silence is somewhat peculiar given a widespread recognition that organisations contribute actively to the ways in which gendered identities are constructed. The gendered identity permissible among managers is very limited indeed: it is that of 'heroic' masculinity. Currently, leadership theories advocate what is called 'post-heroic' leadership, which advocates a gentler, more 'feminine' gendered practice. We showed in Chapters 3 and 4 that all leadership discourses are impregnated with concepts of the hero. This means that claims to a 'post-heroic' perspective must be full of tension. The managers whose stories appear in this chapter show what happens when macho management and heroic leadership meet post-heroic leadership: trauma and anxiety.

Woolbury: Inserting the post-heroic leader into the macho organisation

Woolbury (a pseudonym) is a local authority in the North of England. In the year before this study, 120 of its most senior managers had participated in a major leadership development programme which aimed to change the organisation's culture and ways of operating through shifting towards a post-heroic leadership culture. Eighteen managers were interviewed for this study, using in-depth biographical narrative methods both for data gathering and analysis (Hollway and Jefferson, 2000; Crossley, 2000; McAdams, 1993). The managers were drawn from senior, middle and junior managerial ranks.

The leadership programme which the senior managers had not only commissioned but also participated in had aimed to develop a post-heroic form of leadership within the organisation. Some managers regarded the newer forms of leadership as necessary for purely instrumental reasons, while others regarded them as important for their own sake. Alec (all names are pseudonyms) is typical of the former group. He sees post-heroic leadership as necessary because of market forces and shortages of skilled professionals, leading to 'far more attention being paid to people's working environment and life'. The sense from this interview is of a tension between his feeling compelled—given market pressures—to adopt a more participative and facilitative approach and his preference for a now seemingly out-dated 'command and control' managerial style. He reflects on changes he has had to adopt in his approach to his staff in more recent years, suggesting

> you can't instruct people to do things for you almost like people have got to be wanting to do it and you've got to manage in a way that people want to do it for their own personal satisfaction rather than being told to do it and then reluctantly doing it, because you're paying 'em.

Introducing the 'more modern' styles of leadership, whether for philosophical or instrumental purposes proved to be far more intricate and complex than Alec's lamentation for a seemingly lost age would suggest. This is seen, firstly, in the case of Stuart.

Stuart presents himself as someone who aspires to a more distributive or post heroic leadership approach, yet at the same time he reluctantly admits that not only is he paying little active attention to his team, he is also tending towards the culturally accepted macho management discourse:

> I'm not giving much attention to [the team] because I've more or less drifted off . . . I'm so tied up in the corporate agendas now and fighting all the battles there. Em . . . so I'm less engaged with my staff than I ever have been individually, . . . any actual work that's going on with people on development is happening lower down the food chain, and I'm not really engaged with. I suspect there's not enough of it going on, but er . . . but again, we're a processed organization and a task focussed organization so . . . not a lot of time for that stuff.

Robert's account tells us more about what happens when managers are exhorted to do one thing yet pressures of work ensure they do something very different. His statements illustrate how leadership discourses can be paradoxical and how selves are fragmented and continually in process. He depicts two 'chastening experiences' in his work career that have caused him to challenge his approach and leadership style. The first of these came via his former personal assistant who alerted him to the negative effect his highly macho behaviour was having on his staff. She had told him that rather than arrange to meet him face to face, staff would approach her and ask her to pass on any messages, adding 'just slip him that piece of paper, don't tell him I'm here'. He acknowledges now that his impatience to make a difference to the services for which he was responsible had led to his being feared:

> perhaps in the past what I've done is I've forced in things and been very aggressive about it, and em . . . superficially therefore got the change to work, but it's not been embedded necessarily, so I think I now recognise that I need to be a lot more patient and em . . . I bought myself a relaxation tape!

He could admit, at the time of the interview, that he had found himself perpetuating a practice he'd observed in his previous employment, his second 'chastening experience':

> The organization I was then working for didn't actually care about people, if the truth was known, so if it needed to take someone out, it took them out and I saw that happen and I thought that could happen to me.

Robert now sees himself as having changed. He wishes to practise a more open, post-heroic leadership style:

> One of the things that I attempt to do within the department is to be ... is to ... make sure that ... em ... there's not a sort of hierarchy, particularly with the manual workers, but you know like, they can come and talk to me and I can talk to them, and I don't do that in any demeaning way, I don't 'f and blind' to do it, but equally I don't want there to be any false barriers in the organization.

However, he noted that the personal feedback he received during the leadership development programme was that his staff felt he was not sufficiently visible and available to them, contradicting the account he now gives of himself. Robert's various narratives of himself, as a post-heroic leader who heads up the directorate, as an impatient manager wanting to effect changes more quickly, etc., all compete in his daily work and surface at different points in his interview

The dissonance between how Robert and his staff regard his leadership style is not peculiar to Robert, for the interviews show that each tier of managers regards its leaders poorly. This study found that at every management tier interviewees reported themselves as practising post-heroic forms of leadership, but feeling let down by their senior managers, one tier above, whom they saw as autocratic. One group of managers would state this about their leaders, and those very leaders regarded by their followers as autocratic felt themselves to be post-heroic, but let down by their own autocratic leaders. And so on, up through the management hierarchy, with at each level people reporting a self-perception that was in dissonance with how their followers saw them. Jane's account exemplifies this. She describes the management style in her part of the organisation as follows:

> We seem to have had, within our own function; we seem to have had managers who've been more transactional rather than transformational—quite authoritative in some ways.

Later, she generalises this observation to the whole of the senior management team, when she refers to the

> nature of a lot of senior management who are quite erm ... transactional and autocratic.

She concludes:

> I suppose talking through this has made me realise that we haven't
> got that many transformational leaders in the Council.

When she talks about middle and more junior grades of managers, however, her perspective is quite different:

> People at our level in the organization which is, like, junior to mid-
> dle management are quite happy to meet and get things done and
> make changes and what it is about them up there erm . . . that they
> seem unwilling to share information to erm . . . share ideas, to work
> cooperatively, you know and they were talking about how they are
> in their silos, so they came from different parts of the organization,
> erm . . . but looking up they all had the same view that there's this
> silo mentality and, for some reason, the senior managers aren't open
> to that . . . that sharing and cooperative working, but I . . . it does still
> seems to be there at lower levels in the organization.

Senior managers are therefore presented as the last bastions of a more
old-fashioned, traditional and macho approach to management, and
also as individuals who are preventing the accomplishment of change
and more cross-functional ways of working. By the same token, more
junior managers perceive themselves and their colleagues as far more
amenable to new ideas and approaches.

What these interviews reveal therefore is a belief held by individual
managers that they are attempting to be post-heroic leaders, but they are
let down by their more senior managers and, at the same time, frustrated by ways in which the organisation prevents their being post-
heroic leaders. In Stuart's and Robert's accounts we see such frustration
arising from their having, through pressure of work it seems, to practise
a despised and unwanted managerial self. Another senior manager, Sean,
shows similar negative perspectives on the self as a senior manager. He
argues that senior management (and he includes himself in this definition) are frequently portrayed as remote, judgemental and transactional-
focussed:

> Do you know that one thing about senior management . . . you know
> you fly and squawk and shit on them, and that's the only time they
> ever see top management.

A similarly discomforting clash between the dominant macho management culture and the desired post-heroic leadership culture was contained in the transcripts of both middle level managers (service heads) and front-line (principal and senior) officers. Timothy has been working as a Service Head for the last ten years. He depicts his approach to leadership as one that recognises the need to support and encourage staff and yet, he reflects, this is something he had not paid much attention to in recent years. He recognised that personal and interpersonal relationships suffered because

> you get so entrenched in where you . . . you have to be and the job you have to do that you tend to forget about everything else.

So, managers espouse one thing and practise its opposite, although sometimes under the misapprehension that they are more like post-heroic leaders than those around them believe them to be. But there is also ambiguity in managers' response to post-heroic leadership. Jim, a principal officer, articulates this most clearly. On the one hand, he states how keenly he supports current models of leadership, yet closer analysis of his interview shows that he reveres leaders who were autocratic and very far removed from the type of leader he now believes in:

> So, transformational leadership . . . we didn't do transformational leadership back in [former name of organization] days, but we did do the . . . we did a leadership style—an American leadership style, which I can never remember the name of erm . . . which was very good and actually developed ideas about leadership and vision erm . . . and performance so, he was really . . . he was a great leader, yes, but, in terms of the transformational leadership program, talking about caring for your staff being 60% of the . . . something . . . important in terms of how successful that would be with your staff—that wasn't how he operated and yet, he got significant results, so it's quite intriguing. I've other people who have not inspired me at all and that's because they were probably er . . . technocrats who'd been promoted to a level . . . one level beyond their capabilities.

Jim described how this manager was highly autocratic,

> brilliant in setting direction and had a fabulous knowledge of the organization . . . but basically didn't give a toss about his staff, a very hard face . . . was a bit of a bully.

This exalted manager returned at various points in Jim's transcript, especially as an exemplar in comparison to the Council's current senior managers, who he thought were 'useless'. He said

> genuinely, I couldn't name anybody else in the authority who I would, in the last twenty years . . . who would inspire me.

He went on to add:

> There's nobody at a more senior management to me that I regard as a leader.

He referred to one other autocratic and uncaring leader who had left the Council some years ago, and spoke in glowing terms of the successes he achieved.

The sense gleaned from Jim's narrative, which exemplifies that found throughout this study, is one of confusion and contradiction. On the one hand, he argues in favour of so-called transformational (or post-heroic approaches to) leadership and caring for staff (which he claimed to be passionate about), and on the other, he argues that the most effective leaders he has worked with were two men who were not only highly autocratic, but who had no interest in the staff for whom they were responsible.

Furthermore Jim, a middle manager, claimed to have been damaged by practising transformational/post-heroic approaches to leadership. He states that his preferred style is to be open and approachable:

> I've always been that way, but my big problem was that I couldn't . . . I think looking back, I've never known er . . . I've never set the boundary. There's a boundary into how much you should care for staff and that's always been my problem. I've er . . . I've not set the boundary in the right place. I've allowed it to go too far and then you end up getting compromised . . . can be compromised erm . . . and I think that's been my problem over 20 years as I look back—certainly in the latter years, I've probably allowed myself to be compromised by caring too much for individuals to come back and sort them out when they needed sorting out. Yeah? I . . . both because I understand the problems they've got too well and wasn't prepared to take the action that was necessary to get them back on the straight and narrow, perhaps.

Jim refers several times in his transcript to the 'empty' feeling he has been left with owing to the draining effect of operating in what he perceived as a transformational way, and yet not being recognised for promotion in the organization. He refers to several failed attempts at securing a more senior position, and yet he sees people he regards as less capable then he being promoted to more senior positions. He says this frustration at others' promotions and his inability to secure a more senior job has led to a number of emotional symptoms in him: 'it's come out in frustration, annoyance and anger and irritation.'

So we find within these interviews of managers who have been through an intensive training programme in leadership, in an organisation which espouses post-heroic leadership, what appear to be positive and welcoming responses to the new concepts. We find throughout the organisation managers who feel themselves to be post-heroic leaders yet whose staff report very different interpretations. At the same time we find ambivalence towards and paradox within their discussions about leadership. We find that aims to practise post-heroic leadership are frustrated by organisational demands which mean the traditional, more autocratic, managerial practices prevail. What we are, therefore, seeing are the hugely complex interactions that occur when discourses of leadership are introduced into organisations.

Further, and importantly, the autocratic (heroic) manager and the post-heroic leader are aspects of the identity of each manager, demonstrating the complexities and intricacies of becoming a leader and practising leadership. Our earlier chapters drew on theories which, following Althusser, (1971) suggested that when called to be something we turn, and in turning, become that by whose name we have been hailed. In this chapter we have seen that we are never hailed by just one name but by many, some of which may be contradictory. The managers in this organisation have been called by the macho organisational culture (see below) to be heroic managers, and by the desires for a different culture to be post-heroic leaders, and numerous other identities, all in the same moment. It must be, therefore, that in turning, they know not which way to turn—and the result is a struggle for identity and confusion, if not worst—as different possibilities for identity, some of them compulsory, insist on co-existing in the same psyche.

We will now introduce Trudie, whose account of her experiences as a senior manager in this organisation may tell us something further about these complex organisational interactions between management and leadership.

Compulsory masculinity

Trudie is one of the four female directors employed within the council in a front-line service directorate. We are focusing upon Trudie as she exemplifies the unhappy co-existence of macho-management and post-heroic discourses of leadership, found in all these interviews.

Trudie has strongly articulated ideas about what, to her, represent effective and ineffective leadership in local government organizations, and is lucid in her articulation of these discourses. Strongly committed to making things happen within her directorate, she is also ambitious and has mapped out a trajectory for her career.

Trudie's narrative shows that she has deliberately chosen to adopt a macho managerial style. Her transcript is replete with examples of ways in which she has learnt, in her words, to 'think like a man'. One example is how she abandoned the opportunity of a family holiday (and thus a feminine subject position) the previous year. The sacrifice means that she was available at work to lobby the executive during the informal corridor discussions that culminated in a huge uplift in her budgetary allocation:

> [T]here are phases where you have to do what you have to do and you don't have a work/life balance. I mean, I would love to get away February half-term break and I've got my diary clear. Daren't book it, 'cos that might be the week, sod's law applying, that'll be the week that corridor deals are done on the political budget-making and, you know, the same was true [last year] and I had a week clear and I didn't go and that week, a conversation in the corridor made a million pound's difference and if I hadn't been there, we wouldn't have had a million pounds in the budget, so I know that, so times of year as well, you know. Easter's not a problem, 'cos they're all ... you know, but that ... so there are ... so the nature of the job is such that some things have to take precedence.

'Things', such as the job, take precedence over the non-articulated private realm of the family. This competitive, driven and macho approach was encouraged by an organizational culture that, interviewees argued, placed a premium on achieving targets, delivering the Comprehensive Performance Assessment (CPA) agenda, reinforcing competition between directors for the bigger share of the scarce resources, and perpetuating the 'old boys network' in which key decisions are made outside of the formal organizational arrangements.

By abjuring a 'feminine' perspective and engaging in such 'masculine' behaviours, Trudie constructs herself as a powerful force in a competitive and challenging environment. In doing this she conforms, it would seem, to Marshall's (1984) description of women managers as travellers in a male world, who take on masculine practices in order to conform. However, following Judith Butler's (1990, 1995, 1997) more recent analysis of the performativity of gender (see Chapter 5) and the work of other post-structuralist feminists (see below), it would be more apposite to argue that all managers, male and female, have to actively adopt such an approach. The masculinity that is permissible is very narrow, and may feel uncomfortable for many men who, nevertheless, have to adapt themselves to it. It is just more visible to the observer when it is a woman who does this.

Trudie is very much aware of acting in a macho way. She recounts incidents from a series of regular meetings with peers from other (neighbouring) organisations designed to improve collaborative working relationships. Initially, she said, she adopted a 'caring and helpful approach', but it soon became apparent to her that she 'was doing all of the work and getting none of the influence', so she 'started to be a bit more arrogant . . . and chuck my weight around'. The result, she stated, was that she was listened to by other directors and she became more influential in the decision-making process. Note here that not only had she consciously adopted a 'masculine' stance, but her earlier adoption of a more 'feminine' approach had been just as deliberate a choice.

Trudie has described a macho organisational culture and shown how, in conforming to such a culture, she helps in its perpetuation. This culture was described, and lamented by, numerous managers. Dorothy, for example, a junior manager in a support function, describes how the management style in more recent years has become increasingly macho:

It's a much more macho climate than when I left it . . . em . . . I think in terms of equality it's massively backtracked.

Male managers also talked about this macho culture. Alec, for example, sees a previous 'command and control', and thus macho, model as continuing to influence managerial culture:

You know, it was all set up and they were still using these sort of military terms like 'divisions' and . . . and there was even then in the 80s very much this expectation that you could tell people to do something and that that person would go 'yes sir' and do it and certainly going back beyond that to when I first started working in [place of work] it was like that that there was an expectation that sort of erm . . . because of your position in the hierarchy . . . if you told somebody to do it, they'd respond by doing what you told them and I don't think . . . I don't think that exists in anything like the same way now and I think you've got a completely different model to work with.

Stuart uses a wonderfully evocative metaphor to describe this macho organisational culture. It is that of 'the caveman'—competitive, unthinking, aggressive, heavily controlled, and thus resistant to any changes in leadership style:

I fear we've done this . . . the transformational leadership programme and all that, I don't see the culture of the organization changing as a consequence of that, I see some quite transformational leaders around the place . . . em . . . battering on the walls of the cave to get out, but I don't see it embedding in the organization as a culture.

Principal Officer Joe's depictions of the organisation shows that, inside the cave, there is a focus on faultfinding, blame and failure—or fear of failure. He suggests:

I think in the culture we have now that there's a . . . there's a real danger that people will just . . . you know . . . people will just find fault and . . . and, therefore, you will become more scared if you're not careful, erm . . . as a manager and you start to . . . well, it goes back to performance indicators. You know, we're terrified about declaring this result for this thing and, therefore, we . . . you know, we do our damndest to make sure we can count everything we possibly can towards it and then you start to be . . . it's a sort of fine line between that and then starting to . . . well, I don't mean falsified, but you know what I mean, you start to, sort of, be economical with the truth about something, because you're scared . . . And you start to get diverted from, if you're not careful, what really matters and also, you create a culture . . . well, not . . . sort of . . . fear in a way or . . . or real fear of failure, perhaps, rather than celebration of success.

We have been using the word 'culture' straightforwardly in the above descriptions, as if there is such a thing as a culture which an organisation has. Our post-structuralist stance would argue otherwise: it is one which sees organisations as constructed through discourses and interactions between human and inanimate organisational participants (Burrell, 1988; Cooper and Burrell, 1988; Chia, 1995). The repeated reference in these interviews to a macho organisational culture would be seen, in this perspective, as creating that very thing being described. In other words, there is a dominant discourse of macho masculinity in this organisation which, in circulating and being recounted and repeated, enacted within the psyches and the embodied practices of organisational members, *constructs* a macho organisation. Trudie's seemingly active choice of becoming a male manager in a female body is therefore necessary if she is to achieve the career success for which she strives, but at the same time it contributes to the on-going process of making the organisation macho.

The post-heroic leader meets the heroic manager

We have been examining managers in an organisation that aims to instigate a post-heroic leadership culture in place of its macho management culture. We have shown some of the complexities that arise when competing discourses meet and clash, and how managers suffer when embroiled in the clashing of titans. The organisation has decreed that the manager should be post-heroic, but at the same time requires of him/her that s/he must be heroic. To be a leader, as we showed in Chapters 3 and 4, is to have introduced into one's fantasies of the self the very concept of 'the hero'. It is smuggled in, almost, contained in the discursive baggage. Managers are therefore told they must give up the heroic stance at the same time as they are encouraged to become heroic. The manager can thus be neither one thing nor the other; he turns constantly in a fruitless endeavour to achieve both contradictory positions, of the heroic and the post-heroic. Sometimes some may feel they have won the battle, but their staff tell otherwise. Sometimes some may feel bruised, battered and bewildered by the attempt. Some may just give up and practise management in whatever way comes easiest to hand. Some may 'talk the talk' of post-heroic leadership while abjuring the concomitant practices, and their lack of integrity will ensure they fail as leaders. However, there is disillusionment throughout the organisation about the policy of introducing leadership.

We have seen that in this organisation is constructed a culture that its participants experience as domineering, aggressive, goal-driven, rational and, therefore, macho. This organisation is not alone in this—it is a model that is true of the majority, as we will discuss when we turn to the theories introduced in this chapter.

We have read how ambitious women managers have to ungender themselves, strip themselves of their femininity and act 'like a man'. Male managers are not consciously aware of having to gender themselves using similar mechanisms, but gender theory is adamant that gender is constructed through the practices of gender, that is, of masculinity and femininity (see Chapter 5 and below for a discussion of this body of theory). It follows that those managers with male genitalia have to work as hard at constructing and maintaining their masculinity as those managers with female genitalia who consciously construct a managerial machismo.

Managers thus have the following requirements laid upon them:

• You must, regardless of your biological sex, be masculine.
• You must be a macho, heroic manager.
• You should be a heroic leader.
• You must be a post-heroic leader.

Masculinity and heroic management are closely related, as we will see. Post-heroic leadership, however, is seemingly more 'feminine' in its practices. If managers who work hard to construct the requisite masculinity are then required to articulate a gendered identity that is at odds with this masculinity, the result is, and can only be, confusion and worse. For the organisation, the outcome is a general disillusion about the failure to implement a much-vaunted policy.

To understand these requirements and their effects upon leaders, we will now turn to the theories that explain these hugely conflicting requirements. We will commence with theories about men and masculinities, to show something more of the masculinity that is required of managers, a masculinity which is at odds with the femininity required of leaders. We will then explore how feminist writers regard the machismo of management.

Managers must be masculine and macho

Organization and management theory assumes, although never explicitly, that managers and workers are male, with male stereotypic powers, attitudes and obligations (Acker, 1990; Calás and Smircich, 1992; Martin, 1990). Most of the literature on organisational studies is already about men (think of Taylor's 'Man Management' and Mintzberg's famous chief executives as the most obvious examples) but this focus has been tacit and has not been explored in relation to men as gendered (i.e. how men become men) (Cheng, 1996). Organisational structures, cultures and everyday practices have all been shown to constitute the 'ideal employee', and especially the ideal manager (Fournier and Kelemen, 2001), as a disembodied and rational figure, one which fits closely to cultural images of masculinity. Femininity, associated with embodiment, emotions and sexuality, is regarded as inferior and subordinate to 'male' rationality and out of place in rational organisations.

There is thus strong agreement among those who think about gender in organisations that management is masculine; for masculinity is implicit in the construction of management in that it seeks to be rational, target-driven, performance managed, controlling and rigid. Whitehead, for example, (1996, p. 157) argues that management is gendered male not only through the 'sheer numerical dominance of men as managers' but also 'through the masculinist cultures which prevail in male organizational settings'. He presents an account of male managers speaking from a position of double certainty as both men and managers. He argues that through their work as managers, men invest considerably in notions of masculinity (masculine identity). Collinson and Hearn (1996, 2001, see also Hearn, 1996, 1998, 2000) show in some depth how management is masculine, and how the form of masculinity required by managers is very specific—Anglo-Saxon, middle class and conservative. This is what they call 'hegemonic masculinity', or a form of masculinity that is so dominant it inhibits our being able to conceptualise other forms.

The concept of hegemonic masculinity/masculinities has been contested in more recent writings on masculinities (see Hearn, 2004; Wetherell and Edley, 1999). Nevertheless, it is a notion that is used widely in critical studies of men and masculinity to depict the dominant relations of power between men, as well as to gain insights into the similarities and differences between cultural norms of masculinities and the realities of men's experiences. Connell's work is frequently cited as seminal in the discussion of hegemonic masculinities. In the later edition of his influential book, *Masculinities*, Connell (2005) defends the concept against more recent criticism as a way of 'theorising gendered power relations among men and understanding the effectiveness of masculinities in the legitimation of the gender order' (p. xvii). He argues that within a given society or specific social context, there is a culturally dominant construction of masculinity, which is a hegemonic discourse. This takes us back to the discussion of norms in Chapter 5—hegemonic masculinity is a normative masculinity. It is a 'historically mobile' and fluid concept (Connell, 2005, p. 77) that will inevitably alter in different contexts and societies, and is perceived as an ideal type or, as we have said, societal norm rather than the only form of masculinity available to men. Donaldson (1993) argues that it is this hegemonic model of masculinity which is depicted through practices of popular heroes and role models. Alsop et al. (2002, p. 141) suggest that in Western society, hegemonic masculinity 'is recognised in most literature as hinging on heterosexuality, economic autonomy, being able to provide for one's family, being rational, successful, keeping one's emotions in check and above all not doing anything considered feminine'. Furthermore, critical studies on men have highlighted how white, middle class heterosexual hegemonic masculinities have tended to dominate other masculinities (Collinson and Hearn, 1996, 2001). Whereas working class masculinity, black masculinity and gay masculinity are presented as subordinate or marginal masculinities, each sub-group also produces its own cultural norms of masculinity. Kaufmann (1994) argues that these sub-groups define manhood or the masculine ideal in different ways in accord with the economic and social possibilities of that group. So, for example, if the dominant masculine ideal in Western culture relates to measures of personal success through education, employment or sporting acumen, those men unable to achieve success in these areas (owing perhaps to their social status) may seek other ways to prove their worth through, for example, physical strength or violence or crime.

Notions of hegemonic masculinity in critical studies of men and masculinities tend to embrace two main features (Alsop et al., 2002, p. 142). First of all, hegemonic masculinity is perceived as a cultural ideal and is therefore unavailable to the majority of men. Secondly, while there is fluidity in the subject matter of hegemonic masculinity, the dominant ideals of masculinity reject both femininity and homosexuality. As the demands of hegemonic masculinity are out of reach for most men, it is argued that there is a constant need for men to prove that they are achieving the goals of masculinity and with this, an enduring insecurity attached to manhood.

However, there is much difficulty in defining 'masculinity'. Rather than depicting it as an object, Connell suggests focussing on processes and relationships through which men and women conduct gendered lives. Masculinity, he argues, 'to the extent that this term can be briefly defined at all, is simultaneously a place in gender relations, the practices through which men and women engage that place in gender and the effects of these practices in bodily experience, personality and culture' (2005, p. 71).

Authors exploring men and masculinities follow an earlier feminist line of argument which demonstrates that gender is not given biologically, but is socially constructed (see Chapter 5 for details of this perspective). Genitalia are the signs that show how an embodied person should act in ways that conform to societal presumptions about what it is to be a man or to be a woman, but they do not determine that the person is a man or a woman. Gender is therefore something that is achieved through numerous practices. It is fragile, unstable and needs constant labour to maintain the semblance of what appears to be 'true' gendered identities. Masculinity and femininity, it follows, can be achieved by individuals regardless of whether they are biologically male or female. A woman can be masculine, a man feminine (Benjamin, 1988, 1995, 1998).

That a man becomes a man through the public sphere and work settings outside of the family context (Hearn 1992) is part of the construction of masculinity. A successful career achieved by clear vertical progression through the organizational hierarchy is frequently the means through which men secure a stable masculine identity. The status, benefits and perks are merely external signs of success and power.

Whitehead's writings (1999b, 2001) depict a complex and symbolic connection between men as gendered subjects, management discourse and masculine identities. Discourses of gender inform management discourse, which constitutes masculine and managerial identities that in turn inform wider constructions of gender. Managerial masculinity is characterised by the pursuit of personal success and a need for control. The driven and competitive nature of men's managerial ambition and subsequent behaviours can have significant consequences for both their private lives and their health (Collinson and Hearn, 2005; Kerfoot, 2001; Whitehead 1999, 2001). However, to be a manager is to be a man and to be a man requires such competition and ambition.

It has been noted that men's primary identification is with work (Cheng, 1996), although the works of Whitehead, Hearn and Collinson would suggest that it is the constructions of masculinity that influence such an identification, while this focus upon work in turn constructs masculinity. Cheng (op cit) however observes that as women aspire to similar 'success' in organisations, they too adopt a primary identification with work and hegemonic masculinity (as we have seen in the case of Trudie). Paid work provides for men a strong sense of masculine identity so that men's sense of self, and concomitant sense of 'importance and relevance is reconfirmed daily in our overflowing diaries' (Whitehead, 1999b, p. 116). As an arena with particular historical and gendered associations, managerial work offers numerous opportunities for men to achieve a sense of masculine identity.

In short, management is masculine, but masculinity is not some fixed substance or essence: it is something that is achieved through being worked at. The form of masculinity management takes is narrow and rigid, based on rationality, logic, competitiveness, ambition and abjures any emotions. Managers become men through engaging in masculine, competitive battles for dominance over other staff, male and female. Women who wish for successful managerial careers must similarly become masculine.

This is the norm of gender that informs heroic management. It is the one that Jim describes when he refers to the autocratic leaders who had so impressed him. It is that which Trudie attempts to achieve when acting as masculine as possible. It is what Alec is familiar with and is loathe to lose. This is the understanding of how to be a manager that circulates in the thoughts and the psyches of the managers in Woolbury and many other organisations.

The impact of masculinity upon working lives: The view from feminist writers

Much of the influence for this approach to understanding managers and masculinities comes from post-structuralist feminist perspectives. They call into question gender categories in that they show the errors inherent in treating men and women as two unified groups ('men' and 'women') and undifferentiated categories (in which all men are presumed to be the same, and all women presumed to be the same). The logic of post-structural feminist enquiry is to oppose those things which are supposed to be typical of men or of women. Where men have been regarded as logical, non-emotional, aggressive, occupiers of the public realm, and women the opposite, post-structural feminism, influenced by Foucault and Butler (see Chapter 5) shows how these descriptors not only *create* the genders they supposedly do no more than describe, but become *norms* by which we do not feel we are truly men or truly women if we do not live up to them.

Post-structuralist feminism has emerged out of two centuries of feminist scholarship. Earlier work focused on establishing a voice for women in society; it had its foundations in the eighteenth century scholarship of Mary Wollstencraft, the nineteenth century writings of John Stuart Mill and the mid twentieth century writings of Simone de Beauvoir and Betty Friedan. However, it has been the final third of the last century that has seen feminism emerge to influence and prominence. Most authors emphasise that feminist theory critically addresses the subordination of women with the aim of seeking an end to it. Weedon (1997, p. 1) suggests that feminism

> is a politics, directed at changing existing power relations between women and men in society. These power relations structure all areas of life, the family, education and welfare, the world of work and politics, culture and leisure. They determine who does what and for whom, what we are and what we might become.

This is not the place to outline the history of feminist thinking, and its various schools of thought—interested readers will find many superb texts available (see, for example, Alsop et al., 2002). We have focused on post-structuralist feminist theory because it is part of the body of theory we are using to analyse leadership in this book and it explains well why femininity is so derided at the same time as it is widely practised. Post-structuralist feminism explores how constructions of gender are historically, socially and culturally specific, with the aim of changing oppressive gender relations (Gavey, 1997). The aim here is liberation from oppression for women *and* for men. Attention is focussed on gendered subjectivities and their plurality, ambiguity and fragmented nature within asymmetrical power relations. Women still have less power than (those constructed as) men, still have lower life chances, earn less, have more restrictions placed upon them, than do men, so the priority remains that of liberating women from oppression, but with a wider remit of understanding how men too are caged in by gender.

So, feminist post-structuralist analysis results when gender issues are incorporated into a post-structuralist framework. It offers a means to understand, expose and alter hierarchical social networks that use power to silence and marginalise discourses related to gender. Feminist post-structuralists seek to transform gender dimensions, to develop new ways of understanding sexual differences and to uncover androcentric (where the male is regarded as the norm) biases within socially, politically and culturally established institutions. In relation to the aims of this book, feminist post-structuralism enables fresh light to be shed on leadership theories and the ways in which they gender leaders and followers, and perpetuate those very practices of power and domination which good leadership is (ostensibly) designed to eradicate.

In this perspective, the study of masculinities in organisations is not necessarily about men. It is about the socially constructed performance of gender, in which masculinity can be and is performed by men and women alike. Women who are deemed to be successful managers perform hegemonic masculinity, for the type of behaviour deemed appropriate for managers in contemporary organisations coincides with images of masculinity and thus are centred around rationality, measurement, objectivity, control and competitiveness (Burrell, 1992; Harding, 2003; Oseen, 1997). While men are portrayed as meeting the competences and characteristics that are central to the behaviour of managers in organisations, women are associated with the 'feminine' characteristics of caring, nurturing and sharing that are allegedly more appropriate for the domestic sphere and the reproduction of the home and the family (Gherardi, 1995).

Fournier and Kelemen (2001) identify many studies that show the effort that women have to invest in presenting 'viable public images'. Trudie's strategy (above) of choosing to be masculine is just one of these available options (Brewis, 1999). Several studies have shown how women try to fit in by adopting 'masculine' styles, by being tough and aggressive or by adopting a cold professional approach (Calás and Smircich, 1996; Collinson and Collinson, 1996; Collinson and Hearn, 1996; Fletcher, 2004; Marshall, 1995). Options chosen by other women have included making themselves discreet and invisible through requesting permission to speak in meetings or other behaviours demonstrating a lack of assertiveness, so as to repair the damage done by 'infringement of the symbolic order of gender' (Gherardi, 1995, p. 141).

Feminist writers, therefore, show how anything to do with the feminine is derided and seen not only as second class, but out of place in public arenas such as organisations. This is important, because postheroic leadership calls for the practice of attributes that have long been regarded as 'feminine'.

Managers must be post-heroic leaders

There is much research which suggests that women's styles of management and leadership are more suitable to the organisations of the twenty-first century. For example, Rosener's (1990) research, subsequently developed by other writers in the US and the UK (Alimo-Metcalfe, 1995), has suggested that women's style of leadership differs from that of men; that women are more likely to adopt transformational approaches which are perceived as being of greater significance in present-day organisations. Men, on the other hand, are more likely to describe themselves in ways consistent with transactional leadership behaviours, in exchange relationships in which punishment and reward are seen as prime motivators. This approach has concentrated more on how women's skills have been undervalued by placing emphasis on their (perceived) nurturing and supportive qualities and calling for an increase in the number of women managers and feminine leadership styles. Other researchers have argued that all leaders, male and female, should adopt more feminine leadership styles, leading to worries of a colonisation of the feminine by the male (Brewis, 1999).

Such discussions are located within a theoretical perspective that sees gender as something that is fixed. Rosener (1990, 1997), for example, argues that because men and women are socialised differently, they also manage differently, an approach that has been criticised for essentialising women's differences (Calás and Smircich, 1992). However, these studies should not be dismissed too quickly: we suggest that the problem lies with the interpretation and presumptions surrounding the fixity of gendered identities. If we examine these studies through the theoretical lens we are using here, which argues that men and women alike can and do practise 'masculine' and 'feminine' ways of managing and leading, then we are led to the conclusion that

- masculine styles have long been valorised, and are the norm; and
- feminine styles are now regarded as essential for organisational success.

This is recognised by those who write about post-heroic leadership, who argue that the post-heroic leader possesses, and actively uses, skills and attributes previously seen as feminine, includes connectedness and a team-focussed identity in which the leader asserts the importance of making links with staff and showing a genuine interest in what they do. As Fletcher (2004, p. 654) argues:

> Women are expected to teach, enable and empower others without getting anything in return, expected to work interdependently while others do not adopt a similar stance, expected to work mutually in non-mutual situations and expected to practice less hierarchical forms of interacting even in traditionally hierarchical contexts.

So, the post-heroic leader must be nurturing, empowering, supportive and thus—in a nutshell—feminine.

Now we have been arguing that gendered attributes are not the domain of one sex, they should not be divided arbitrarily into 'male' and 'female' and are practised by women and men. The problem we have highlighted is that it is masculine attributes, those of macho-management, that are dominant and regarded as most desirable. For example, Judy Wacjman's study of management in five male-dominated multinational corporations concluded that 'macho management' and traditional managerial hierarchies were still very much part of the organisational landscape, sustained by a culture of fear and uncertainty that was generated by continuous change. Wacjman argues that

> [T]he business context of almost continuous restructuring and job losses has greatly intensified pressures for senior managers and means that insecurity about the future is pervasive . . . The logic of survival results in heightened individualistic competition for a dwindling number of job opportunities. In this economic climate, both men and women feel the need to conform to the male stereotype of management because it is still, in practice, the only one regarded as effective.
>
> (1996, p. 345)

This leads to a commitment to working long hours and displaying aggressive and competitive behaviours in which men are privileged as the objects of leadership and the operators of the tools of leadership (Sinclair, 1998).

The macho approach is represented through more traditional leadership behaviours (embodied in early studies of leadership, and reinforcing trait, style and charismatic approaches) and appears to draw more strongly from hegemonic masculinist discourses of leadership, reinforced through the subject position of a competitive, controlling and self-reliant individualist.

The macho or heroic manager (or leader) is thus utterly seductive for managers—perhaps too hard to resist. Research evidence affirms that striving to identify with this form of masculinity is likely to lead to employment security and material success. Put in this way, masculinity 'is as seductive as it is anxiety making' (Brewis and Linstead, 2004, p. 79). In Woolbury, too, managers talked about the necessity of conforming to its macho culture, as we have seen. The necessity to conform may mask a desire to conform.

Conclusion

Managers are now told that they have to become post-heroic leaders, but at the same time the fantasy of being a hero, and thus masculine, has been tapped into. They are told, in effect, to be more feminine, to show characteristics they have previously understood they should hide when they are at work, and at the same time are energised by the masculinity of 'the hero'. They are told to demonstrate attributes that belong to the inferior (to women), and at the same time experience a desire for the superiority of the alpha male.

This, we propose, is why we found such dissonance in the managers studied. They were struggling with the requirement that they adopt three highly conflicting identities—the macho managers, the macho hero and the feminine leader—at one and the same time. Each of these is at once compelling and coercive, fluid and constraining. The interviewees had to be both macho manager and gentle (feminine) leader at one and the same time. They had to be open, caring and emotional, and at the same time closed, distant and rational.

The result was that managers experienced great anxiety (in a psychodynamic sense—see Ford (2007) for a full account). They were unhappy, tense, stressed and uncertain about the future. Part of the anxiety created appears to be associated with what Brewis and Linstead (2004) have identified as a hidden fear at the heart of managers who continue to acknowledge a preference for more macho management and leadership practices. On the one hand, this way of managing provides affirmation and security, as this masculine approach is still deemed to be representative of modern management (Kerfoot, 2000). On the other hand, sustaining this identity can in itself be an exhausting project on which individuals constantly have to work to demonstrate their abilities to expand, affirm and maintain managerial control.

Thus, both men and women managers in organisations are likely to be motivated to identify with masculinity, and to be 'seduced by a masculinist way of being' (Whitehead, 1999b, p. 27). When introduced to post-heroic leadership, however, they are told that they must identify with femininity *at the same time* as identifying with two extreme versions of masculinity. Furthermore, much of the discussions about post-heroic leadership are appealing. They speak to managers of the value of discarding some derided practices, and promise to free them to manage in ways that conform to culturally validated 'good' ways of relating to other people, concepts that many managers may feel very happy with. It is the clash of gendered cultures that cause anxiety.

Managers, male and female, have long been told to be 'real [managerial] men'. The current turn in leadership tells them to be 'real, caring, women' and 'real, heroic men'. The first requires distance, the second interrelationships and empathy and the third self-sacrifice. The first demands rationality and objectivity, the second self-knowledge and care for others and the third a combination of the two. Managers are now charged with the task of being both masculine and feminine. The evidence from Woolbury is that the incompatibility of this charge is causing anxiety. We turn in the next chapter to an analysis of the effects of leadership discourses upon the psyche.

7
The Psyche and Leadership

Introduction

In Chapter 5 we drew on a study of leadership development to show that 'Great Man' and charismatic theories of leadership still inform organisational practices. We concluded that leadership therefore presents a norm which is so difficult to achieve that it can only have negative consequences for leaders, while it simultaneously creates categories of people who are 'abnormal' and who are thus second class, inferior and denigrated. In Chapter 6 we demonstrated that the people we call 'leaders' or 'managers' must simultaneously be both leaders *and* managers. As this calls on them to behave both in masculine and feminine ways, they do not know which way to turn and the result is anxiety. The theoretical perspectives we used in those chapters, queer theory and post-structuralist gender theories, draw on psychoanalytical theory to assist the development of understanding of what it is to be a person living in the West in the twenty-first century. In this chapter we turn explicitly to psychoanalytical theory itself and apply some of its insights to leadership.

We are doing this firstly because the theories we use in this chapter can tell us much more about the issues we have been discussing in Chapters 5 and 6. Secondly, we wish to follow the warnings from queer theory of the need to explore how the academy contributes to the maintenance of inequalities. Thirdly, the vast majority of leadership theory is based either on armchair theorising or upon survey-type studies which are not only limited in their scope but often poorly operationalised. The study of Woolbury we reported in Chapter 6 is one of the few in-depth qualitative studies of the development of leadership in organisations, and that study shows the intricacies and complexities of the context into which leadership is inserted. Leadership theories are often developed with only a simple organisational context in mind. Finally, and related to this last point, we are extremely concerned at the naivety of much leadership theory, development and training, and the deleterious effects on populations that can be caused by a misuse of inadequately thought-through theories. In this chapter our aim in particular is to grapple with poor theory adopted from psychology for use in leadership studies. We are concerned that the theory of the self used by many leadership writers, just like the theory of the organisation, is superficial and inadequate. Owing to its over-simplifying of that most complex of creatures, the human being, such theory unwittingly offers as a cure something which may rather prove to be a poison. This chapter reveals the reasons for our disquiet.

Unlike in other chapters we are not here drawing on original research. Our focus now is on how leadership is theorised and written about, so we are turning instead to an analysis of one of the latest theories of leadership, known as authentic leadership (AL), and how that model of leadership is conceptualised and written about. AL is currently gaining adherents on both sides of the Atlantic, and many readers of this book may find themselves on training courses in AL. It is based on a body of theory known as 'positive psychology' whose focus is on looking for the positive aspects of life. As optimists, we are pleased to see such an approach being used to balance the overemphasis on the negative in some other bodies of theory. However, where a theory is developed that ignores much of the reality of what it is to be a human subject, we *have* to interrogate it to find out the possible impact of an application which ignores, rather than dealing with, the negative.

AL is of interest for another reason. In common with most mainstream theories of leadership, it presumes that the relationship between leader and follower is vital to improving organisational functioning, and it explores ways of 'improving' the means through which the leader influences the follower. However, the claims made regarding interactions between leaders and followers are presumptions not supported by empirical research or closely argued theoretical development. We will bring in interactions between leaders and other people into our analysis, as all people have psyches, and an unconscious, and it is the interaction of psyches in relationship that are the unexamined underpinnings to the presumptions of leadership theory.

There are several competing schools of psychoanalytical theory. All theories have their foundations in the work of Sigmund Freud, who was the first person to clarify the existence of an unconscious that influences the conscious mind. We are drawing on the school of thought known as object relations theory. This theory, like all theories influenced by Freud, argues that the unconscious as well as the conscious evolves in the first months of life. What happens in those early years may appear to be forgotten, but memories of childhood events are stored in the unconscious. Throughout life various triggers bring up those memories into the preconscious and influence how we behave and respond, albeit that we do not often know the suppressed reasons that are influencing our actions and responses. Psychoanalytical theory is therefore a body of theory of how we come to be human subjects. In this chapter we are drawing upon objects relations theory, an influential body of theory based on Freud's insights.

In exploring AL through an object relations perspective, we show that the model contains the seeds of its own destruction. Were there to be attempts to implement it in practice, there could be dire consequences for people at work. Although the critique of this one model cannot become a generalised critique of all theories of leadership, we suggest the analysis may say something more generally about theories of leadership, and thus this critique allows us to say something more about followers.

The theory of authentic leadership

In 2005 there were special issues on AL in both the *Leadership Quarterly* and the *Journal of Management Studies,* attesting to its increasing popularity and influence. Its focus is part of what Fineman (2006, p. 270) calls 'the "positive" neohumanistic turn in organizational theorizing', that is, a move towards emphasising the need for, and ways of developing, positive emotional states in the workplace. This 'seductive discourse' (ibid.) draws upon positive psychology and a somewhat limited reading of the writings of the founding father of philosophy, Aristotle.

The history of the emergence and development of authentic leadership theory, so far as we can discover, is as follows. One of the leading writers on leadership, Bass, used the term in 1999 to qualify aspects of the theory of transformational leadership for which he is noted. He inserted concepts of authentic leadership into his original model following critiques relating to the darker side of charisma and the potential for narcissistic and authoritarian managers to masquerade as transformational leaders. Along with Steidlmeier (Bass and Steidlmeier, 1999, p. 181) he argued that the 'truly transformational' leader would be highly moral: to be otherwise would result in inauthentic or *pseudo*-transformational leadership. Thus, 'self-aggrandising, fantasising, pseudo-transformational leaders can be branded as immoral. But authentic leaders, as moral agents, expand the domain of effective freedom, the horizon of conscience and the scope for altruistic intention' (op cit, p. 211).

This statement signals the emergence of the AL model, for it is following publication of that paper that the AL model has been discussed in the works of such writers as Avolio and Gardner (2005); Gardner et al. (2005); Luthans and Avolio (2003) and Shamir and Eilam (2005). These writers trace its emergence not to Bass's work but to Greek philosophy and the notion of being true to oneself, of being 'genuine' and 'reliable'. The claim to such a long pedigree is common among organisation theorists, who seem to seek legitimacy for their ideas by claiming such a long heritage (Harding, 2003). It is the work of Avolio and Gardner (2005) and Gardner et al. (2005) that we primarily focus on here, for these two papers in the special edition of *The Leadership Quarterly* promise to become the foundational papers in the field. The former paper summarises the AL model while the latter develops 20 propositions in relation to the theory.

Definitions of authenticity in these foundational papers are somewhat vague. It appears to be related very much to what post-structuralist theorists call the monad of Western philosophical thought: the ontologically fixed entity having an inner self securely bounded from the exterior world. By this is meant that each person is an island unto themselves, born with a personality that is not affected by its interactions with others. This person looks out at the world from a body in which the self is located, secure in the belief of who they are and that they will never change. This person suffers no existential angst, never wakes and looks in the mirror to ask the question: who am I? Authentic leadership theory is thus located in a binary, or pair of opposites, of inside/outside. There is me, inside my body, and I look outward at you and the rest of the world.

The theory argues that authentic leaders will be moral persons who, being moral, will be good 'on the inside'. It follows that through revealing their inner goodness such people will be authentic leaders. The immoral person may try to hide their inner evil, may try to give the impression of being 'good', of being moral, but will be found out by those who seek to 'unlock the mask' behind which 'pseudo' or inauthentic leaders hide. Authentic leaders are

> deeply aware of how they think and behave and are perceived by others as being aware of their own and others' values/moral perspectives, knowledge, and strengths; aware of the context in which they operate; and who are confident, hopeful, optimistic, resilient, and of high moral character.
>
> (Avolio, Luthans, and Walumbwa, 2004, quoted in Avolio and Gardner, 2005, p. 321)

They will pursue 'an integrated set of goals that reflect personal standards of conduct', will be 'intrinsically motivated' so that they 'often become so engrossed in their work that they are motivated solely by a sense of curiosity, a thirst for learning, and the satisfaction that comes from accomplishing a valued task/objective', resulting in 'the total immersion of the self at work' (Gardner et al., 2005, p. 355). They will selectively disclose aspects of themselves to others so as to 'create bonds based on intimacy and trust', and will encourage others in the organisation to do the same (op cit, p. 357).

There is the potential for such an authentic leader to adapt how they present themselves, but they will remain authentic, it seems, so long as they accurately reflect aspects of their inner selves. One of the papers in the special edition edited by Avolio and Gardner (2005) argues that both leaders and followers associate authenticity with sincerity, honesty, and integrity, but leaders can control how others see them through (a) being consistent in words and deeds for to be inconsistent is to be inauthentic and (b) presenting different faces to different audiences (Goffee and Jones, 2005). They assert that

> [A]uthentic leaders seem to know which personality traits they should reveal to whom, and when. Highly attuned to their environments, authentic leaders rely on an intuition born of formative, sometimes harsh experiences to understand the expectations and concerns of the people they seek to influence. They retain their distinctiveness as individuals, yet they know how to win acceptance in strong corporate and social cultures and how to use elements of those cultures as a basis for radical change.
>
> (Goffee and Jones, 2005, p. 88)

Presenting one's self differently to different audiences thus remains authentic so long as it is done not to manipulate but to accurately reflect aspects of the leader's inner self.

The theoretical foundations for such a self are found in humanistic psychology. This branch of psychology, Avolio and Gardner (2005) argue, reinforces the idea that authentic individuals have compatible understandings of themselves and their lives, 'unencumbered by others' expectations for them ... [so that] they can make more sound personal choices' (Avolio and Gardner, 2005, p. 319). They illustrate this by distinguishing between sincerity and authenticity. Sincerity, they argue, differs from authenticity. Sincerity is defined as the extent to which external expression of feelings and thoughts are related to the sense of self that is experienced 'within'. Sincerity, it seems, is an intersubjective experience which must, it follows, depend upon the existence of an external 'other'. Authenticity, by contrast, is seen as 'self-referential' (p. 320), not requiring the explicit involvement or relationship with others but instead, as Erickson (1995, p. 125) argues, 'existing wholly by the laws of its own being'.

It is thus the inner, core self that is addressed in descriptions of authentic leadership: the leader must be 'genuine' in that s/he must be self-aware and must, through self-knowledge, show the external world their essential, true selves. As Avolio et al. (2004, p. 802) claim, 'the more people remain true to their core values, identities, preferences and emotions, the more authentic they become.' The essential, true self of an authentic leader is inherently good, it would seem. Such a genuine leader will cope with 'unique stressors facing organizations throughout the world today' (Avolio and Gardner, 2005, p. 316).

The theory, therefore, argues that authentic leaders must be prepared to reveal themselves through their practices and behaviours, and the self that is revealed must be the authentic self. Persons who would be leaders must therefore know themselves. The model is summarised by 20 propositions (Gardner et al., 2005) which start with

Proposition 1. Critical elements from the personal history of authentic leaders, including influential persons who model authenticity and pivotal trigger events, serve as positive forces in developing leader self-awareness.

(Gardner et al., 2005, p. 349)

And end with

Proposition 20a. Followers of more as opposed to less authentic leaders will experience higher levels of workplace well-being.

Proposition 20b. Employee engagement arising from authentic follower behaviour will promote increases in workplace well-being among followers.

Proposition 20c. Workplace well-being contributes to elevated levels of veritable and sustainable follower performance.

(Gardner et al., 2005, p. 367)

The model can thus be summarised as one which focuses firstly on how the authentic leader may develop authenticity in himself/herself, and then moves to demonstrate how such an individual will influence followers and thus the organisation.

Leaders and followers

A leader, by definition, requires followers. Gardner et al. (2005) articulate the relationship between authentic leaders and their followers very clearly. There is a presumption that the authentic leader will, in modelling his/her self-awareness, self-regulation and authenticity, foster the development of authenticity in followers. Through this, their well-being will be improved, and 'sustainable and veritable performance' will be achieved; in other words, the organisation will achieve higher rates of performance and will be a nicer (veritable) place in which to work. Followers, too, must be 'authentic', that is, must know who they are and reflect this self-knowledge to others. There is no room, in this model, for self-knowledge to reveal anything that is not positive. The individual is not allowed a dark side. We will ask later whether such a person could possibly exist, for are we all, each and every one of us, not flawed in some way? Do we not all have realms that are private to ourselves which we do not wish to share with others? And, indeed, can anyone have such perfect self-knowledge? Theories ranging from the popular 'Johari's window' to the abstract work of the philosopher Judith Butler argue that we cannot. Johari's window, much used in training courses, asserts that the individual has, in addition to aspects of the self known to the self and known to others, aspects of the self known to the self but not known to others, aspects of the self unknown to him/her but known to others, and further aspects that neither the individual nor others knows about (http://en.wikipedia.org/wiki/Johari_window, accessed 4 January 2008). Butler (2005), meanwhile, argues that it is the very fact that we cannot know ourselves fully which qualifies the possibilities of fully ethical accounting of the self. These are just the first of the questions that arise when reading about AL. We will introduce others below.

How is authenticity in followers to be achieved? Authentic leaders, we are told, will 'heighten the self-awareness and shape the self-regulatory processes of followers' (Avolio and Gardner, 2005, p. 326). These processes will facilitate followers' 'greater clarity about their values, identity, and emotions and, in turn, move towards internalized regulatory processes, balanced information processing, transparent relations with the leader and associates, and authentic behavior' (ibid.). The follower, in short, will model himself/herself on the leader. Further, we are told that 'one of the central premises' of this theory is that 'both leaders and followers are developed over time as the relationship between them becomes more authentic (op cit, p. 327). This is because

> [A]s followers internalize values and beliefs espoused by the leader their conception of what constitutes their actual and possible selves are expected to change and develop over time. As followers come to know who they are, they in turn will be more transparent with the leader, who in turn will benefit in terms of his or her own development.
>
> (Ibid.)

This, the authors stress, is a *relational* developmental process, with both follower and leader each shaping the other's development. It is the leader's character, example and dedication that will achieve this, through energising followers by 'creating meaning and positively socially constructing reality for themselves and followers' (op cit, p. 330). The keen reader will observe the disparity between the *relational* process between leaders and followers used at this point, and the adamantly *non-relational* definition of authenticity noted above. Such internal inconsistencies litter the model.

There are some warnings about poor followers. Notably, followers who are low in self-clarity may come to so much identify with an authentic leader that they take on that leader's characteristics as their own (Gardner et al., 2005, p. 360). In this case they will be inauthentic as those characteristics are not their own and do not reflect their core selves. Leaders of such people should encourage them to look inwards so as to develop self-knowledge and outwards to the core values of the group. Gardner et al. expect that such people will internalise core organisational values, and thus they will 'achieve the high levels of self-clarity and autonomy that accompany authenticity' (ibid.). It is in this phrase that we see that authenticity and organisation are so intertwined that *authenticity refers to the inability to distinguish between the self and the organisation*.

Objects relations theory

The AL model is located within theories of the self that have a very long pedigree. Indeed, Lawler (in review) suggests Avolio et al. are echoing (albeit not so poetically) the words of Polonius, in Shakespeare's Hamlet, 'to thine own self be true'. In the early twentieth century, the theory of a core self residing within a constructed social world gained precedence largely due to the works of theorists such as William James, George Herbert Mead, Herbert Blumer and, later, Irving Goffman. Arguably the most influential of these, Mead, wrote in 1934 that it is impossible to conceive of a 'self' arising outside of social experience. This socially grounded self is dynamic, based on the premise that a sense of self emerges from interactions between individuals. This self was not intended to be a mere puppet of the social, for individuals were viewed as actively and intentionally adapting themselves to social demands. Goffman's theory of the dramaturgical self (1959) located the individual more firmly within social interactions, rituals and context of interaction. Goffman's work, as the following quote shows, could inform authentic leadership, but it would do so with a more critical and analytical edge:

> The individual in ordinary work situations presents himself and his activity to others [through] the ways in which he guides himself and his activity to others, the ways in which he guides and controls the impression they form of him, and the kinds of things he may and may not do while sustaining his performance before them.
>
> (Goffman, 1959, p. xi)

This is a self that is a 'relatively recent phenomenon, born of a unique combination of individual agency, optimism and democracy' (Holstein and Gubrium, 2000, p. 4). It is one that has been subjected to decades of attention focussed on 'self-awareness, self esteem . . . an embattled self cascades from all quarters' (op cit, p. 10). It is, indeed, a self whose suffering is recognised.

As each chapter of this book makes clear, our own preference, located within a European philosophical and psychoanalytical tradition, is for post-structuralist theories which argue against the possibility of there being anything such as a core self. We do not wish to debate authentic leadership from this perspective, however, for the result would be little more than a battering of paradigms incommensurably between ourselves and proponents of AL. Rather more productive, and indeed more apposite, is an analysis that uses object relations theory. Indeed, Jessica Benjamin, whose works we draw on in this chapter, has somewhat reconciled post-structuralist and constructionist accounts of the self (Benjamin, 1995, pp. 12–13). She needs to do this as psychoanalytical theory is predicated upon the existence of an inner self, a notion disavowed by post-structural theorists who argue that the self is always a process of becoming, behind which there is no core, or inner self.

Benjamin suggests that we should not confuse the category of the thinking subject with that of the self as a locus of conscious and unconscious subjective experiences. That is, we should distinguish between subject (that which we call 'I') and self (that which we call 'me'). We should think of the *subject* as a locus of experience that need not be centrally organised, coherent or unified but which allows continuity and awareness of different states of mind and that can feel more or less real, more or less alive, more or less aware of a sense of individuality. This subject may not be unitary but will have multiple positions and voices. The self, meanwhile, has a singularity that Bollas (1993) refers to as his or her aesthetic or unique idiom (Bollas, 1993). This is a being who is separately embodied and thus would appear to have an individual psyche (Benjamin, 1995, p. 13) but whose boundaries are permeable so that it is constantly assimilating and incorporating the 'outside' (1998, p. 79).

Authentic Leadership and Object Relations Theory

The AL model is of an inherently intersubjective encounter between leaders and followers, for the follower is presumed to become 'authentic' through interaction with the leader. In this, AL is similar to other recent theories of leadership in its focus upon the intersubjective. This makes the use of object relations theory particularly fruitful, for it is a school of thought located within psychoanalytical theory that explores how 'objects', including people and experiences as well as inanimate objects, become incorporated into the psyche and, therefore, the self. The theory emerged from analyses of encounters between psychoanalysts and analysands, how each became an object for the other, and the resulting dialectical intra- and intersubjective relationships that allow articulation of the self (Bollas, 1987).

In this chapter we draw largely on the works of Jessica Benjamin and Christopher Bollas. This analysis will show that the AL model is inoperable in practice. This is partly because the model presumes that authentic leaders and followers, when they look inwards, see core organizational values—we saw this in the discussion of AL leaders as people who would totally immerse themselves in their work. If this is so, that is, if internalisation of core organisational values results in authenticity, then *authenticity and organisation are so intertwined that authentic leaders (and followers) are people who cannot distinguish between the self and the organisation.*

This is disquieting, for it means leadership theory can be seen to be a form of control over employees (managers and staff). This is of particular concern to us given that we have summarised in Chapter 4 and elsewhere

(Ford and Harding, 2007) the ways in which leadership training courses, of which there are many, may performatively achieve changes in the selves of managers, opening them and the staff they work with to more subtle and potentially irresistible forms of control. Thus our first charge against the AL model is that an approach which claims the high ground of morals is itself immoral, for it is designed to bend people further to the organisational grindstone without their knowing they are so bent.

However, that accusation presumes the psyche can be reduced easily to an organisational cog in which subjectivity is lost, something which object relations theory, as we will show, suggests is impossible. This leads us to a conundrum, for how can we charge a theory with the crime of allowing more subtle means of control if the crime is, from its inception, impossible? We will argue that if managers are encouraged to develop themselves as authentic leaders, as they may well be, the results for themselves and their staff could be traumatic. Rather than a means of control the theory is shown to be a means of instigating psychological suffering. This is because the AL model presumes the existence of individuals who are so lacking in any shortcomings, they appear saintly. The leaders written about are flawless, perfect, rejoicing in the knowledge of an inner self that has nothing to hide, no traumas, no imperfections, in short, no human characteristics. We posed the question above: are there any people who can claim, honestly and truthfully, such perfection? Psychoanalytical theory acknowledges that the 'human condition' is one of suffering, where inevitably flawed individuals yearn and search for a lost sense of utter belonging (Jones and Spicer, 2005; Roberts, 2005). Indeed the ancient Greeks recognised this. Aeschylus told a story of the earth having been inhabited by round creatures that had two heads, four arms, four legs and two sets of genitalia. They grew so confident that they threatened the gods, who put them in their place by smiting them in half. The resulting creatures each had one head, one pair of arms and legs and one set of genitalia each. Since then, these creatures, who are the humans we now know, have searched the world looking for their lost other half.

It is to psychoanalytical theory that we therefore turn to explore what happens to the AL model (and similar models of leadership) when the non-saintly individual is introduced. In doing this we mimic what may happen in training courses. There are now numerous opportunities to go on courses to develop one's authentic leadership capabilities. We have in mind as we write this a person who is keen to develop their leadership capabilities, and who packs their bag and sets out for a three-day, intensive course in authentic leadership. There they will be taught more about developing self-knowledge and showing that self to others. We assume that the person who is packing their bags is a normal individual, who has had a reasonably happy childhood and is set to be a success in the world. This person, however, will not be flawless. What then happens when s/he is told they must be unblemished? In this chapter we use object relations theory, and particularly the works of Jessica Benjamin and Christopher Bollas, to explore the impact upon our hypothetical traveller. We will show that by refusing to acknowledge that all individuals are less than saintly the AL model, if introduced into organisations, would result in trauma for the people working in organisations.

The intrasubjective and intersubjective

Object relations theory argues that the self is formed through the internalisation of 'objects', both animate (such as people) and inanimate (such as works of art) that are absorbed into the psyche. With Freudian roots, it emerges out of the theories of Melanie Klein (1948, 1975), Wilfred Bion (1961) and Donald Winnicott (1964). Arguably the two most influential object relations theorists writing at present are Christopher Bollas (1987, 1993, 1995, 2007) and Jessica Benjamin (1988, 1995, 1998).

For Bollas (1995) the self is a continuously moving experience, a psychic texture formed over many years by countless experiences that contribute to a store of mental contents, some of which cannot be put into words and may not even be easily accessible by the conscious mind. These mental contents comprise introjected objects, both animate and inanimate and include, as we have argued elsewhere (Harding, 2003), discourses. Bollas suggests that the individual begins life

> as a peculiar but unrealized idiom of being, and in a lifetime transforms that idiom into sensibility and personal reality. Our idiom is an aesthetic of being driven by an urge to articulate its theory of form by selecting and using objects so as to give them form.
>
> (1995, p. 151)

But, the self 'does not seem to arise out of a person's episodic experiences' (p. 160), it is not the sum of its parts, rather it is 'an aesthetic intelligence' (p. 166) or an 'aesthetic movement that can be felt psychically' (p. 172). The self is an 'internal object' that is

> fashioned from several sources: from an inner feel of the authorizing aesthetic that gives polysemous (not unitary) shape to one's being;

from an inner feel of internal objects which are the outcome of the other's effect upon one's self; from the shape of discrete episodes of self experience.

(1995, p. 173)

This 'internal object', this 'phenomenon of the real', is, he argues, the result of the self moving through the experiences of its life as a unique set of evolving theories that generate insights, questions and new perspectives about its self (1995, p. 69). The theories arise from the effect of objects upon the self: people, music, artworks, artefacts, whatever, they 'move through' the individual like ghosts, inhabiting the mind, conjured up when their names are evoked (1993, pp. 56–7) in the conscious or unconscious thought processes through which the self dreams its self into being. Thoughts of objects indeed form countless trains, thousands of ideational routes, leading to an explosive creation of meanings which meet up with new units of life experience (1995, p. 55), mostly when the self is, literally, 'lost in thought'. The individual is thus inhabited by inner structures which form highly condensed psychic textures: thus the self can be 'substantially metamorphosed by the structure of objects; internally transformed by objects that leave their traces within us' (1993, p. 59).

Such an account of the self is important in analysing leadership for it allows some understanding of the interactions between self and other, and between self and discourses of leadership and how the self is formed through such interactions. However, Bollas's analysis is largely of the intrapsychic—relationships within the psyche. Jessica Benjamin's account introduces intersubjectivity to the analysis, something that is vital if we are to understand relationships between leaders and followers.

The failure of differentiation, the refusal of subjectivity

Reading Hegel's master/slave dialectic through a Freudian lens, Benjamin argues that all encounters with others bring with them the potential for relationships of domination and subordination. This makes her account even more useful for studying organisations which, being hierarchical structures, are inescapably places in which relationships of domination and submission are played out. Indeed, the very terms 'leaders' and 'followers' bespeak of a hierarchy in which one is dominant and the other, the follower, has to bend his/her will to that of the leader.

The German philosopher Georg Wilhelm Friedrich Hegel (1770–1831) developed the famous thesis, the master/slave dialectic, which informs much Western writing today. In Hegel's thesis, the slave is a means to the satisfaction of the master's desire not only for the overt tasks he carries out but because the slave allows the master to recognise himself, his self, as master. Without a slave there can, of course, be no slave master. In Hegelian dialectics there occurs a 'profound reversal' (Kain, 2005, p. 47) whereby the dominant consciousness, that of the master, becomes dependent upon the subordinate consciousness for recognition. This is because the master cannot be a master without recognition from the slave, who calls the master by his name of 'master'. However, the slave is nothing, is worthless, is utterly inferior, so what price recognition from such a subservient being? The master's 'reality and importance' (op cit, p. 48) becomes 'hollow and inessential' (ibid.) when he recognises that he depends upon such an abject being to know his own superiority. The slave, meanwhile, through hard work and fear, becomes self-referential and through 'an autocreative act, the slave's negation itself becomes negated' (Carr and Zanetti, 1999, p. 329). In other words, the slave is able to recognise his own existence and becomes aware of who he is. He thus becomes superior to the master. It is this thesis that informs Benjamin's writing.

The AL model presumes an intersubjective encounter between leader and follower in which the follower is inspired by the leader to become authentic in her/his own turn. Benjamin's thesis allows us to analyse the interaction between the authentic leader and follower as one in which the leader must deny subjectivity to the follower. The analysis will show the impossibility of the follower absorbing the AL's example into the account of the self. It will show, indeed, that in attempting to be authentic inauthenticity must be introduced, resulting in the destruction of the follower and the despair of the leader.

Benjamin's account starts from the perspective that rather than being monads (or islands) the subject can exist only through interactions with others (1988, p. 17). Whereas Bollas's work explores the *intra*subjective, or activities within a single psyche (although see Bollas (2007) for a more intersubjective perspective), Benjamin explores interactions between two psyches. Bollas's account would help us analyse our hypothetical leadership trainee as s/he travels alone to the training venue, while Benjamin's helps us analyse the interactions between the trainee and the people s/he meets while at the venue. Her account is thus of an *intersubjective* dynamic in which the other whom the self meets is also a self, a subject in his or her own right, who is different and yet alike and is capable of sharing similar mental experiences. The intersubjective encounter is important for Benjamin because it 'reorients the conception of the psychic world from a subject's relations to its object toward a subject meeting another subject' (p. 19).

Here, mutuality of recognition is utterly important, but as each subject seeks both freedom and belonging, the encounter between two subjects is fraught. Hegel, in *The Phenomenology of Spirit*, showed that the self's wish for absolute independence conflicts with the self's need for recognition. In trying to establish itself as an independent entity, the self must yet recognise the other not as a mental representation but as a subject like itself, if the self is to be recognised by the other. In other words, when two people meet, each must recognise that the other is an individual in their own right, rather than an object there to satisfy the individual's own needs. The meaning of this is obvious to anyone who has been approached at a conference or meeting by someone who introduces themselves and then talks solely about themselves and their work for the next 20 minutes—we are there to suit that other person's needs and they have no interest in us as individuals whatsoever.

However, in psychoanalytical terms, we each of us feel that we are absolute and to recognise that we are not unique compromises that essential part of the psyche. This is captured by Hegel in the master/slave dialectic—the master wishes the slave to recognise him as master, but does not wish to be affected by that recognition. That we must recognise the other's subjectivity immediately compromises the self's absoluteness and poses the problem that the other could be equally absolute and independent, wanting recognition from us. Each self wants to be recognised and yet to maintain its absolute identity: the self says, 'I want to affect you but I want nothing you do or say to affect me; I am who I am.' Each needs the other and this mutual wish undercuts that affirmation (Benjamin, 1995, pp. 36–7). The self that had begun in a state of 'omnipotence' must acknowledge the other, but such acknowledgement denies the absoluteness of the self. The need for recognition therefore entails what Benjamin calls 'this fundamental paradox', which is that

> at the very moment of realizing independence we are dependent upon another to recognise it. At the very moment we come to understand the meaning of 'I, myself', we are forced to see the limitations of that self. At the moment when we understand that separate minds can share the same state, we also realise that these minds can disagree.
>
> (1988, p. 33)

Intersubjective theory thus perceives the relationship between self and other as a constant exchange of influence with a dynamic tension between sameness and difference, but one that is always fraught at the same time as it is life-giving. There is a 'paradoxical balance' between oneness and separateness (Benjamin, 1988, p. 49).

This is further bedevilled by the intrapsychic in which *I* may misapprehend *you*, for I may fail to recognise you as an independently existing subject and see you instead as a 'fantasy extension of my wishes and desires' (1988, p. 125). In this encounter of two subjectivities, one party may not see the other as independently existing and desiring but see that person instead as the incorporator of his/her own wishes, agency and desire. (Think of the person at the conference lunch who drones on and on, using us as their audience but seeing us only for our use value and not as people in our own right.) One may withdraw into private fantasy (bored, we switch off) or both may share a mutual fantasy in which they fail to recognise each other (we talk about ourselves as the other talks about himself/herself, but as two monologues rather than a dialogue). 'The distinction between my fantasy of you and you as a real person is the very essence of connection' Benjamin writes (1988, p. 71), but the intrapsychic may intervene in intersubjective interactions and inhibit connection (1988, p. 125).

The self which cannot relate to what Kleinian theory calls 'the whole object' (Benjamin, 1998, p. 90) is the omnipotent self determined on destroying (psychically) its object through refusing to allow the object its subjectivity. (The bore at the conference lunch in effect destroys us as individuals—we have to escape and interact with others to have our individuality restored.) Benjamin warns that 'the adumbration of inter-subjectivity must continually retain the awareness of the other's liability not to survive it' (1998, p. 93). In other words—we need to constantly monitor how we interact with others if we are not to become the bore who drives people away to where they can have their own sense of themselves, our having destroyed it.

Applying this theory to AL leads us to suggest that AL requires the leader to deny, and thus destroy the follower through denying him/her subjectivity. A person who is destroyed in this way has no option but to leave, to seek recognition elsewhere, if they are to survive as healthy selves. The evidence for our suggestion is found in Propositions 14, 15a and 15b (Gardner, Avolio et al., 2005, pp. 360–1), which divide followers into those having 'high' and those having 'low' 'self-clarity', or understanding of the self.

The follower who has more self-knowledge will 'identify with and emulate the leader' (op cit, p. 360) while those with lesser understanding of the self will take one of two directions. They may come to depend on the leader who, through his/her greater self-knowledge, will encourage the follower to develop greater self-knowledge. This type of leader will encourage

> internalization of the core organizational values, allowing [followers] to achieve the high levels of self-clarity and autonomy that accompany authenticity.
>
> (p. 360)

They will do this through

> modeling self-discovery processes, shifting them away from personal identification with and dependence on the leader to identification with the collective and autonomy, and ultimately, internalization of the core values and mission of the collective.
>
> (p. 361)

Those lacking self-knowledge or having 'low self-concept clarity' and so suffering from 'inner confusion' may 'reject the leader as a source of influence', but over time,

> consistent, genuine, and respectful behaviour by the leader may elicit feelings of trust that likewise trigger the process of self-discovery, identification, and value internalization.
>
> (p. 361)

There is no room here for any self that is not aligned with the leader and thus the organization. The authors argue that any person who retains their own opinions and feelings will suffer from 'inner confusion', a telling phrase which suggests that to insist on agency, to demand the right to freedom of thought, is to be confused. Such 'confusion' will be overcome by the gentle persistence of the leader who will ensure that everyone in the organisation, when they look 'inside' themselves, will see only the organization. The individual subject is allowed no subjectivity beyond that required by the organization.

The follower, this suggests, is an object to the subject of the leader. The follower is denied subjectivity, is not allowed to be an I. In psychoanalytical terms, the leader, in denying subjectivity, *destroys* his/her followers. The adult who does not survive will, if it is free to do so, absent itself, leave to seek encounters with others that allow her/him their subjectivity. Those who remain, denied subjectivity, serve their part in confirming the leader's omnipotence, with dire consequences, as we will now show.

For Benjamin, the ideal, healthy interaction between two subjects is one in which there is always a necessary tension between self-assertion (this is me, this is I) and a mutual recognition that allows self and other to meet as sovereign equals. The self can be confirmed only through the recognition the other gives. Assertion and recognition, she writes (1988, p. 12), constitute the poles of a delicate balance that is integral to 'differentiation', or the individual's development as a self that is aware of its distinctness from others. Such a balance is difficult to sustain: failure results in domination. This leads to the question of whether any relationship in which one person is 'leader' and one 'follower' can ever be one that is not a relationship of domination.

Domination (1988, p. 52) begins with the attempt to deny dependency. No one can truly extricate her- or him-self from dependency on others, from the need for recognition, but if this dependency results in a breakdown of differentiation, then the self will be assimilated to the other, or the other to the self, and internalization replaces interaction or exchange with others (p. 73). The outcome is a numbness that comes from 'false' differentiation, a numbness akin to solitary confinement, what Benjamin (p. 83) calls the 'sterility of modern rationality', and a 'particularly modern form of bondage' whose aim is isolation from others. Breakdown of differentiation occurs because the fragile balance of the tension between self and others is sustained only through mutual recognition of the other's subjectivity. There is no such recognition in the AL model—indeed there is the requirement for just that lack of differentiation that Benjamin warns against. Leaders must not differentiate themselves from the organisation, and followers must not differentiate the self from that of the leader's self. Everyone must become exact copies of the organisation.

Take, for example, Propositions 17a, 17b and 17c (Gardner, Avolio et al., 2005, p. 364). Here, 'authentic leader-follower relationships' are most likely to emerge when there is 'high congruence' between leaders' and followers' concepts of who they are, how they ought to be, and how they would ideally like to be (17a). Proposition 17b states that the most authentic people will become leaders, and followers will work enthusiastically with these persons (thus becoming more like them), while 17c states that authentic leaders will, through facilitating followers' own authenticity, 'enable them to fill their needs for autonomy, competence, and relatedness' (p. 164). However, the leader does this through 'boost[ing] followers' identification with the collective' (op cit). It is claimed that the result, over time is that 'followers come to learn what the leader values and desires and how those values and desires match with their own' (p. 365). They thus trust the leader implicitly. The aim is a 'better fit between work roles and salient self-goals of the authentic self' (p. 366) which leads to that work-place well-being described by the authors as eudaimonic well-being, from the Greek philosophic term for human flourishing. This is summarised in propositions 20a, 20b and 20c which argue that immersion in the organ-isation, resulting from authentic leadership, has positive effects which 'compound one another and spread through social contagion processes' (p. 367). There are thus 'high levels of trust, intimacy, cooperation and alignment of goals' (p. 364). In other words, the job of the authentic leader is to ensure that everyone in the organisation subsumes themselves with-in a collectivity that will not tolerate difference. Everyone must conform: there is no possibility of being recognised as an individual.

This lack of recognition of the self as a subject denies the contradicto-ry desires for freedom and interdependence, for wanting to be subordi-nated and at the same time wanting to be free to leave, as explored by Benjamin (1998). The child submits to the parents' control because of the child's need to be nurtured, but at the same time the child yearns for freedom. These desires are re-lived throughout adult life, Benjamin argues, and are brought to encounters in which the promise of domina-tion offers security, albeit a security that stifles the need for freedom. The leader who denies the follower's desire to refuse leadership, and indeed the theorists' refusal of any contradictory desires in the people who would be leaders, must result in domination rather than leadership.

The outcome for the leader must be dire: if followers are but a reflec-tion of the self then the leader will either be plunged into 'unbearable aloneness' or will escape into merger with like-self beings (1998, p. 96) where anyone who is different is destroyed. The authentic leader is actu-ally charged with a merger with like-self beings, indeed with making others like-self. Gardner, Avolio et al. (2005) and Avolio and Gardner (2005) refuse the possibility of any dissent—over time, as we have shown above, they presume that any recalcitrance will be overcome through followers identifying with the (authentic) leader. Benjamin shows that this will result in destruction—the individual who conforms, as required by the authentic leader, will suffer a psychic death. Proposition 17b, as noted above, states that leaders who are the 'most authentic' will emerge. Read through Benjamin's lens, what this means is that the leaders who emerge will be those who are utterly absorbed into the organisation. They will lack subjectivity but will seek to dominate through making others as much like the (organisational) self as possi-ble. Destruction is the only outcome.

Our arguments so far are as follows. Our reading of AL using object relations theory shows that the authentic leader is one who is so totally absorbed into the organisation that s/he is an object lacking subjectivity. This leader's role is to ensure that followers are themselves no more than objects, with all claims to subjectivity denied. The outcome can only be domination and destruction. Our hypothetical leadership trainee would, if persuaded by the arguments put forward on the AL training course, seek to develop a self which resembles very much that of the young infant. The infant believes itself to be ruler of the universe, and capable of bending everything in the universe to its will. The universe is its mother or carer and its crib. It does not recognise that its carer and its crib are outside its self—it has not yet attained sufficient maturity to have grasped the distinction between its self and others. The idea that an individual can, through the very power of their self-knowledge, persuade others to become like them, is as unformed a presumption as the infant's that s/he controls the world.

But this is not all that will happen to our hypothetical trainee. We will look now at projection and projective identification, concepts developed by Melanie Klein and important in object relations theory.

Rendering the other abject

Klein proposed that two psychological mechanisms, splitting and projection, develop in very early infancy and continue to inform psychic life throughout adulthood. Splitting and projection allow the self to cope with unpleasant emotions. They emerge out of total dependency on a caregiver (usually the mother) who is seemingly unpredictable as she both gives nurture and comfort and apparently withholds it. This ambiguous relationship is encountered in the first external object the infant is aware of, the mother's breast. The breast is perceived as being 'good' because it satisfies hunger, but because it does not always do this it is also 'bad'. Klein hypothesised that the infant is not able to cope with the extreme anxiety caused by having the same object be both good and bad. Consequently, as a defence against this anxiety it splits its feelings of love and hate and projects them onto a 'good breast' and a 'bad breast', respectively. Over time, the infant begins to recognise the breast and subsequently the mother as a whole object with the ability to both frustrate and satiate. The infant introjects or internalises its relationship to the good and bad breast, so that their influence remains. Other 'objects' such as the mother's smile are similarly internalised. The infant thereby creates two mothers—a good one to attend to its needs and a bad one on whom to be resentful. This mechanism of splitting enables the infant, and in later life the adult, to cope with anxiety by separating the self from painful feelings.

Further, the parts of the self that are feared as bad are split off and projected onto others, usually an object or person (Hollway and Jefferson, 2000). This is the second mechanism, referred to as projective identification, identified by Klein (1948). The person at whom the projection is 'aimed' (transference) can often find themselves feeling and acting in ways which are not authentic to themselves but derive from the other's projected characteristics which have been unconsciously assumed (counter-transference) (Hollway and Jefferson, 2000).

Klein is a controversial figure, but if we follow the generations of interpreters who support her stance, then there can be no such thing as the authentic leader dreamt of in the pages of the texts that seek to describe him/her. Rather, there are individuals who suffer levels of anxiety bound up in their search for belonging. There is no hiding place from these anxieties—no one is immune from them. They are unconscious so not available to conscious thought. No matter how deeply authentic leaders look, they cannot gaze into their unconscious (see Butler, 2005). Instead, they will see others around them who are not measuring up to the norms of authenticity, but those they charge with inauthenticity may be innocent carriers of the putative authentic leader's disavowed flaws. The leader, too, will be the recipient of followers' anxieties. To write anxiety and other forms of trauma out of the workplace, as the AL model seeks to do, is to do a great disservice both to the theory and to the people working within organisations.

Benjamin shows some of the ways in which this dishonouring of the complexities of the psyche, in a relationship in which one of the parties must deny its own flaws, may work themselves out. Following Klein, she suggests that the denied flaws will either be projected onto the not-I or turned against the self (1998, p. 99). To avoid this the leader would have to acknowledge both their own and others' destructiveness, something the authentic leader who, by definition, has no imperfections, is prevented from doing. Benjamin warns (1998, p. 100), that the postulation of a self who can assume both 'goodness' and 'badness', and also recognition and negation of the other, is the 'only ground for a critique of the subject's inability to recognize the other' (1998, p. 100). Citing Young's (1990) work, Benjamin (1998, p. 101) argues that the 'autonomous, self-enclosed subject who always knows itself, its desires, a unity rather than heterogenous and multiple being' is more likely to produce chauvinism and nationalism than respect for otherness.

That recitation bears marked similarity to the definition of authentic leadership. This reading thus suggests that by failing to recognise the legitimacy of an outside other, that other (the follower) becomes a repudiated and threatening abject other. Far from being authentic, this model of leadership is chauvinistic, dictatorial, unable to brook opposition, destructive of psyches and selves and thus utterly dangerous.

Our hypothetical trainee would be in for a traumatic time if s/he attempted to incorporate all the recommendations of the course they have attended.

Conclusion

Using object relations theory, we suggest that the theory which calls itself 'authentic leadership' is a theory of a leader who is so totally absorbed into the organisation that s/he is an object lacking subjectivity. This leader's role is to ensure that followers are themselves no more than objects, with all claims to subjectivity denied. The relationship is not one of leader/follower, but of domination/suppression. The tensions established through attempting to practise this form of authenticity are such that turmoil, abjection, trauma and psychic death will result. The authentic leader would breed a sick organisation.

In Chapter 5 we suggested that leadership development is concerned with the elevation of unachievable norms, by which leaders are rendered malleable and followers abject. Leadership development is achieved through participating in courses which involve developing insights about the self. These insights can be invaluable. They can help us understand how others see us, and the impact of our own actions, conscious and unconscious, on other people. We are therefore not being critical of those courses for what they do, but for what they aim to do. In this chapter our concern has grown, for courses in authentic leadership would feature even more strongly ways of developing self-knowledge. The aim now would be of seeing the self as flawless, and with this could come the arrogant requirement that colleagues and staff share in that narcissistic hero worship, and indeed are forced to emulate it.

The self participants would reflect upon would, furthermore, be an organisational self, one devoid of agency or freedom of thought. Trainees would be encouraged to progressively deny (and thus suppress) any negative aspects they found in themselves, until they could look at themselves and see only a saintly (organisational) self reflected back at them. This self would be denied subjectivity—it would become an object to the organisation's subject.

A participant in an authentic leadership course would thus be encouraged to suppress all the negative qualities of the self, but those rejected aspects may well be projected onto other, less powerful, others. These others would come to be regarded as deeply flawed. There is no possibility of agency in the AL model, no possibility of freedom of speech or thought: to demand such things would result in being seen as inauthentic and thus unsuitable for the organisation. There is no possibility of subjectivity in AL, no chance to assert that I am me: there is only the position, and this is that of the brainwashed object. Only the leader, and thus the follower (and in recent models of leadership all leaders are also followers) who mimics the organisation and its demands will be regarded as acceptable.

The claim to authenticity is thus undermined by the psychic dynamics instigated by that very claim. The authentic leader would be an individual who caused acute distress in those working with him/her, and who suffered such distress himself/herself.

We have chosen one of the most recent theories of leadership for our analysis, but we suggest that it has relevance for the majority of other leadership theories, for they all must presuppose intersubjective relationships between leaders and followers. They all, we suggest, possess highly inadequate theories of the subject and thus they play around with the people of whom they write as if they are objects, pawns, on an organisational chequered board. These theories have a performative impact—they bring things into being, through the power of their written words (Butler, 1997) and through the courses which train people. They thus encourage the reduction of people working in organisations, managers, leaders, staff and followers, to the status of objects, having no subjectivity, existing only to affirm the selves of more powerful subjects. We thus call on leadership theory to take cognisance of Benjamin (1998, p. 195), when she writes:

> Without concrete knowledge, empathy, and identification with the other subject—with the other's needs, feelings, circumstances, and history—the self continues to move in the realm of subject and object, untransformed by the other. The self says 'You cannot affect or negate my identity, you can only be the object of my assertion.' What is absent is the tension of recognizing the outside other as both different *and* alike.

If there are to be theories of leadership, then we conclude by calling for the theorists to think first about the real people whose lives they may affect.

Thankfully, however, we showed in Chapter 6 that organisations are extraordinarily complex places, and the possibilities of transferring AL into practice without, at least, major amendments, are small.

Part II Deconstructions: Closing Notes

Part I introduced leadership and also post-structuralist theory. It showed how leadership offers a form of identity, or practices of the self, for leaders, instigated by the very terms 'leader' and 'leadership'. That first section was descriptive, laying out the possibilities for what will happen to people who encounter the requirement that they be leaders and practise leadership. In the three chapters of Part II, we have explored how the performativity of the terms 'leader' and 'leadership', in providing the subject positions discussed in Part I, constructs forms of the self that are very different from what the rhetoric of leadership would have us believe.

In Chapter 5 we drew on data from a study of leadership development to queer the concept of leadership. We showed in that chapter that the 'Great Man', charismatic leader lives on, in the form of its influence over current understandings of leadership in organisations. That chapter argued that leadership is a norm to which all leaders must aspire. It is a norm which states that leaders should be charismatic and should possess a *je ne sais quoi* that is augmented by self-knowledge. Not only are the stakes so high that this norm is unattainable, it also has a self-defeating aspect at the centre of its arguments. This is because if all leaders became extraordinary, there would be no ordinary person against whom to measure the self as leader. So leadership theory, this queer reading argues, must set up in leaders dynamics that cause them to feel as if they are not good enough, that they are doomed to failure as leaders. At the same time, leadership brings into existence 'followers', the binary opposite on which leadership rests. Followers must be that against which leadership measures and assesses itself.

In Chapter 6 we introduced gender theory to the exploration of an empirical study of managers in an organisation that had recently undergone a leadership development programme. We followed a history of thinking about gender which argues that organisations actively 'gender' their members along certain, highly restricted lines. We showed the extreme unease among managers regarding their capacity to be leaders. There was paradox, uncertainty, confused interpretations, disillusionment and denial. There were not many people who did not want to practise post-heroic leadership, but the barriers to doing so seemed insurmountable. However, there had ensued a battle for identity among managers, who turned both to the machismo of the traditional management culture, and at the same time towards the gentler, more feminine perspectives of post-heroic leadership. The result was anxiety.

Chapter 7 explored the latest model of leadership through the lens of psychoanalytical theory, countermanding the psychological theory used in developing understanding of what is called Authentic Leadership. In that chapter we argued that were organisations to introduce authentic leadership as advocated by its many supporters, the result would be dire for managers and staff. This is because authentic leadership (a) rests on a highly simplistic understanding of the human subject; (b) requires that the leader be inauthentic, even while claiming authenticity, and (c) sets up dynamics that are so destructive that the only way to survive psychically is to leave.

These chapters also alluded, where possible, to the role of followers in these theories. It was argued that leadership cannot exist without followers, and that leadership theory therefore *creates* followers. Followers are, however, the binary opposite of leadership, and thus they are called into being as 'followers' (rather than, say, staff or employees) so that leaders may know themselves as leaders. To be a follower is, therefore, to be the obverse of the leader. To be a follower is to be regarded as inadequate, lacking, in need of external guidance, untrustworthy and so on. Leadership thus contains the seeds of its own destruction, for in establishing something that is supposed to motivate people to work harder it sets up the dynamics by which their disillusionment will persuade them of the lack of any value to working harder, or to being loyal to the company.

This reading, at this point, is a reading by prophets of doom. We do not intend it necessarily to be read that way. It can be seen that there is much merit in some of the arguments surrounding leadership. That managers should climb down from their hierarchically privileged forms of autocracy over staff cannot be criticised. That they should be more concerned with the well-being of staff is another benefit to leadership theory. That managers should gain better understanding of the effect they have on others cannot be criticised, so long as that knowledge is used to the good of managers and staff. However, much current theory and practice of leadership, we are suggesting, is based on practices and developments which ensure dominance of the negative aspects of leadership, thus overriding potential benefits and making working lives more onerous, less satisfactory and more oppressive than they are currently.

Are there ways of avoiding the dark side of leadership outlined in this book? We suggest there are, and turn, in our closing chapter, to exploring possible ways of building on the positive aspects of leadership while throwing out its more oppressive aspects.

Part III Towards Emancipatory Leadership Development?

8
Conclusions: Towards Emancipatory Leadership?

Introduction

The concerns about leadership that led us to write this book were the following:

1. There is a huge body of literature on leadership and yet the vast proportion of it is located within one narrow theoretical perspective designed to improve profitability, efficiency and effectiveness in organisations.
2. Research into leadership is often fragmented, poorly conducted, at times trivial and frequently based on management/guru academics and practitioners, who have a vested interest as they are keen to promulgate their latest solutions to the 'dilemmas of leadership' (Collinson and Grint, 2005, 5).
3. There is no consensus on how to define leadership so it would be easy to dismiss it out of hand, but it has become such an authoritative discourse in both academic and organisational settings that it is too important to ignore (Collinson and Grint, 2005; Ford, 2007; Sinclair, 2005).
4. Leadership theory constructs a model of 'the leader' that is impossible to achieve. It represents the leader as a singular subject, a 'monad', who is objective, rational and secure unto himself/herself. Managers and leaders are, however, people (not robots) and so they have complex identities.
5. Despite all these huge limitations on the theories and practices of leadership, the terms 'leader' and 'leadership' have a performative impact, that is, they bring things into being, so 'leaders' and 'leadership' have become part of the identities and practices of managers.

6. We were furthermore struck by the virtual absence of post-structuralist thinking about leadership, despite the strengths and influence of post-structuralist theory.

7. Another absence was critical and reflexive approaches that pay attention not only to the individual as *leader* but also to the context of *leadership*: the situations, events, institutions, ideas, social practices and processes that all need to be taken into account. This is despite classical leadership theory having argued the need for a contingency approach that takes context into account. 'Context' appears to have been very narrowly defined, and ignored in many later theories of leadership.

We aimed to address these issues in the writing of this book. It is addressed to leadership theorists, current and future managers and leaders, and those who teach or train them, who may have felt some stirrings of misgivings about leadership. Often this may have been experienced as little more than an uneasy feeling that something is wrong, an uncomfortable niggle of doubt which, when probed, cannot be articulated. This book cannot explain all such doubts and does not attempt to, but it has aimed to allow articulation of some of those qualms. It has adopted one particular theoretical stance, post-structuralism; other theoretical positions would have given different interpretations of the suspicions and feelings that things are not quite right. What we hope the book has done is give credibility to those little niggles of doubt, and to ask that they be listened to.

Our analysis started, in Part I, with demonstrating how the terms 'leader' and 'leadership' actively construct the leaders of which they speak. We moved on to showing that this construction is not like an assembly kit whereby 'the leader' emerges if all the relevant parts are assembled in the right way. We showed that the words themselves carry multiple and ever-shifting meanings, and are informed by many other terms. The 'hero' was a term we encountered several times in our discussions. The notion of 'the leader' is so heavily impregnated with notions of heroism that we cannot understand leadership without understanding something about the myths of heroic deeds. Meanwhile, leaders in the twenty-first century are also required to be nice people, open with their emotions and in touch with their 'inner selves', possessing self-knowledge so that they know who they are. This is a person who is very much involved in interactions with others, and whose identity is formed in part through those interactions.

The leader who emerges from the construction process is, therefore, a complex individual, with a past, a present and a future, who, in each moment of their interactions with others, will construct and dispose with, a self that is always in flux, always developing. The constructions will be various and many, the responses similarly so.

In Part II we explored the negative, or dark, aspects of the performativity of the terms 'leaders' and 'leadership'. We showed how leadership is a norm that controls leaders, by making them strive to be something that is utterly unachievable. We argued that the very presence of leadership renders others, 'followers', abject. We demonstrated that organisations now require managers to be both macho managers and more feminine leaders, so managers/leaders do not know which way to turn as whatever they do they will get it wrong. Finally, we showed the major flaws in the latest leadership theory. We demonstrated how its simplistic presumptions of what it is to be a human being could, if taken up fully, result in huge pain and misery for believers in its prescriptions and the unfortunates who have to follow them. These three chapters dealt with leaders as if they are persons who are gendered and who have psyches. This is important, for it is impossible to be a person who has no gender and has no psyche, yet much leadership theory appears ignorant of such banal, yet vital, observations.

Through all these discussions the follower has appeared and disappeared. We have not done sufficient justice to the place of the follower, although we have shown that the very existence of leadership relies on making some people abject, so that leadership may carry the seeds of its own destruction in that it destroys rather than elevates. We have also alluded to the problems for leaders of being both leaders and followers. We have suggested that leaders will flick-flack between a position of superiority in one encounter and then a position of abject inferiority in another; and they will be told they are special at one moment, and then that one is bereft of the ability to manage one's own day at the next. The response can be only a psychic juggling act in which the integrity of the self, one's 'ontological security', must be challenged.

We hope that the discussions in the preceding seven chapters have allowed a language to be given to some of the niggles, worries and concerns about what is done with these words 'leader' and 'leadership'. We have shown that leadership is far from the simple verities often assumed by writers and trainers, and how the processes of translating this vague thing 'leadership' into practice are beset with difficulties. Indeed, much of our arguments suggest the impossibility of any such thing as leadership.

We have argued furthermore that the leadership course which is supposed to develop and expand possibilities of being creates the opposite of what it intends. The programmes and courses that encourage an openness and reflexivity of the self do this, we have argued, in order to control and exploit the leader, to bind him/her more tightly to the corporation. We are not alone in making these arguments. A special issue of *Leadership Quarterly* (June 2007) has been dedicated to a discussion of 'Destructive Leadership', in recognition that there is an emerging (yet nascent) body of inquiry focusing on the negative aspects of leadership, and what can be called its so-called darker side (Popper, 2001; Tierney and Tepper, 2007).

But . . . So what?

However, we cannot dismiss a major cultural movement out of hand. To do so would leave many asking 'so what?'.

So what, if leadership has negative effects—I still have to go on training courses and practise leadership.

So what if I now have a language in which I can better understand my concerns—I still am told that I have to lead other people.

So what—I still have to teach people how to be leaders; I still have to run training courses.

This chapter tackles these 'so what' questions. It does this by exploring one way of putting the knowledge and skills gained from training in and practising leadership to good effect in the daily round of organisational work. Leadership training courses traditionally encourage the development of self-knowledge, as we have shown throughout this book. There are advantages to developing greater self-knowledge. We come to understand better our impact on other people, what may trigger us to behave in ways we may later regret, why we respond negatively to some people and positively to others, etc. If we perhaps better understand the impact we each have on other people, and get to know how we can make other people feel worse about themselves (even if we do not set out to do that) then we can improve the quality of working life in organisations. Furthermore by getting to know ourselves better we can be gentler on ourselves when we fail to live up to the expectations we have of ourselves. If we categorise ourselves as 'intraverts' in the Myers-Briggs/Jungian sense, we can stop beating ourselves up because we do not seem to have the confidence our extravert friends and colleagues have. If we think of ourselves as extraverts, we can stop tormenting ourselves with the idea that others hate us whenever we are alone for any length of time.

Leadership theory suggests these types of insights are required by leaders in order to develop more efficient, profitable and effective organisations. In that sense, becoming a nicer person, easier to work with, less destructive of others, is for instrumental purposes only—to improve organisational outcomes. Our perspective is that excellent working relationships should be an end in themselves, not a means to an end (of higher profits or greater efficiency). So, we are against self-knowledge because it is required by the organisations in which we work—that is exploitation at the level of the psyche. We are in favour of self-knowledge both for its own ends and to improve relationships with ourselves and with the people with whom we work. In the absence of, and no prospects of, any revolution that would fundamentally change working lives, leadership should be something that improves interactions between managers, professional staff, knowledge workers and all employees. It should improve the quality of working life in general. If profits improve as a result, well that is a by-product, not the primary goal. People within organisations are more than resources: they are human beings with all the requirements and entitlement to respect and dignity which that phrase involves.

We too should practise what we preach. Having alerted readers to the potential impact of leadership upon their psyches and their souls, it would be unethical to do nothing to change leadership development. Thus it behoves us to set out some principles by which leadership development may come to be a form of liberation from the oppressive organisational structures and practices that control, demean and diminish staff and managers.

The problem is that it is exceedingly difficult to reach agreement about how to achieve such a thing. We have debated the merits of discussing the sort of micro-emancipations advocated by Gibson-Graham (1996), which would involve seeking small, local-level revolutions in the workplace. We have discussed the merits of Foucault's ethics of the self, explored in his last works (Foucault, 2006). While we are keen on the potential of such works, we opted, in the end, for pragmatism. What we discuss here is an approach to leadership development developed by the first author of this book.

Our starting point is that the workplace is a social environment which could and should provide far more than a wage or salary: it should provide sociality, a sense of self, of identity and numerous possibilities for the full expression of our humanity. All these should be, we emphasise again, a major objective of organisations. The revolution we call for is that people in organisations are ends in themselves, rather than means to ends. Leadership development programmes should therefore be designed with people as ends in mind. They should take the people, leaders, who are given power over others, and ensure they never abuse that power but use it wisely to limit, so far as is possible, the damage organisations can do to people, including themselves.

In the final part of this chapter we, therefore, hijack leadership development programmes and suggest ways in which the development of greater self-knowledge may be turned towards the ends of improving life at work. We call such a programme 'Emancipatory Leadership Programmes'.

Emancipatory leadership programmes

We need to keep in mind, as we think about leadership development, the lessons from this book. We need to be aware of the ways in which languages construct that of which they speak, in this case, the leader and leadership, and aim to change the ways in which leadership is spoken about. This can be done, in part, through introducing into these ways of speaking alternative languages that allow for different possibilities of being. We should challenge the unachievable norms of leadership, offering in place of a super-hero a model of a flawed individual in interactions with others. We should reconcile the conflictual nature of management and leadership, and should be careful of the psyche, which is fragile. In all this, we should be alert to the ways in which others are seen as the inferior other, and ways in which the self can, in its turn, be reduced to an abject status, through encouraging exploration of the impact of the self on others and others on the self. We should never forget that selves are formed through interactions with others, and these interactions always take place within contexts made available through and limited by the discourses which make it possible to speak and to act.

What follows is based very much upon the work of Jackie Ford, who is pioneering work in ethical leadership programmes. It refers to ideas arising out of the development of narrative 360 discussions, which focus on reflexive dialogue and narrative to examine and build relationships within management and leadership processes (Ford and Lawler, 2003, 2006). This has led to the design of a diagnostic approach known as the '360 degree narrative approach'. This is an approach to developmental feedback founded on qualitative research theory and methods. It relies on dialogue between those giving and receiving feedback, based on individual reflection, leading to shared understandings, with recognition and value placed on differences of interpretation of management and leadership. It provides the opportunity for a deeper exploration of management and leadership potential between trainer and participant than is provided in other approaches to leader development. The approach provides a framework for a dialogue, or series of discussions, which individuals can reflect on and discuss further as they identify and clarify their own personhood, their impact on others and others' impact on them.

There is a danger that this approach can be turned to a cynical use—to the making of a profit through bastardising the critical voice that has been incorporated into the approach. We hope that the years of reading, thinking, theorising and research that have gone into the narrative approach make it inaccessible to anyone wishing to do such a thing, but recognise the naivety of that hope.

This is only one way of taking up the challenges outlined in this book. As a revolution it just would not register at all, but in the limitations of the current contexts of capitalism, it is a small step towards change. Its aims, following Fournier and Grey (2000, 20), are to endeavour to 'free individual subjects from the power relations within which they are inscribed, including their own subjectivity'.

The trainer's voice—offering new accounts

In the first part of the book, we explored how language worked to construct the identity *of* the leader *for* the leader. It showed how various discourses of leadership interact with each other in the construction of the self as leader. In Chapter 4 we further showed that when participants enter a training room they bring with them numerous imaginings of 'the leader', including myths and stories about heroes and heroism. These numerous meanings form part of the discourses that construct leadership. There are at least two other myths of leadership, found in texts and discussions, that the trainer, versed in discussions of leadership, will bring to the encounter. These are the transcendental (literally above everything, including emotions, requirements of the flesh, spirituality, etc.) and the homogeneous (the same as each other, like peas in a pod) manager. These contradict the multiple, competing and ambiguous constructions that form selves, but they are the illicit contraband smuggled into training rooms, and they form the identities advocated for leaders.

Our first recommendation is that teachers and trainers identify the presuppositions that underpin their practices, and in particular the ways in which these presuppositions become presented as norms to whose achievement participants should aspire. In short, teachers and trainers should make it clear that leaders are human, and not superhuman.

Ditching the homogeneous and transcendental leader

Orthodox accounts in organisation studies present leaders as superhuman or transcendental beings, with no variety between them at all. The depiction of transcendence is apparent through the portrayal of leaders as individuals who surpass all known limitations of what is humanly possible. They are presented as heroic and distant beings who are almost completely disconnected from everyday human experience and interaction, and relieved from the circumstances that daily interaction and exchange would expect. They are rational, devoid of emotions, all-knowing and capable of moving mountains. At the same time, management and leadership theories presume the existence of 'the perfect manager'. This manager is perfectly formed and has no need of interaction with others. He/she never suffers doubts or uncertainties, is always rational and logical, and uses emotions wisely in the pursuit of organisational interests, so even emotions are treated rationally.

This is the model of the manager that underpins most management theory. Its homogeneity is at odds with the endless variety of narratives and practices of the self presented by managers. Managers are social beings who form concepts and practices of the self, indeed their managerial identities, through interactions with others. They are often emotional, are riven with desire, find the limitations on the emotions they can express oppressive, experience huge anxieties and uncertainties (Ford, 2007) and are, in a nutshell, human beings with all that that involves.

Now, this may seem like 'common sense'. Of course every manager is different from all other managers. However, the continuing dominance of uncritical and positivist accounts of leadership serves to promote hegemonic masculine discourses (see Chapter 6) which feature this transcendental, homogeneous manager or leader. This is the model of the leader that participants will encounter when they participate in a development programme. It is the model they are taught to desire to emulate.

Cooper (1999) argues that the model arises from a disengaged, objective, disinterested research stance which leads to 'standard accounts' in which transcendence and homogeneity are smuggled in. This is possible for researchers dealing with constants such as inert matter, chemical reactions and physical forces and may be useful in some aspects of social interactions. However, the social worlds in which leaders work is too complex, and leaders themselves too multifarious, to constrain them within a model which presumes transcendence and homogeneity.

The result is texts, lectures and training courses replete with 'standard accounts' of leadership, of models, characteristics, standards and competences, that do not reflect the huge diversity of 'lived experience' of managerial life in all its settings. These so-called standard accounts overlook the extent to which the world we inhabit is a human one, 'whose structure, articulation and very existence are functions of human agency' (Cooper 1999, p. 58).

But these standard accounts do things, as we showed in Chapters 2 and 5: they construct worlds, and so they present norms of managerial behaviour. The manager must not step outside the narrow confines dictated by these implicit presumptions. The ubiquity of this account in management literature and in development programmes adds to the considerable dissonance and tension felt by managers for no one can live up to such idealisations (Harding, 2003). Many current accounts of leadership studies appear to take too lightly, if they treat of it at all, the insecurity, anxiety and ambiguity in the lives of managers (Ford and Harding, 2004; Ford, 2007). Through ignoring these feelings they actively *create* these feelings. Managers are told they should be confident, secure and very clear about what they are doing, and why they are doing it, in all circumstances. That is impossible in practice—who could live up to such a paragon? By failing to live up to an over-ambitious norm, managers feel themselves to be failures.

Our approach is one which argues that context, individual biographies and idioms of the self (Bollas, 1996) cannot be ignored as leadership, indeed work in general, involves interpersonal relationships. We bring our selves, our psyches, our histories, our idiosyncrasies, our ways of talking and thinking and acting, to these workplace relationships. If we bring all those aspects of the self uncritically to the workplace, and are then encouraged to behave as if we are transcendental, homogeneous beings whose impact on others is justified by our positions as leaders or managers, then we may do untold harm to others. Indeed, stories of organisations are littered with the harm done to the majority by the minority who occupy powerful positions. So, reflexivity on the part of managers is important if they are to know how they interact with others and with themselves, why they interact with others in the ways they do, and the impact this has on self and others.

Leadership development programmes therefore need to make it very clear to participants that there is no such thing as a transcendental leader, so no need to strive for such an impossible position. Similarly, homogeneity is impossible to achieve, and its value questionable in any case. By exposing the unwritten presumptions that underpin theories of management and leadership the trainer or teacher will allow the voicing of alternative, more subjectivist approaches that allow for local contextual understandings and relational and intersubjective understandings. This may free leaders to speak out as individuals rather than following 'group think'.

Thus we recommend that there should be a continual striving to avoid the homogeneity that is imposed upon managers and leaders when current concepts of management and leadership are trotted out as the ideal which all managers should strive to achieve. Similarly, there is a need, if participants are to reflect on the self, to reject the notion of the transcendental manager or leader. This may be difficult, for although the notion of transcendence is a normative ideal, it is an attractive one. It states that you or I, if singled out as a potential leader, can feel omnipotent and thus above reproach (see the discussion on authentic leadership in Chapter 7). Such a feeling of perfection would make it very difficult to explore the impact one has on other people, for the belief in one's own perfection prevents our seeing any negative impact on others. Rather, we will see any negativity as something arising from them, from our Other.

In and outside the training room—different accounts of the psyche

As we discussed in Chapter 4, the majority of leadership development programmes use psychometric measures, such as the MBTI and the 360-degree model of leadership development, to assist in the development of self-knowledge. We argued in Chapter 4 that such measures, while providing knowledge about the self and how we are seen by others, limit the possibilities of the selves we can be. They are often influenced by the work of Carl Jung, one of Freud's disciples.

Now, we have suggested these have some uses, so long as they are used for the individual's own good, and for the good of those with whom they interact, at the same time as they have numerous limitations. What we now go on to advocate, however, is changes in the ways in which these insights are used when leaders interact with the consultants responsible for assisting the leaders' development during one-to-one feedback. The psychometric measures allow participants to tell themselves something about themselves, but little about interactions with others, and how those others are vital in the constructing of the self. Collinson (2005, 2006) has argued the need for a post-structuralist approach that recognises the dynamics of leadership as a social process, and which encourages individuals and organisational members to inter-relate in ways that encompass new forms of intellectual and emotional meaning. The aim is to discover more meaningful and constructive ways of relating and working together. In this concluding chapter we tease out what form such interrelationships should take when going beyond the psychometric measures. Our approach is to use theories of the self as an on-going project of construction, in keeping with writers who encourage rigorous debate on ways in which Critical Management Studies can inform management education (see for example, Reynolds, 1997, 1999).

We are recommending therefore that more relational and inter-connected approaches be used in leadership development courses. These should acknowledge the impact of dominant ideas about management and leadership on the self, but also the ways in which participants inter-act with others, and the ways in which those interactions are constitutive of the self. We advocate an approach that is located more in the work of Sigmund Freud than Carl Jung. However, we advocate it carefully, for the intention is not to engage in a psychoanalytic encounter, nor indeed in a therapeutic or counselling one, but to use the development of concepts of the self in a way that is challenging and also productive.

The approach we adopt is to encourage managers to undertake a critical analysis of the leader and the personhood of the leader (through explo-ration of biography, experiences etc.) and of leadership (the sociological implications). We combine these two approaches and argue the case for a psychosocial understanding of the practices of leaders and leadership.

Leadership development programmes encourage the development of self-knowledge. However, individuals are not ahistoric beings without a multiplicity of experiences that inform who they are in the present. Each person has a complex history in which events have had an impact on them and who they are, and how they practise, in the present. There is therefore a need for leadership development to facilitate participants in taking a fresh look at their biography and experiences to date, at how they narrate the self, and get to know better both themselves and the impact they have upon others. This is, of course, a reflexive approach of the type recommended to academics as they carry out their research. It presumes that reflection on the self can provide insights into how per-sonal experiences have informed narratives of the self and how these narratives influence every action and interaction in which we are involved (Ford, 2007).

Reflexivity has become a central concept in post-structuralist theoris-ing and its application to practice. It is not a new concept. Gadamer argued in 1975 that critical reason requires an on-going self-critical activity that goes beyond the self and embraces historical, social and moral contexts. Hawes (1998, 100) depicts this as 'a process of turning one's gaze back on oneself for the purpose of permitting the other to become known through a dialogical process of differentiation'. Reflexive analysis in this reading goes beyond the individual and explores the social and intellectual unconscious embedded in analytical tools and operations (Bourdieu, 1992). This process of critical reflexivity encourages individuals to see themselves and their worlds in ways that were hitherto not visible to them, and begins to explore the 'nitty-gritty of real life' (Bourdieu, 1992, p. 199). As Bourdieu (1992, p. 199) argues:

> When you apply reflexive sociology to yourself, you open up the possibility of identifying true sites of freedom, and thus of building small-scale, modest, practical morals in keeping with the scope of human freedom which, in my opinion, is not that large.

This reflexivity therefore has two aspects (Benjamin, 1995):

• Intrasubjective approaches which explore the psyche, and how the self comes to be a self in interaction with others.
• Intersubjective, relational approaches, that explore the impact upon each self when two or more people interact.

In combining the personal (inside the mind, so to speak) with the social (interactions with others) the aim of this approach is development of a critical, subjectivist account that lends itself to the development of more reflexive, situated and dialogical methods of relating to people at work. In short, we are starting to explore an ethics of the self. By 'dialogical' is meant, literally, dialogue, but the subject who is engaging in dialogue with others will also have numerous discourses at work constructing their own subjectivities (how we speak to ourselves), and it is necessary to 'tune into' these discourses through which we speak to ourselves so as to understand how the self is constructed. We have noted two of these: the homogeneous manager and the transcendental leader, discourses so subtle and so persuasive we may hardly notice they are speaking through us and influencing our thoughts and actions.

Through engaging in dialogical interactions, the ways in which the transcendental model of the manager or leader influences self-perceptions and practices becomes clear: is this a norm that is striven for? No one can be that manager, but that does not prevent people striving (and failing) to be that manager or leader. The impact of their striving, on self and others, may be highly negative.

In terms of practicalities, or how to engage with participants during leadership development using critical dialogical interactions, a narrative 360 process may be used, and/or more critical, psychosocially informed development interventions such as those described in Ford and Harding (2007) and Ford and Lawler (2007). These help participants develop understanding of how, through their interactions with others, they have an impact on those others but also upon themselves. They also explore the personal histories they bring to those interactions, and how these influence the ways they act in the present.

This is achieved through an iterative process of exploring the leadership role, gaining new insights from analysing one's past (histories as well as actions, roles and relationships) and a clear recognition of the constraints and opportunities open to them. In such accounts it becomes clear that leadership is not an individual and heroic quest, but a performance delivered within a social, organisational context; a performance that it would be wrong to classify as largely unconnected to personal history or character (Sinclair and Wilson, 2002).

What is important in this process are issues about listening and learning from others (so-called followers, as well as friends, peers, colleagues and others); two-way feedback dialogue and being in tune with colleagues; encouragement of constructive dissent (Grint, 2005, p. 40), and challenging prejudices, stereotypes and the status quo. This involves an exploration of both the interpersonal (which comes from leaders achieving a better understanding of the impact of the self, drawing from their own biographical and reflexive understandings, plus narrative 360); and also the intrapersonal, which is both the dialogical and relational, building on the reflexive and interpersonal. It seems to be a way to relate 'leaders' (the intrapersonal, or in contemporary discourse, human capital) with 'leadership' (the interpersonal, or social capital). Rather than talking about 'leaders' and 'followers', therefore, we are talking about the people charged with the task of leadership and how they relate to the others with whom they work. Our aim is to cease the use of the word 'followers', for the reasons explored in this book.

Leaders—the intrapsychic realm

While it would be wrong to use self-knowledge, and in particular the kind of in-depth, personal knowledge we are advocating here, for the ends of the organisation, it can be of great value if those given power over others gain better understanding of themselves. Without this, are not organisations giving power to people, telling them to use that power, and then letting them loose regardless of their capacity for misusing that power? We have found that it is important for leaders to draw on their biographical understandings and recognise the importance of knowing their interpersonal skills and dynamics, and thus what makes them into the people they are. This allows later exploration of the impact they—as leaders—have on other people.

The approach we have found useful is critical reflexive analysis, as noted above. The question of reflexivity has, in more recent years, been identified as central to critical management studies, because it draws on post-structural and social constructionist suppositions to highlight the contradictory and problematic nature of explanation—that we construct the very accounts we think describe the world (Cunliffe, 2002; Hardy et al., 2001; Perriton, 2000). While the different approaches to critical reflexivity vary, most aim at encouraging both a reconstruction of the focus of the reflection, as well as a deeper critique and questioning of how we account for our experiences (Alvesson and Wilmott 1996).

We encourage managers to undertake a more critical and reflexive account of their past actions and to give more consideration to some of the constraints and opportunities that may be buried in many of these accounts. This goes beyond the reflective practitioner approach advocated by Schon and others (Schon, 1983; Ghaye and Lillyman 1996), which essentially adopts a functionalist approach to reflection, and invites the leader to make connections and test understanding through seeking patterns, logic and order in their experiences. Individuals should be encouraged to gain more critical insights into their selves by seeking new meaning and understandings of their backgrounds and personal histories, and to use these understandings in further dialogical exchanges with other individuals in their leadership relationship. The intention is that the active pursuit of reflexive consideration of individual's biographies, experiences, career histories and relationships will encourage greater awareness of ways in which they constitute, maintain and thereby retain some control over their realities and sense of who they are, and how they account for their experiences and personal development.

Leadership—the interpersonal

Consideration of intrapersonal influences alone is not sufficient for managers to make sense of their selves and their roles as leaders because such an analysis, devoid of any understanding of context, would be narcissistic. There is a need for more exploration and understanding of the overall dynamics of the community as a whole within which leaders and others engage and work. As we discussed in Chapter 7, any parties involved in a leadership dynamic are implicated in these interactions and so an exploration of leadership entails recognition of the social context of the interaction as well as of the individuals concerned. The leader, in short, is an individual located within a particular environmental context. Here we have the psychosocial environment, in which both the psyche of the individual and the sociological context must be accounted for.

A dialogical approach to leadership development should be critical, reflexive and intersubjective, and recognises embodiment and the investment of emotion, by all in the organisation, in the encounters between leaders and others (Collinson and Grint, 2005; Elliot and Reynolds, 2002; Gold et al., 2002; Rumens, 2005; Sauko, 2002). The intention is to reinforce and promote the importance of reflexive and dialogical relationships across all encounters in individuals' working lives, as people consider their impact on others, others' impact on them, and the various and many things which influence these mutual interactions. The leader should be mindful, thoughtful and considerate in all her interactions.

Dialogical exchanges present the opportunity of moving away from universal understandings to examine the unique elements which unfold in personal exchanges. This enables people to go beyond the idea that the leader is a leader and a follower a follower, and to explore how these prescribed roles are enacted jointly, as well as recognise the active participation of many others in our working lives. The aim is development of a shared view of activities which goes beyond what exists currently so as to examine what might be created collectively. The problem, of course, is continuing inequalities in salary, status and hierarchy. So long as there are such distinctions, these ideas may seem as a romantic sop to the elite in organisations. However, it is not the elite we are talking of here, but managers in the lower levels of the organisation. Indeed, if Katz and Shotter (1996,p. 920) are right, and this process creates new links and associations between events, then the approach takes on something of the consciousness raising that was so successful to second-wave feminism. Managers are often amazed to discover that their work could be seen as oppressive to others: by making them aware that they have such a negative effect on others, and at the same time are themselves subjected to oppressive working regimes, then the micro-changes that contributed to changes in women's status may start taking place throughout organisations.

> It is only by being able, through dialogue with others, to create end-less new links and connections between events that individuals are able to present their selves and their 'worlds' to one another. It is in such living moments between people, in practice, that utterly new possibilities are created, and people 'live out' solutions to their prob-lems they cannot hope to 'find' solely in theory, in intellectual reflec-tion on them.
>
> Katz and Shotter (1996:920)

This process then encourages development but on a broader scale than traditionally considered. The focus here is not on skills or compe-tence development, but the development of 'knowing of a third kind', that is, not developing knowledge by adding to facts—knowing *that*, or skills—knowing *how*—but 'knowing from within' (Shotter, 2005, p. 122). Exploring this *intersubjective* relationship, Klugman (1997, p. 298) argues that

> [M]ultiple models of subjectivity which allow (us) to modulate between one conception and another may broaden our ability to make meaning of . . . subjective experience and the sense of self and identity that is so closely linked to that experience.

The means of understanding the subjective experience of others is only possible, Klugman argues, through inter-subjectivity, but we add to this the necessity of exploring inter-subjectivity within its numerous and var-ious organisational contexts. We have shown, for example, that managers at Woolbury (Chapter 6) worked in an organisational culture which was antithetical to the leadership styles they were being urged to develop. However, those managers were participants in the construction of such a culture, so their using 'culture' as a reason for the failures of leadership changes in Woolbury need to be explored further, to find out how they use notions about a macho managerial culture in their constructions of their identities, and how these then prevent them doing something which, at first sight, they seemed keen to practice. This type of question-ing can be assisted by use of the *dialogic reflexivity* referred to above.

The active encouragement of reflexive and dialogical space enables managers to become more aware of how they constitute, maintain and thereby retain some control over their realities and identities.

Engagement in a critical, relational and reflexive dialogical approach encourages managers and staff alike to a deeper critique and questioning of how they account for their experiences (Cunliffe, 2002; Finlay, 2002; Hardy et al., 2001; Perriton, 2000; Reynolds, 1997, 1999). This goes beyond the reflexive considerations of biographies and draws on the situated and negotiated nature of experiences, through using reflexivity as 'intersubjective reflection' (Finlay, 2002, p. 215), so as to more fully explore the dynamics of individual's identities. It of course important to acknowledge the power imbalance between the leader and follower. Frank (2005) identifies this imbalance in the researcher participant relationship and this is also true of the role of leader and follower in organizational life. This approach involves adoption of a more reflexive, dialogical influence, in which both leaders and followers (and it is important to remember that managers occupy both subject positions) are in constant motion, becoming, changing and adapting during their working lives (Chia, 1996; Cunliffe, 2002; Frank, 2005). Managers are steeped in the continuous construction of their multiple identities through their numerous interactions with others, and it is this dialogical and reflexive process that needs to be incorporated into leadership experiences (Ford and Lawler, 2003, 2006). Multiple perspectives, identities and interpretations are therefore made available in the construction of the self (Ford 2006).

In summary, using a reflexive dialogical approach provides greater opportunities to encourage deeper insights by examining individual responses and interpersonal dynamics, and through this to open up knowledge of barely conscious motivations. This is done while retaining a sense of movement and multiplicity of identities that are lost through the fixing and coding of managers that more conventional approaches to an understanding of and development in leadership appear to encourage. The intention is to build on joint conversations between leaders and their staff, peers, boss and others in the employment relationship as well as taking account of the particular institutional contexts in which the relationships take place and the multiple and shifting narratives of the self that are produced in these relationships.

The critical voice that can inform more reflexive dialogical practices may be one way of encouraging a leadership that turns away from the demands of coordination and control, and towards relational practices that disrupt the complacency of many mainstream approaches and encourage leaders to face up to difficult issues in their working lives. The encouragement of self-reflexivity and critical questioning of taken for granted aspects of the experiences of managers may facilitate a determined critique among managers that can lead to resistance to organisational control. This may be possible through active interpretation of storied accounts of peoples' experiences and reflexive dialogical critique in which many interpretations can be surfaced.

Conclusion

Leadership is here to stay, at least for a while. It could have the potential to do good, but as it is currently constructed it has an equal or greater potential to do damage. The damage is both to leaders themselves, in the narrow and controlling identity of leader that is made available, and to those who make leadership possible—followers. Those of us working in educating and training leaders, and those of us who may indeed be leaders, can work to reduce the potential for such harm. That should be the least of our objectives.

References

Acker, J. (1990) 'Hierarchies, bodies and jobs: A gendered theory of organizations'. *Gender and Society* 4, no. 2, 139–58.

Adler, N. (1999) 'Global Leaders: Women of Influence' in Powell, G. (ed.), *Handbook of Gender and Work*. Thousand Oaks, CA: Sage.

Alimo-Metcalfe, B. and Lawler, J. (2002) 'Leadership Development in British Companies: Lessons for the NHS' *Journal of Management in Medicine* 15, (5), 387–404.

Alimo-Metcalfe, B. (1995) 'An Investigation of Female and Male Constructs of Leadership and Empowerment'. *Women in Management Review* 10, no. 2, 3–8.

Alimo-Metcalfe, B. (1998) *Effective Leadership*. London: Local Management Board.

Alimo-Metcalfe, B. and Alban-Metcalfe R. J. (2001) The development of a new transformational leadership questionnaire. *The Journal of Occupational & Organizational Psychology* 74, no. 1, 1–27.

Alimo-Metcalfe, B. and Lawler, J. (2001) 'Leadership development in British companies: Lessons for the NHS'. *Journal of Management in Medicine* 15, no. 5, 387–404.

Alimo-Metcalfe, B., Ford, J., Harding, N. and Lawler, J. (2000) *Leadership Development in British Companies at the Beginning of the 21st Century*. London: Careers Research Forum.

Alsop, R., Fitzimons, A. and Lennon, K. (2002) *Theorizing Gender*. Cambridge: Polity Press.

Althusser, L. (1971) *Lenin and Philosophy and Other Essays*. New York and London. Monthly Review Press. Available on-line at http://www.marx2mao.com/Other/LPOE70NB.html. Date accessed: 20th January, 2007.

Alvesson, M. (2002) *Understanding Organizational Culture*. London: Sage.

Alvesson, M. and Kärreman D. (2000) 'Taking the linguistic turn in organizational research: Challenges, responses, consequences'. *Journal of Applied Behavioral Science*, 36, 2, 136–58.

Alvesson, M. and Sveningsson, S. (2003) 'The great disappearing act: Difficulties in doing "leadership"' *The Leadership Quarterly* 14, 359–81.

Alvesson, M. and Willmott, H. (1996) *Making Sense of Management: A Critical Introduction*, London: Sage.

Alvesson, M. and Willmott, H. (2002) 'Identity regulation as organisational control: Producing the appropriate individual'. *Journal of Management Studies* 39, no. 5, 619–44.

Antaki, C. and Widdicombe S. (eds) (1998) *Identities in Talk*. London: Sage.

Austin, J. L. (1962) *How to Do Things with Words*. Oxford: Oxford University Press.

Avolio, B. J., Gardner, W. L., Walumba, F. O., Luthans, F. and May, D. R. (2004) Unlocking the mask: A look at the process by which authentic leaders impact follower attitudes and behaviours. *The Leadership Quarterly*, 15, 801–23.

Avolio, B. J. and Gardner, W. L. (2005) Authentic leadership development: Getting to the root of positive forms of leadership. *The Leadership Quarterly* 16, 315–38.

Barbalet, J. M. (2001) *Emotion, Social Theory, and Social Structure: A Macrosociological Approach*. Cambridge: Cambridge University Press.

Barthes, R. (1972) *Mythologies*. London: Paladin Grafton Books.

Bass, B. (1990*) Bass & Stodgill's Handbook of Leadership* (3rd ed). New York: The Bass, B. and Steidlmeier, P. (1999) 'Ethics, character, and authentic transformational leadership behavior'. *Leadership Quarterly* 10, no. 2, 181–217.

Beardsworth, R. (1996) *Derrida & the Political*. London: Routledge and Kegan Paul.

Bellavita, C. (1991) 'The public administrator as hero'. *Administration and Society* 23, no. 2, 155–85.

Benjamin, J. (1988) *The Bonds of Love: Psychoanalysis, Feminism and the Problem of Domination*. New York: Pantheon.

Benjamin, J. (1995) *Like Subjects, Love Objects. Essays on Recognition and Sexual Difference*. New Haven: Yale University Press.

Benjamin, J. (1998) *Shadow of the Other: Intersubjectivity and Gender in Psychoanalysis*. New York: Routledge.

Benn, S. I. and Gaus G. F. (1983) 'The Public and the Private: Concepts and Action' in Benn S. I. and Gaus G. F. *Public and Private in Social Life*. London: Croom Helm, 3–30.

Bennis, W. (1959) 'Leadership theory and administrative behavior: The problem of authority'. *Administrative Science Quarterly* 4, 259–60.

Bennis, W. (1989) *Why Leaders Can't Lead*. Oxford: Jossey-Bass.

Bennis, W. and Nanus, G. (1985) *Leaders: The Strategies for Taking Charge,* New York: Harper and Row.

Bion, W. (1961) *Experiences in Groups and Other Papers*. London: Tavistock Institute.

Blackler, F. and Kennedy, A. (2004) 'The design and evaluation of a leadership programme for experienced chief executives from the public sector'. *Management Learning* 35, no. 2, 181–203.

Boje, D. M., Alvarez, R. C. and Schooling, B. (2001) 'Reclaiming Story in Organisation: Narratologies and Action Sciences' in Westwood, R. and Linstead, S. (eds), *The Language of Organisation*. London: Sage.

Bollas, C. (1987) *The Shadow of the Object: Psychoanalysis of the Unthought Known*. London: Free Association Books.

Bollas, C. (1993) *Being a Character: Psychoanalysis and Self Experience*. London: Routledge.

Bollas, C. (1995) *Cracking Up: The Work of Unconscious Experience*. London: Routledge.

Bollas, C. (1996) *Forces of Destiny: Psychoanalysis and Human Idiom*. London: Free Association Books.

Bollas, C. (2007) *The Freudian Moment*. London: Karnac Books Ltd.

Bourdieu, P. (1992) *Invitation to Reflexive Sociology*. Chicago: University of Chicago Press.

Bowles, M. (1997) The myth of management: Directions and failure in contemporary organizations'. *Human Relations* 50, no. 7, 779–803.

Bowring, M. A. (2004) Resistance is *not* futile: Liberating captain janeway from the masculine-feminine dualism of leadership. *Gender, Work and Organization* 11, no. 4, 381–405.

Boyne, G. (1996) 'The intellectual crisis in public administration: Is public management the problem or the solution?'. *Public Administration* 74, 679–94.

Brewis, J., Hampton, M. P. and Linstead, S. (1997) Unpacking Priscilla: Subjectivity and identity in the organization of gendered appearance. *Human Relations* 50, no. 10, 1275–304.

Brewis, J. and Linstead, S. (2004) 'Gender and Management' in Linstead, S., Fulop, L. and Lilley, S. *Management and Organization: A Critical Text.* London: Macmillan, 56–92.

Brewis, Jo (1999) 'How Does It feel? Women Managers, Embodiment and Changing Public Sector Cultures' in Whitehead, S. and Moodley, R. (eds), *Transforming Managers: Gendering Change in the Public Sector.* London: UCL Press.

Briggs Myers, I., McCaulley, M. H., Quenk, N. L. and Hammer, A. L. (1998) *MBTI Manual.* Palo Alto, California: Consulting Psychologists Press Inc.

Brower, R. A. (1971) *Hero & Saint: Shakespeare and the Graeco-Roman Heroic Tradition.* Oxford: Clarendon Press.

Brown, A. (2001) 'Organization studies and identity: Towards a research agenda'. *Human Relations* 54, no. 1, 113–21.

Bryman, A. (1992) *Charisma and Leadership in Organisations,* London: Sage.

Bryman, A. (1996) 'Leadership in Organizations', in S. R. Clegg, C. Hardy and W. A. Nord (eds), *Handbook of Organization Studies.* London: Sage.

Bryman, A. (2004) 'Qualitative research on leadership: A critical but appreciative review'. *Leadership Quarterly* 15, no. 5, 721–891.

Budgeon, S. and Roseneil, S. (2004) 'Editors' introduction: Beyond the conventional family'. *Current Sociology* 52, no. 2, 127–34.

Burrell, G. (1992) 'The Organization of Pleasure' in Alvesson, M. and Wilmott, H. (eds), *Critical Management Studies,* London: Sage.

Burrell, G. (1998) Modernism, 'Post-Modernism and Organizational Analysis: The Contribution of Michel Foucault' in McKinlay, Alan and Starkey, Ken(eds), *Foucault, Management and Organization Theory.* London: Sage, 14–28.

Butler, J. (1995) 'Burning Acts: Injurious Speech', in Haverkamp A. (ed.), *Deconstruction is/in America: A New Sense of the Political.* New York: New York University Press, 149–80.

Butler, J. (1990) *Gender Trouble.* London: Routledge, Chapman and Hall.

Butler, J. (1993) *Bodies that Matter.* New York: Routledge.

Butler, J. (1996) 'Imitation and Gender Insubordination' in Morton, Donald (ed.), *The Material Queer: A LesBiGay Cultural Studies Reader.* Westview Press; Colorado, 180–92.

Butler, J. (1997) *Excitable Speech: A Politics of the Perforamtiave.* New York: Routledge and Kegan Paul.

Butler, J. (2004) *Undoing Gender.* New York: Routledge.

Butler, J. (2005) *Giving an Account of Oneself.* New York: Fordham.

Butterfield, D. and Grinnell, J. (1999) '"Re-viewing" Gender, Leadership and Managerial Behavior: Do Three Decades of Research Tell Us Anything' in Powell, G. (ed.), *Handbook of Gender and Work.* Thousand Oaks, CA: Sage.

Calás, M. and Smircich, L. (1992) 'Using the F word: Feminist Theories and the Social Consequences of Organizational Research' in Mills, A. J and Tancred, P. (eds), *Gendering Organizational Analysis.* New Park, CA: Sage.

Calás, M. and Smircich, L. (1996) 'From the Woman's Point of View: Feminist Approaches to Organizational Studies' in Clegg, S., Hardy, C. and Nord, W. (eds), *Handbook of Organization Studies.* London: Sage.

Calás, M. B. and Smircich, L. (1991) 'Voicing seduction to silence leadership'. *Organization Studies* 12, 567–602.

Cameron, D. (2000) *Good to Talk?: Living and Working in a Communication Culture.* London: Sage.

Campbell, D. (2000) *The Socially Constructed Organization.* London: Karnac Books.

Campbell, J. (1949) *The Hero with a Thousand Faces.* New York: Pantheon Books.

Carr, A. and Zanetti, L. A. (1999) 'Metatheorising the dialectics of self and other: The psychodynamics in work organizations'. *American Behavioral Scientist* 43, 3245–7.

Case, P. and Phillipson, G. (2004) 'Astrology, alchemy and retro-organizational theory: An astro-genealogical critique of the Myers-Briggs type indicator'. *Organization* 11, no. 4, 473–95.

Catley, B. and Jones, C. (2002) 'Deciding on violence'. *Reason in Practice: Journal of Philosophy of Management* 2, no. 1, 23–32.

Chemers, M. and Ayman, R. (1993) *Leadership Theory & Research.* London: Simon and Schuster.

Cheng, C. (ed.) (1996) *Masculinities in Organisations.* Thousand Oaks: Sage.

Chia, R. (1995) 'From modern to postmodern organizational analysis'. *Organization Studies* 16, no. 4, 579–604.

Chia, R. (1996a) 'Metaphors and Metaphorization in Organizational Analysis: Thinking beyond the Thinkable' in: Grant D. and Oswick C. (eds), *Metaphor and Organizations.* London: Sage, 127–45.

Chia, R. (1996b) 'The problem of reflexivity in organizational research: Towards a postmodern science of organization'. *Organization* 3, no. 1, 31–59.

Clark, T. and Salaman, G. (1998) 'Telling tales: Management gurus' narratives and the construction of managerial identity'. *Journal of Management Studies* 35, no. 2, 137–61.

Clarke, J. and Newman, J. (1993) 'The right to manage: A second managerial revolution'. *Cultural Studies* 7, no. 3, 427–41.

Clarke, J. and Newman, J. (1997) *The Managerial State: Power, Politics and Ideology in the Remaking of Social Welfare.* London: Sage.

Collins, D. (2000) *Management Fads and Buzzwords: Critical-Practical Perspectives* London: Routledge.

Collinson, D. (2005) 'Dialectics of Leadership'. *Human Relations* 58, no. 11, 1419–42.

Collinson, D. (2006) 'Rethinking followership: A post-structuralist analysis of follower identities'. *Leadership Quarterly* 17, 179–89.

Collinson, D. and Collinson, M. (1996) 'It's only dick: The sexual harassment of women managers in insurance sales'. *Work, Employment and Society* 10, 29–56.

Collinson, D. and Grint, K. (2005) 'Editorial: The Leadership Agenda', *Leadership* 1, no. 1, 5–9.

Collinson, D. and Hearn, J. (eds) (1996) *Men as Manager, Managers as Men. Critical Perspectives on Men, Masculinities and Managements.* London: Sage.

Collinson, D. and Hearn, J. (2001) 'Naming Men as Men: Implications for Work, Organisation and Management' in Whitehead, S. and Barrett, F. (eds), *The Masculinities Reader.* Cambridge: Polity.

Collinson, D. and Hearn, J. (2005) Men and Masculinities in Work, Organizations and Management. In: M. S. Kimmel, J. Hearn and R. W. Connell (eds), *Handbook of Studies on Men and Masculinities*, Thousand Oaks: Sage, 289–310.

Connell, R. W. (2005) *Masculinities* (2nd edn). Cambridge: Polity Press.

Cooper, D. (1999) *Existentialism: A Reconstruction* (2nd edn). Oxford: Blackwell.

Cooper, R. (1989) 'Modernism, postmodernism and organisational analysis 3: The contribution of Jacques Derrida'. *Organization Studies* 10, no. 4, 479–502.

Cooper, R. (1990) 'Organization/Disorganization', in Hassard, J. and Pym, J. (eds), *The Theory and Philosophy of Organizations: Critical Issues and New Perspectives*. London: Routledge and Kegan Paul, 167–97.

Cooper, R. and Burrell, G. (1988) 'Modernism, postmodernism and organizational analysis: An introduction'. *Organization Studies* 9, no. 1, 91–112.

Cooper, R. and Law, J. (1995) 'Organization: Distal and proximal views'. *Research in the Sociology of Organizations* 13, 237–74.

Council for Excellence (2002) *Managers and Leaders: Raising our game*. Council for Excellence in Management and Leadership.

Couto, R. A. (1991) 'Heroic Bureau'. Administration and Society 23, no. 1, 123–147.

Crossley, M. (2000) *Introducing Narrative Psychology: Self, Trauma and the Construction of Meaning*. Buckingham: Open University Press.

Crotty, M. (1998) *The Foundations of Social Research: Meaning and Perspective in the Research Process*. London: Sage.

Cunliffe, A. (2002) 'Reflexive dialogical practice in management learning'. *Management Learning* 33, no. 1, 33–61.

Currie, G. and Brown, A. D. (2003) 'A narratological approach to understanding processes of organizing in a UK hospital'. *Human Relations*, 56, no. 5, 563–86.

Currie, G., Boyett, I. and Suhomlinova, O. (2005) 'A panacea for organizational ills? Transformational leadership within secondary schools in England'. *Public Administration* 83, no. 2, 265–96.

Davies, B. and Harre, R. (2001) 'Positioning: The Discursive Production of Selves' in Wetherell, M., Taylor, S. and Yates, S. *Discourse Theory and Practice: A Reader*. London: Sage.

Davies, C. (1987) 'Viewpoint: Things to come–The NHS in the next decade'. *Sociology of Health & Illness* 9, no. 3, 302–17.

Day, P. and Klein, R. E. (1983) 'The mobilisation of consent versus the anagement of conflict: Decoding the Griffiths report'. *British Medical Journal* 287, 1813–15.

Deetz, S. (2003) 'Reclaiming the legacy of the linguistic turn'. *Organization* 10, no. 3, 421–9.

Denzin, N. K. and Lincoln, Y. S. (1998) *Handbook of Qualitative Research*. London: Sage.

Denzin, N. K. and Y. S. Lincoln, (eds) (2002) *The Qualitative Inquiry Reader*. Thousands Oaks, California: Sage.

Derrida, J. (1976) *Of Grammatology*. Baltimore, MD: Johns Hopkins University Press.

Derrida, J. (1978) *Writing and Difference*. London: Routledge and Kegan Paul.

Derrida, J. (1979) 'Signature Event Context'. *Glyph* 1, 172–97.

Derrida, J. (1981) *Dissemination*. London: Athlone Press.

Derrida, J. (1987) *The Truth in Painting*. Chicago, IL: University of Chicago Press.

Derrida, J. (1988) *Limited Inc*. Evanston, IL: Northwestern University Press.

Derrida, J. (1992a) 'Afterw.rds: or, at least, less than a letter about a letter less', in N. Royle (ed.), *Afterwords*. Tampere, Finland: Outside Books, 197–203.

Derrida, J. (1992b) *Acts of Literature*. New York: Routledge and Kegan Paul.

Derrida, J. (1994) *Specters of Marx: The State of Debt, the Work of Mourning, and the New International.* New York: Routledge.

Derrida, J. (1996) 'As if I were Dead: An interview with Jacques Derrida' in Brannigan, J., Robbins, R. and Wolfreys, J. (eds), *Applying: To Derrida.* Basingstoke: Palgrave Macmillan, 212–26.

Derrida, J. (1998) *Monolingualism of the Other; or, The Prosthesis of Origin.* Stanford, CA: Stanford University Press.

Derrida, J. (2000) 'Et Cetera . . . : (and so on, und so weiter, and so forth, et ainsi de suite, und so überall, etc.)' in Royle, N. (ed.), *Deconstructions: A User's Guide.* Basingstoke: Palgrave Macmillan, 282–305.

DH (2002) *Code of Conduct for NHS Managers.* Dept of Health, HMSO.

DH (2002) *NHS Leadership Qualities Framework.* NHS Leadership Centre, Dept of Health.

DHSS (1983) *NHS Management Inquiry* (DA(83)38). Stanmore Middlesex: DHSS (Leaflets).

Donaldson, M. (1993) 'What is hegemonic masculinity?'. *Theory and Society* 22, 643–57.

Doty, M. (1993) *Firebird.* New York: HarperCollins.

Downs, A. (1997) *Beyond the Looking Glass.* New York: Amacom.

Easterby-Smith, M., Thorpe, R. and Lowe, A. (1991) *Management Research: An Introduction,* London: Sage.

Edmonstone, J. and Western, J. (2002) 'Leadership Development in Health Care: What do we know?'. *Journal of Management in Medicine* 16, no. 1, 34–47.

Elliot, C. and Reynolds, M. (2002) 'Manager-Educator Relations from a Critical Perspective'. *Journal of Management Education* 26, no. 5, 512–26.

Ellis, C. and Bochner, A. (2000) 'Autoethnography, Personal Narrative, Reflexivity: Researcher as Subject' in Denzin, N. and Lincoln, Y. (eds), *Handbook of Qualitative Research.* Thousand Oaks, CA: Sage.

Erickson, R. J. (1995) 'The importance of authenticity for self and society'. *Symbolic Interaction* 18, no. 2, 121–44.

Exworthy, M. and Halford, S. (eds) (1999), *Professionals and the New Managerialism in the Public Sector.* Buckingham: Open University Press, 50–65.

Fineman, S. E. (ed.)(1993) *Emotion in Organisations.* London: Sage.

Fineman, S. E. (2000) *Emotion in Organizations.* (2nd edn) London: Sage.

Fineman, S. (2006) 'On being positive: Concerns and counterpoints'. *Academy of Management Review* 31, no. 2, 270–91.

Finlay, C. (2002) 'Negotiating the swamp: The opportunity and challenge of reflexivity in research practice', *Qualitative Research* 2, no. 2, 209–30.

Fletcher, J. K. (2004) 'The paradox of postheroic leadership: An essay on gender, power and transformational change'. *Leadership Quarterly* 14, 647–61.

Fletcher, J. K. and Kaeufer, K. (2003) 'Shared Leadership: Paradox and Possibility' in Pearce, C. J. and Conger, J. (eds), *Shared leadership: Reframing the Hows and Whys of Leadership.* London: Sage.

Flynn, R. (1992) *Structures of Control in Health Management.* London: Routledge and Kegan Paul.

Ford, J. (2004) 'A Feminist Critique of Leadership and Its Application to the UK NHS' in Learmonth, M. and Harding, N., *Unmasking Health Management.* New York: Nova Publishers.

Ford, J. (2006) 'Discourses of leadership: Gender, identity and contradiction in a UK public sector organization'. *Leadership* 2, no. 1, 77–99.

Ford, J. (2007) *Managers as Leaders: Towards a Post-Structuralist Feminist Analysis of Leadership Dynamics in UK Local Government*. Unpublished PhD thesis.

Ford, J. and Harding, N. (2003) 'Invoking Satan or the ethics of the employment contract'. *Jo. Management Studies* 40, no. 5, July. 1131–50.

Ford, J. and Harding, N. (2004) 'We went looking for an organization but could only find the metaphysics of its presence'. *Sociology* 38, no. 4, 815–30.

Ford, J. and Harding, N. (2007). 'Move over management: We are all leaders now?'. *Management Learning* 38, no. 5, 475–93.

Ford, J. and Harding, N. (2008) 'Fear and loathing in Harrogate *or* an exploration of the mutual constitution of organisation and members'. Organization 15, no. 2, 233–50.

Ford, J. and Lawler, J. (2003) 'Leadership and Narrative: Subjective perspectives'. Proceedings of 2nd International Conference on Studying Leadership, University of Lancaster, December 2003.

Ford, J. and Lawler, J. (2006) 'A Narrative Approach to Development'. Paper for symposium on Continuous Professional Development, *British Academy of Management Conference*, September 2006.

Ford, J. and Lawler, J. (2007) 'Blending existentialist and constructionist approaches to leadership studies: An exploratory account'. *Leadership and Organisational Development Journal* 28, no. 5, 409–25.

Foucault, M. (1970) *The Order of Things*. London: Allen Lane.

Foucault, M. (1979) *The History of Sexuality*, vol. 1. London: Allen Lane.

Foucault, M. (1986) *The History of Sexuality*, vol. 2. Harmondsworth: Viking.

Foucault, M. (1992) *The History of Sexuality*, vol. 3. London: Penguin.

Foucault, M. (2006) *Psychiatric Power. Lectures at the College de France 1973/74*. New York: Palgrave.

Fournier, V. (1998) 'Stories of Development and Exploitation: Militant voices in an enterprise culture'. Organization 5, no. 1, 55–80.

Fournier, V. and Kelemen, M. (2001) 'The crafting of community: Recoupling discourses of management and womanhood'. *Gender, Work and Organization* 8, no. 3, 267–90.

Fournier, V. and Grey, C. (2000) 'At the Critical Moment: Conditions and Prospects for Critical Management Studies'. *Human Relations* 53, no. 1, 7–32.

Fox, N. J. (1997) 'Texts, frames and decisions over discharge from hospital: A deconstruction'. *Social Sciences in Health* 3, no. 1, 41–51.

Frank, A. (2005) 'What is dialogical research and why should we do it?' *Qualitative Health Research* 15(7): 964–74.

Frug, G. E. (1984) 'The ideology of bureaucracy in American law'. *Harvard Law Review* 97, no. 6, 1276–388.

Fuery, P. and Mansfield, N. (2000) *Cultural Studies and Critical Theory*. Oxford: Oxford University Press.

Fulop, L. and Linstead, S. (eds), (1999) *Management: A Critical Text*, London: Palgrave Macmillan.

Fulop, L. and Linstead, S. (1994) *Management: A critical text*, Australia: Macmillan.

Fulop, L., Linstead, S. and Dunford, R. (2004) 'Leading and Managing' in Linstead, S., Fulop, L. and Lilley, S. (eds), *Management and Organization: A Critical Text*. London: Palgrave Macmillan.

Fuss, D. (2001) 'Theorizing Hetero- and Homosexuality' in Seidman, Steven and Alexander, Jeffrey C. (eds), *The New Social Theory Reader: Contemporary Debates*. Routledge: London.

Gabriel, Y. (1999) *Organizations in Depth: The Psychoanalysis of Organizations*. London: Sage.

Gardner, W. L., Avolio, B. J., Luthans, F., May, D. R. and Walumbwa, F. (2005) '"Can you see the real me?" A self-based model of authentic leader and follower development'. *The Leadership Quarterly* 16, 343–72.

Gasché, R. (1995) 'Possibilizations, in the Singular' in Haverkamp, A. (ed.), *Deconstruction is/in America: A New Sense of the Political*. New York: New York University Press, 115–24.

Gavey, N. (1997) 'Feminist Poststructuralism and Discourse Analysis' in Gergen, M. and Davis, S. *Toward a New Psychology of Gender: A Reader*. London: Routledge, 49–54.

Gemmill, G. and Oakley, J. (1992) 'Leadership: An Alienating Social Myth?'. *Human Relations* 45, no. 2, 113–29.

Gennep, A. V. (1960) *The Rites of Passage*. Chicago, University of Chicago Press.

Gergen, K. (1994) *Realities and Relationships: Soundings in Social Constructionism*. Cambridge MA: Harvard University Press.

Gergen, K. (1985) 'The social constructionist movement in modern psychology'. *American Psychologist* 40, 266–75.

Gergen, K. (1991) *The Saturated Self: Dilemmas of Identity on Contemporary Life*. New York: Basic Books.

Gergen, K. (1992) 'Organization Theory in the Postmodern Era' in Reed, M. and Hughes, M. (eds), *Rethinking Organization: New Directions in Organization Theory and Analysis*. London: Sage, 207–26.

Gergen, K. (1994) *Realities and Relationships: Soundings in Social Constructionism*. Cambridge MA: Harvard University Press.

Gergen, K. (1999) *An Invitation to Social Construction*. London: Sage.

Ghaye, T. and Lillyman, S. (1996) *Learning Journals and Critical Incidents: Reflective Practice for Healthcare Professionals*. London: Mark Allen.

Gherhardi, S. (1995) *Gender, Symbolism and Organizational Cultures*. London: Sage.

Gibson-Graham, J. K. (1996) *The End of Capitalism (as we knew it). A Feminist Critique of Political Economy*. Malden, Massachusetts: Blackwell.

Giddens, A. (1984) *The Constitution of Society: Outline of the Theory of Structuration*. Cambridge: Polity Press.

Giddens, A. (1991) *Modernity and Self-Identity: Self and Society in the Late Modern Age*. Cambridge: Polity Press.

Goethals, G., Sorenson, G. and Burns, J. (eds) (2004) *Encyclopaedia of Leadership* London: Sage.

Goffee, R. and Jones, G. (2005) 'Managing authenticity: The paradox of great leadership'. *Harvard Business Review*. December 2005, 86–94.

Goffman, E. (1959) *Presentation of Self in Everyday Life*. London: Allen Lane, The Penguin Press.

Gold, J., Holman, D. and Thorpe, R. (2002) 'The role of argument analysis and story telling in facilitating critical thinking'. *Management Learning* 33, no. 3, 371–88.

Goleman, D. (1996) *Emotional Intelligence: Why It Can Matter More Than IQ*. London: Bloomsbury.

Goleman, D. (2002) *The New Leaders: Transforming the Art of Leadership into the Science of Results*. London: Little, Brown.

Greenleaf, R. (1997) *Servant Leadership: A Journey into the Nature of Legitimate Power and Greatness*. New York: Paulist Press.

Grey, C. (1999) ' "We are all Managers Now"; "We always were": On the Development and Demise of Management'. *Journal of Management Studies* 36, no. 5, 561–85.

Grint, K. (1997) *Leadership: Classical, Contemporary and Critical Approaches.* Oxford: Oxford University Press.

Grint, K. (2000) *The Arts of Leadership,* Oxford: Oxford University Press.

Grint, K. (2005) *Leadership: Limits and Possibilities,* Hampshire: Palgrave Macmillan.

Halberstam, J. (1998) *Female Masculinity.* Durham and London: Duke University Press.

Halford, S. and Leonard, P. (1999) 'New Identities? Professionalism, Managerialism and the Construction of Self' in Exworthy, M. and Halford, S. (eds), *Professionals and the New Managerialism in the Public Sector.* Buckingham: Open University Press, 102–21.

Halford, S. and Leonard, P. (2001) *Gender, Power and Organizations.* London: Macmillan.

Ham, C. (1995) 'The Grey Suits Deserve Better Treatment'. *The Independent,* 10 June, 15.

Hancock, P. and Tyler, M. (2001) *Work, Postmodernism and Organization: A Critical Introduction.* London: Sage.

Harding, N. and Learmonth, M. (2000) 'Thinking critically: The case of health policy research'. *Technology Analysis & Strategic Management* 12, no. 3, 335–41.

Harding, N. (2003) *The Social Construction of Management: Texts and Identities.* London: Routledge.

Hardy, C., Phillips, N. and Clegg, S. (2001) 'Reflexivity in organisation and management theory: A study of the production of the research subject'. *Human Relations* 54, no. 5, 531–60.

Harrison, S. (1988) *Managing the NHS: Shifting the Frontier.* London: Chapman and Hall.

Harrison, S. (1994) *National Health Service Management in the 1980s: Policymaking on the Hoof?* Aldershot: Avebury.

Harrison, S. (1999) 'Clinical Autonomy and Health Policy: Past and Futures', in Exworthy, M. and Halford, S. (eds), *Professionals and the New Managerialism in the Public Sector.* Buckingham: Open University Press.

Harrison, S. and Pollitt, C. (1994) *Controlling Health Professionals: The Future of Work and Organization in the NHS.* Buckingham: Open University Press.

Harrison, S., Hunter, D., Marnoch, G. and Pollitt, C. (1992) *Just Managing: Power and Culture in the NHS.* Basingstoke: Palgrave Macmillan.

Hawes, S. (1998) 'Positioning a Dialogic Reflexivity in the Practice of Feminist Supervision' in Bayer, B. and Shotter, J. *Reconstructing the Psychological Subject: Bodies, Practices and Technologies.* London: Sage, 94–110.

Hearn, J. (1992) *Men in the Public Eye: Critical Studies of Men and Masculinities.* London: Routledge.

Hearn, J. (1993) 'Emotive Subjects: Organizational Men, Organizational Masculinities and the (De)construction of "Emotions"' in Fineman, S. (ed.), *Emotion in Organizations.* London: Sage, 142–66.

Hearn, J. (1996) ' "Is Masculinity Dead?" A Critical Account of the Concepts of Masculinity and Masculinities' in Mac an Ghail, M. (ed.), *Understanding*

Masculinities: Social Relations and Cultural Arenas. 202–17, Milton Keynes: Open University Press.

Hearn, J. (1998) 'Theorizing men and men's Theorizing: Men's discursive practices in Theorizing Men'. *Theory and Society* 27, no. 6, 781–816.

Hearn, J. (2000) 'On the complexity of feminist intervention in organizations'. *Organization* 7, no. 4, 609–24.

Hearn, J. (2004) 'From hegemonic masculinity to the hegemony of men'. *Feminist Theory* 5, no. 1, 49–72.

Hennessy, R. (1995). 'Queer Visibility in Commodity Culture' in Nicholson, L. and Seidman, S. *Social Postmodernism: Beyond Identity Politics.* Cambridge: Cambridge University Press, 142–83.

Hochschild, A. R. (1983). *The Managed Heart: Commercialization of Human Feeling.* Berkeley, University of California Press.

Hollway, W. and Jefferson, T. (2000) *Doing Qualitative Research Differently: Free Association, Narrative and the Interview Method.* London: Sage.

Holstein, J. A. and Gubrium, J. F. (2000) *The Self We Live By: Narrative Identity in a Postmodern World.* New York: Oxford University Press.

Homer (1980) *The Odyssey.* Oxford: Oxford University Press.

Hourihan, M. (1997) *Deconstructing the Hero: Literary Theory and Children's Literature.* London: Routledge.

House, R., Hanges, P., Javidan, M., Dorfman, P. and Gupta, V. (2004) *Culture, Leadership and Organizations.* London: Sage.

Huczynski, A. (1993) *Management Gurus: What Makes Them and How to Become One.* London: Routledge.

Hughes, K. (1999) From Anorexia Nervosa to Anorexic Practices: The Process of Subject Constitution in the Therapeutic Encounter. *Sociology and Social Policy.* Leeds: University of Leeds.

Hughes, O. E. (1994) *Public Management and Administration: An Introduction.* Basingstoke: Palgrave Macmillan.

Hunter, D. J. (1984) 'NHS management: Is Griffiths the last quick fix?'. *Public Administration* 62, 91–4.

Hunter, D. J. (1988) 'The impact of research on restructuring the British national health service'. *The Journal of Health Administration Education* 6, no. 3, 537–53.

Hunter, D. J. (1994) 'From Tribalism to Corporatism: The Managerial Challenge to Medical Dominance' in Gabe, J., Kelleher, D. and Williams, G. (eds), *Challenging Medicine.* London: Routledge, 1–22.

Hunter, D. J. (1996a) 'Managers Myths and Malaise'. *Health Services Journal* 106, no. 5513, 21.

Hunter, D. J. (1996b) 'The changing roles of health care personnel in health and health care management'. *Social Science and Medicine* 43, no. 5, 799–808.

Jackson, W. T. H. (1982) The Hero and the King: An epic theme. New York: Columbia University Press.

Jagose, A. (1996) *Queer Theory.* Melbourne: Melbourne University Press.

Jameson, F. (1991) *Postmodernism, or, The Cultural Logic of Late Capitalism.* London: Verso.

Jameson, F. (1998) *The Cultural Turn: Selected Writings on the Postmodern 1983–1998.* London: Verso.

Jameson, F. (2000). 'Imaginary and Symbolic in Lacan' in Hardt M. and Weeks K. *The Jameson Reader.* Oxford: Blackwell.

Johnson, B. (1981) 'Translator's Introduction'. In Derrida, J. *Dissemination*. London: Athlone Press.

Jones, C. (2004) 'Jacques Derrida', in Linstead, S. (ed.), *Organization Theory and Postmodern Thought*. London: Sage, 34–63.

Jones, C. and Spicer, A. (2005). 'The sublime object of entrepreneurship'. *Organization* 12, no. 2, 223–46.

Kain, P. J. (2005) *Hegel and the Other*. New York: State University of New York Press.

Katz, A. and Shotter, J. (1996) 'Hearing the Patient's "Voice": Towards a Social Poetics in Diagnostic Interviews'. *Social Science and Medicine* 43, no. 6, 919–31.

Katzenbach, J. and Smith, D. (1993) *The Wisdom of Teams: Creating the High Performance Organization*, Harvard School Press, Boston, MA.

Kaufmann, M. (1994) 'Men, Feminism and Men's Contradictory Experiences of Power' in Brod, H. and Kaufmann, M. (eds), *Theorising Masculinities*. Thousand Oaks, CA: Sage, 142–63.

Kerfoot, D. (2000) 'Body Work: Estrangement, Disembodiment and the Organizational Other' in Hassard, J., Holliday, R. and Willmott, H. (eds), *Body and Organization*. London: Sage.

Kerfoot, D. (2001) 'The Organisation of Intimacy: Managerialism, Masculinity and the Masculine Subject' in Whitehead, S. and Barrett, F. (eds), *The Masculinities Reader*. Cambridge, MA: Polity Press, 233–52.

Kerfoot, D. and Knights, D. (1993) 'Management, masculinity and manipulation: From paternalism to corporate strategy in financial services in Britain'. *Journal of Management Studies* 30, no. 4, 659–77.

Kets deVries, M. (2006) *The Leader on the Couch: A Clinical Approach to Changing People and Organizations*. CA: Jossey-Bass.

Klein, M. (1948) *Contributions to Psycho-Analysis 1921–1945*. London: Hogarth Press.

Klein, M. (1975) *Envy and Gratitude, and Other Works 1946–1963*. London: Hogarth Press.

Klein, R. (1995) *The New Politics of the NHS*. (3rd edn) London: Longman.

Klugman, D. (1997). 'Existentialism and constructivism: A bi-polar model of subjectivity'. *Clinical Social Work* 25, no. 3, 297–13.

Knights, D. and Willmott, H. (1992) 'Conceptualizing leadership processes: A study of senior managers in a financial services company'. *Journal of Management Studies* 29, no. 6, 761–82.

Kotter, J. (1990) 'What leaders really do'. *Harvard Business Review*. May–June, 103–11.

Laclau, E. (1996) *Emancipation(s)*. London: Verso.

Laclau, E. and Mouffe, C. (2001) *Hegemony and Socialist Strategy: Towards a Radical Democratic Politics*. (2nd edn) London: Verso.

Lasch, C. (1979) *The Culture of Narcissism*. New York: Warner.

Lawler, J. (In review) The Concept Of 'Authenticity' In Leadership: An Existential View.

Lawler, S. (2002) 'Narrative in Social Research' in May T. (ed.), *Qualitative Research in Action*. London: Sage, 242–58.

Learmonth, M. (1997) 'Managerialism and Public Attitudes towards NHS Managers'. *Journal of Management in Medicine* 11, no. 4, 214–21.

Learmonth, M. (1999) 'The NHS manager: Engineer and father? A deconstruction'. *Journal of Management Studies* 36, no. 7, 999–1012.

Learmonth, M. (2003) *Rereading NHS Management.* Unpublished PhD Thesis: University of Leeds.

Learmonth, M. (2004) 'The violence of trusting trust chief executives: Glimpsing trust in the UK national health service'. *Qualitative Inquiry* 10, no. 41, 581–600.

Learmonth, M. (2005) 'Doing things with words: The case of "management" and "administration"'. *Public Administration* 83, no. 3, 617–37.

Learmonth, M. and Harding, N. (eds) (2004) *Unmasking Health Management: A Critical Text.* New York: Nova Science.

Lee, H. (2007). Why Sexual Health Promotion Misses its Audience: Men who have Sex with Men Reading the Texts. *Journal of Health Organization and Management* 21: 2, 205–219.

Lee, H., Learmonth, M. and Harding, N. (2008) 'Queer(y)ing public administration'. *Public Administration* 86, no. 1, 1–19.

Linstead, S., Fulop, L. and Lilley, S. (2004) *Management and Organization.* Hampshire: Palgrave Macmillan.

Llewellyn, S. (2001) '"Two-way windows": Clinicians as medical managers'. *Organization Studies* 22, no. 4, 593–623.

Luthans, F. and Avolio, B. J. (2003) 'Authentic Leadership: A Positive-Developmental Approach' in Cameron, K. S., Dutton, J. E. and Quinn, R. E. (eds), *Positive Organizational Scholarship.* San Francisco: Barrett-Koehler, 241–61.

Malamud, R. (1980) 'The Amazon Problem' in Hillman, J. (ed.), *Facing the Gods.* Dallas: Spring Publications, 47–66.

Mangham, I. and Pye, A. (1991) *The Doing of Management,* Oxford: Blackwell.

Manz, C. and Sims, H. P. (1992) 'Becoming a Super-Leader' in Glaser, R. (ed.), *Classic Readings in Self-Managing Teamwork,* King of Prussia, PA: Organization Design and Development Inc.

Marshall, J. (1984) *Women Managers: Travellers in a Male World.* Chichester: Wiley.

Marshall, J. (1995) 'Gender and management: A critical review of research'. *British Journal of Management* 6 (Special Issue), SS3–S62.

Martin, J. (1990) 'Deconstructing organizational taboos: The suppression of gender conflict in organizations'. *Organization Science* 1, no. 4, 339–59.

McAdams, D. (1993) *The Stories We Live By: Personal Myths and the Making of the Self.* New York: Guilford Press.

Mouffe, C. (1995) 'Post-Marxism, Democracy and Identity'. *Environment and Planning D. Society and Space* 13, no. 3, 259–66.

Newman, J. (2000) 'Beyond the New Public Management? Modernizing Public Services' in Clarke, J., Gewirtz, S. and McLaughlin, E. (eds), *New Managerialism, New Welfare?* London: Sage, 45–61.

Northouse, P. G. (2001) *Leadership: Theory & Practice.* (2nd edn) London: Sage.

Oakley, A. (1972) *Sex, Gender and Society.* London: Temple Smith.

Oseen, C. (1997) 'Luce Irigaray, sexual difference and theorizing leaders and leadership'. *Gender, Work and Organization* 4, no. 3, 170–84.

Parker, A. and Sedgwick, E. K. (1995). 'Introduction: Performativity and Performance' in Parker, A. and Sedgwick, E. K. *Performativity and Performance.* New York: Routledge, 1–18.

Parker, M. (2000) *Organizational Culture and Identity: Unity and Division at Work.* London: Sage.

Parker, M. (2002) 'Queering Management and Organization'. *Gender, Work and Organization* 9, no. 2, 146–66.

Parker, M. (2004) 'Structure, Culture and Anarchy: Ordering the NHS', in Learmonth, M. and Harding, N. (eds), *Unmasking Health Management: A Critical Text*. New York: Nova Science, 171–85.

Parker, M. and Dent, M. (1996) 'Managers, Doctors and Culture: Changing an English Health District'. *Administration and Society* 28, no. 3, 335–61.

Pateman, C. (1983). 'Feminist Critiques of the Public/Private Dichotomy' in Benn, S. I. and Gaus, G. F. *Public and Private in Social Life*. London, Croom Helm, 281–303.

Perriton, L. (2000) 'A reflection of what exactly? A provocation regarding the use of critical reflection in Critical Management Education', paper presented at the *Second Connecting Learning and Critique Conference*, Lancaster University, July 2000.

Petchey, R. (1986) 'The Griffths reorganisation of the national health service: Fowlerism by stealth?'. *Critical Social Policy* 17, no. 3, 87–101.

Peters, T. J. and Waterman, R. H. (1982) *In Search of Excellence: Lessons from America's Best-run Companies*. New York: Harper Row.

Petersen, A. (1998) *Unmasking the Masculine; 'Men' And 'Identity' In A Sceptical Age*. London: Sage.

Peterson, L. W. and Albrecht, T. L. (1999) 'Where Gender/Power/Politics Collide: Deconstructing Organizational Maternity Leave Policy'. *Journal of Management Inquiry* 8, no. 2, 168–81.

Pfeffer, J. (1977) 'The Ambiguity of Leadership'. Academy of Management Review 2, no. 1, 104–112.

Pfeffer, J. (1981) *Power in Organizations*. London: Pitman.

Pinch, A. (1996) *Strange Fits of Passion. Epistemologies of Emotion, Hume to Austen*. Stanford, CA: Stanford University Press.

Pollitt, C. (1993) *Managerialism and the Public Services: Cuts or Cultural Change in the 1990s?* (2nd edn) Oxford: Blackwell.

Popper, M. (2001) 'The dark and bright sides of leadership: some theortical and practical implications' in J. M. Burns, G. Sorenson and L. Matusak (eds), *Concepts, challenges and realities of Leadership*. College Park, MD: Academy of Leadership.

Potter, J. (1996) *Representing Reality: Discourse, Rhetoric and Social Construction*. London: Sage.

Probyn, E. (1999) 'An ethos with a bite: Queer appetites from sex to food'. *Sexualities* 2, no. 4, 421–31.

Probyn, E. (1993) *Sexing the Self*. London: Routledge.

Rapaport, H. (2003) *Later Derrida: Reading the Recent Work*. London: Routledge and Kegan Paul.

Reynolds, M. (1997) 'Towards a critical Management Pedagogy' in Burgoyne, J. and Reynolds, M. (eds), *Management Learning: Integrating Perspectives in Theory and Practice*. London: Sage, 312–28.

Reynolds, M. (1999) 'Critical reflection and management education: Rehabilitating less hierarchical approaches'. *Journal of Management Education* 23, no. 5, 537–53.

Roach, J. (1995) 'Culture and Performance in the Circum-Atlantic World' in Parker, A. and Sedgwick, K. E. *Performativity and Performance*. New York: Routledge, 45–63.

Roberts, J. (2005) The Power of the imaginary in disciplinary processes'. *Organization* 12, no. 5, 619–42.

Ronai, C. R. (1999) 'The next night Sous Rature: Wrestling with Derrida's Mimesis'. *Qualitative Inquiry* 5, no. 1, 114–29.

Roseneil, S. and Seymour, J. (1999) *Practising Identities: Power and Resistance*. New York: St. Martin's Press.

Rosener, J. (1990) 'Ways women lead'. *Harvard Business Review*, Nov–Dec: 119–25.

Rosener, J. (1997) *America's Competitive Secret: Women Managers*, Oxford: Oxford University Press.

Royle, N. (2000) 'What is Deconstruction?' in Royle N. (ed.), *Deconstructions: A User's Guide*. Basingstoke: Palgrave Macmillan, 1–13.

Rumens, N. (2005) 'Extended Review: Emotion in Work Organisations'. *Management Learning* 36, no. 1, 117–28.

Said, E. (1978) *Orientalism*. New York: Pantheon.

Sauko, P. (2002) 'Studying the self: From the subjective and the social to personal and political dialogues'. *Qualitative Research* 2, no. 2, 244–63.

Schon, D. A. (1983) *The Reflective Practitioner: How Professionals Think in Action*, New York: Basic Books.

Sculley, J. and Byrne, J. A. (1987) *Odyssey: From Pepsi to Apple*. London: Collins.

Sedgwick, E. K. (1991) *Epistemology of the Closet*. New York: Harvester Wheatsheaf.

Sedgwick, E. K. (2003) *Touching Feeling: Affect, Pedagogy, Performativity*. Durham, NC: Duke University Press.

Sedgwick, E. K. and Parker, A. (eds) (1995) *Performativity and Performance*. New York: Routledge and Kegan Paul.

Seidler, Victor J. (1994) *Unreasonable Men: Masculinity and Social Theory*. London: Routledge.

Seidman, S. (1997) *Difference Troubles; Queering Social Theory and Sexual Politics*. Cambridge: Cambridge University Press.

Seidman, S. (2001) 'From Identity to Queer Politics: Shifts in Normative Heterosexuality' in Seidman, Steven and Alexander, Jeffrey C. (eds), *The New Social Theory Reader. Contemporary Debates*. Routledge: London, 353–61.

Shamir, B. and Eilam, G. (2005). '"What's your Story?" A life-story approach to authentic leadership development'. *The Leadership Quarterly*, no. 3, 395–417.

Shotter, J. (2005) 'Inside the moment of managing: Wittgenstein and the everyday dynamics our expressive-responsive activities'. *Organization Studies* 26, no. 1, 113–35.

Silverman, K. (1988) *The Acoustic Mirror: The Female Voice in Psychoanalysis and Cinema*. Bloomington: Indiana University Press.

Sims, H. and Lorenzi, P. (1992) *The New Leadership Paradigm*. CA: Sage.

Sinclair, A. (1998) *Doing Leadership Differently*. Melbourne: Melbourne University Press.

Sinclair, A. (2005) *Doing Leadership Differently*. Rev edn. Melbourne: Melbourne University Press.

Sinclair, A. and Wilson, V. (2002) *New Faces of Leadership*. Melbourne: Melbourne University Press.

Smircich, L. and Morgan, G. (1982) 'Leadership: The management of meaning'. *Journal of Applied Behavioral Science* 18, no. 3, 257–73.

Stearns, P. N. (1994) *American Cool: Constructing a Twentieth-Century Emotional Style*. New York: New York University Press.

Stewart, R. (1989) *Leading in the NHS: A Practical Guide*. London: Macmillan.

Stogdill, R. M. (1950) 'Leadership, Membership and Organization', *Psychological Bulletin*, 47: 1–14.

Stogdill, R. M. (1974) *Handbook of Leadership: A Survey of the Literature.* New York: Free Press.

Storey, J. (2004) *Leadership in Organizations: Current Issues and Key Trends.* London: Routledge.

Strong, P. and Robinson, J. (1990) *The NHS under New Management.* Milton Keynes: Open University Press.

Thorne, M. L. (1997) 'Myth-management in the NHS'. *Journal of Management in Medicine* 11, no. 2, 168–80.

Tierney, P. and Tepper, B. J. (2007) 'Introduction to the leadership quarterly special issue: Destructive leadership'. *Leadership Quarterly* 18, no. 3, 171–73.

Timmins, N. (1998) 'A Tale out of School, or Reflections on the Management of the National Health Service' in Best, R. and Maxwell, R. (eds), *The Quest for Excellence:What is Good Health Care—Essays in Honour of Robert J. Maxwell.* London: Kings Fund, 67–76.

Tourish, D. and Pinnington, A. (2002) 'Transformational leadership, corporate cultism and the spirituality paradigm: An unholy trinity in the workplace?' *Human Relations* 55, no. 2, 147–72.

Traynor, M. (1999) *Managerialism and Nursing: Beyond Oppression and Profession.* London: Routledge and Kegan Paul.

Turner, V. (1974) *Dramas, Fields, and Metaphors: Symbolic Action in Human Society.* Ithaca, NY: Cornell University Press.

Van Maurik, J. (2001) *Writers on Leadership.* London: Penguin Business.

Wajcman, J. (1996) 'Desperately seeking differences: is management style gendered?'. *British Journal of Industrial Relations* 34, no. 3, 339–49.

Warner, M. (1994) Fear of a queer planet: Queer Politics and Social Theory. Minnesota: University of Minnesota Press.

Watson, T. (1994) *In Search of Management.* London: Routledge.

Watson, T. (2001) *In Search of Management: Culture, Chaos and Control in Managerial Work.* Rev. edn. London: Thompson Learning.

Weedon, C. (1997) *Feminist Practice and Poststructuralist Theory.* (2nd edn) Oxford: Blackwell.

Westwood, R. and Linstead, S. (eds) (2001) *The Language of Organization.* London: Sage.

Wetherell, M. and Edley, N. (1999) 'Negotiating Hegemonic Masculinity: Imaginary Positions and Psycho-Discursive Practices'. *Feminism and Psychology* 9, no. 3, 335–56.

Wetherell, M., Taylor, S., et al., (eds) (2001) *Discourse Theory and Practice: A Reader.* London: Sage.

Whitehead, S. (1996) 'Men managers and the shifting discourses of post compulsory education'. *Research in Post-Compulsory Education* 1, no. 2, 151–68.

Whitehead, S. (1999) Contingent Masculinities: Disruptions to 'Man'agerialist Identity, in Roseneil, S. and Seymour, J. (eds), *Practising Identities,* Basingstoke: Palgrave Macmillan Press, 107–133.

Whitehead, S. (2001) *Men and Masculinities: Key Themes and New Directions in the Sociology of Management,* Cambridge: Polity.

Willmott, H. (1998a) 'Towards a New Ethics? The Contribution of Poststructuralism and Posthumanism', in Parker, M. (ed.), *Ethics and Organizations.* London: Sage, 76–121.

Willmott, H. (1998b) 'Re-cognizing the Other: Reflections on a "New Sensibility" in Social and Organizational Studies', in Chia, R. (ed.), *In the Realm of Organization: Essays for Robert Cooper*. London: Routledge and Kegan Paul, 213–41.

Wilson, F. (1996) 'Research note: Organization theory—Blind and Deaf to Gender?'. *Organization studies* 17, no. 5, 825–42.

Winnicott, D. (1964) *The Child, The Family and the Outside World*. Harmondsworth: Penguin Books.

Wistow, G. and Harrison, S. (1998) 'Rationality and rhetoric: The contribution to social care policy making of Sir Roy Griffiths 1986–1991'. *Public Administration* 76, 649–68.

Wood, M. (2005) 'The fallacy of misplaced leadership'. *Journal of Management Studies* 42, no. 6, 1101–21.

Wood, M., Ferlie, E. and Fitzgerald, L. (1998) 'Achieving clinical behaviour change: A case of becoming indeterminate'. *Social Science and Medicine* 47, 1729–38.

Wood, M. and Case, P. (2006) *Editorial—Leadership Refrains: Again, Again and Again'. Leadership* 2, 2: 139–45.

Wray-Bliss, E. (2002) 'Abstract ethics, embodied ethics: The strange marriage of Foucault and positivism in labour process theory'. *Organization* 9, no. 1, 5–39.

Wright, P. (1996) *Managerial Leadership*. London: Routledge.

Young, R. J. (2004) *White Mythologies: Writing History and the West*. London: Routledge.

Yukl, G. (1994) *Leadership in Organisations*. (3rd edn) New Jersey: Prentice Hall.

Zaleznik, A. (1997) 'Managers and leaders: Are they different?' *Harvard Business Review* 55, no. 5, 67–78.

Žižek, S. (1989) *The Sublime Object of Ideology*. London and New York: Verso.

Index